Clarity Over Conformity

From Relationships to Authentic Self and Lasting Peace

Megan Elizabeth Victoria, PhD

Clarity with Dr Megan™

ISBN 979-8-9941802-0-4

Published by Clarity with Dr Megan™
www.claritywithdrmegan.com
@claritywithdrmegan

To the United States of America,
for the opportunities I would have lacked elsewhere.

To Jason,
for always being my rock
and bearing witness to my internal tugs-of-war.

And to Dan,
for being the catalyst of my return home to self.
The version of you that rises only in my presence,
the one that had pulled you deeper than you had intended,
will forever live in my heart.

Others' weights are not mine to carry.
~ Megan Victoria

Contents

Before You Begin

This story is about my journey towards self-discovery through romantic connections.

As people I had crossed paths with recognized my accomplishments despite many hurdles, they suggested that I write a book. While that idea intrigued me, I kept convincing myself that no one would care to read about a stranger's life—until a revelation hit me: I can tell my story from the inside out.

It is not what had happened to me; it is how I took advantage of those experiences to find inner peace.

This isn't a how-to guide or a novel with fictional characters and plots designed to hook. It is an unfiltered story about how I walked through my life raw, confused, and even heartbroken, trying to make sense of things with only my lived experience as my guide.

I'm sharing my memories through my perspective. It'll take you through my deeply personal journey in the order of how my internal growth evolved, with some parts illuminated more than others to reflect the significance of their impact on shaping the person I am today.

Names have been intentionally left out to keep the focus on my emotional and internal experiences. Some details have been condensed or rearranged for coherence and flow. Certain moments or individuals have been omitted to highlight what's most relevant and important. I have made a conscious decision to leave out psychological labels or clinical jargon because I want this story to feel human—not academic. Using the word "guy" instead of "man" at applicable places has also been a deliberate choice to mirror their level of emotional maturity.

I hope that you find yourself in my stories and gain the clarity that I once wished for in my younger self.

PART I: THE HYPOTHESIS

CHAPTER 1: CLOSE CALL

The shattered windshield caught me off guard when I woke up from a nap in my car on Interstate 95.

Wonderful! I need a new windshield on top of everything else I've got going on!

The center console must have popped open during my sleep because my phone wasn't inside.

That's strange; I left it there to charge.

I searched everywhere until I found it on the passenger-side floor, buried under a pile of my belongings.

I dialed 911 this time, and you should be proud of me! As you read on, you'll find out why.

"911, what's your emergency?"

"I crashed my car on I-95." The first time talking since waking up, I realized I was chewing on bits of glass.

"Did you hit a semi?"

"I... hit a semi???"

That's when I noticed a semi-truck stopping on the freeway's shoulder ahead of me.

Thursday at 3 am, a vehicle or two continued their travel past me... until I heard blaring sirens and saw flashing red, white, and blue lights converge in my rearview mirror.

Finally, someone stopped for me!

A policeman pointed his flashlight at me and asked if I could unbuckle my seatbelt and step out. He opened my car door as I obeyed his instructions without hesitation—it never crossed my mind that I wouldn't be able to. Standing next to the remains of my rear-engine Porsche, I realized the entire front end had disappeared!

I suppose I must purchase more than just a new windshield.

Firefighters and paramedics planned to transport me to the hospital in an ambulance for a checkup, but I refused. After some generic questions and paperwork, they requested again to take me in. Thankfully, a policeman spoke up for me by reminding them I had already said "no."

These kind gentlemen were even gracious enough to drive me home, which was only two miles down the road from the scene... I had already completed ninety-nine percent of my two-hundred-mile drive home successfully. They even shed light on how lucky they thought I was based on their experience—people rarely walk away from a wreckage that extreme.

I informed my insurance company of what had happened as soon as I set foot in my condo. I was on the phone with them for so long that I didn't even notice the sky turning until sunlight began to press through the curtain. Thus, I texted my boss regarding my late arrival.

Given my morning news viewing habit, what made this morning unique was that I noticed more fatal car accidents being reported. This might have been a fact, or my attention shifted towards them. Regardless of the reason, one realization was undeniable: I could have been one fatality.

It took a month for the initial shock to wear off. I then reflected on how fortunate I was to have survived the ordeal. First responders described what they saw as a miracle, and my insurance company supported their belief by claiming my car as a total loss.

Yet, I walked away with only a small knee bruise, a few minor facial cuts, and some glass pieces in my mouth. It then hit me: I woke up inside the wreckage of my car, yes, but also of everything I had been carrying.

Why, Universe? Why did you save me? What more do you

want me to do? Please, enlighten me.

Had I remained asleep in the driver's seat that morning, I would have harbored zero regrets. You see, I had run out of goals to achieve before that accident. I had done everything: restarting my life alone in a new country, being a business owner, owning exotic cars, modeling, serving in the United States (US) Marine Corps (Marines), earning my Doctor of Philosophy degree (PhD), and being part of a law enforcement agency that I had never dreamed of joining since I was a little girl.

I became a homeowner, even. Despite financial stability, I remained a renter because I had always shunned permanence, like tattoos, spouses, or children, so my personal beliefs never aligned with the need to stay in one location long enough to buy a home.

After COVID-19, however, an unexpected high rent increase at my apartment, a short renewal notice because of a sudden change in property management, and a lack of affordable rentals in the area forced me to look into the real estate buyers' market. Luckily, I found a decent condominium for sale just a block away and became a first-time homeowner in a flash.

My rental and new-home keys overlapped for a short two weeks, so I thought I would move all my belongings bit by bit alone in my compact car. After already giving weekdays to my full-time job and weekends to modeling gigs, I never imagined there would be any problem bigger than just sleep loss.

I had mustered the strength to handle the move by myself because I would ask no one to carry my metaphorical or physical load. I was holding it together without sleep for weeks until my body decided to claim its much-needed rest, though mistimed and misplaced: behind the wheel on a freeway during my three-hour drive home from a runway show.

Ironically, the vehicle's collision, spin, and eventual standstill reflected my life's trajectory. I had been persevering through every shock and turn until the disorder itself induced a period of calm.

With the debris scattered across the freeway and shattered glass in my mouth, the question that surfaced wasn't, *"Am I okay?"*

It was, *"Why am I still here?"*

On the surface, the wreckage seemed fitting for a Porsche advertisement. Yet underneath, it unveiled a tale of someone who had been exhausted for ages—physically, emotionally, and spiritually—when her form faltered, the vicinity slowed to inquire what she had lacked the strength to ask, *"What's wrong with me? Why does it feel like nobody wants me to be their one and only? Am I not enough? What more must I achieve for someone to choose me above all else?"*

Every goal I had set my mind to, I reached, except for romantic relationships. Despite my efforts, this area proved troubling. I was so tired of trying and failing that I would rather immerse myself in more modeling opportunities outside of full-time job obligations, to the point where sleep became a luxury I couldn't afford.

That's it! That's the reason I was saved: I never got to experience being chosen. I dreamt of sharing a life with my true love, my soulmate. The Universe kept me alive for this. I know it!

PART II: THE VARIABLES

CHAPTER 2: CONFORMITY

I used to attribute my failed romances to luck or fate: every past relationship followed the same predictable pattern, regardless of my partner's look, age, background, or personality.

Let me tell you about them.

First Love

Dating had always been taboo in my family, even as I was entering university at 19. I was confined to my home for much of my childhood. My sole role was to be a daughter; any other purpose would make me feel guilty.

Right when I was introduced to dial-up internet, I encountered a guy six years my senior through I-Seek-You, or ICQ. Do you recall that platform? He became my "first love" in a heartbeat. I use the term "love" loosely here because, as you'll see, it was anything but.

What actions might a young girl hiding a boy from her family pursue? She got creative! Given her long commute between home and school and long hours spent teaching piano on the weekends, she extended her schedule here and there to see him so her mother wouldn't notice.

Exclusivity remained unmentioned because seeing someone was a fresh and unknown concept. I sought little from others, if any at all. Nobody had taught me to evaluate or discern. I didn't date him because he was right for me; I was with him because he had selected me. It never struck me that I was allowed to choose. He declared me his girlfriend at the conclusion of our first date. Since he had courted me from the start, I thought we belonged as one... a reasonable implication coming from a girl brought up unseen and unloved. My younger self didn't lack intelligence or worth; she lacked context. She had no reference point for healthy desire, mutuality, or slow-building intimacy.

I remember only bits and pieces of that relationship: we shared meals, shopping trips, and travel itineraries. He showered me with lavish gifts... even gave me a credit card linked to his account—I thought that was love.

At some point, he quit his job as a private investigator to join a multilevel marketing (MLM) company that recruited people to grow some sort of fungus. It appeared unusual, yet my naivety led me to embrace it. He let me know he had invested his life savings to join that company for me, as he otherwise would not have quit the job he loved. I experienced a combination of emotions: I was honored to possess the qualities to influence another person's decisions, but I was also puzzled... I didn't ask him to alter his life path for me.

Perhaps love means sacrificing for others? Though it feels... off.

My former self was too emotionally immature to dive deeper into the reasoning. How was I supposed to cope given the weight regarding another's path? I had just begun to learn about relational connections; he soon handed me a guilt trip while I was still trying to find my footing. I was too busy trying to play catch-up socially, emotionally, and romantically... while balancing the grief of losing my father, my mother's dependency, the academic load as a new college student, and occupational stress from being newly hired as a piano teacher by a well-known music school.

But now I see that wasn't genuine love; it was emotional leverage. What I absorbed from that relationship wasn't just the memory of dates or gifts, but the beginning of a pattern: being cast into someone else's story as the reason for their risk or pain.

Parallel to that relationship, I was pursuing an opportunity to attend graduate school abroad once I would finish my bachelor's degree. Since English is the only language I speak, my choices came down to Australia, Canada, or the US. Mismatched school years excluded Australia, whereas cold climate eliminated Canada. After a friend's return from her San Diego trip, highlighting her feeling of safety walking alone after dark, I decided on the US.

I then traveled to San Diego during a summer break to tour a few college campuses and later got a student visa sponsorship for a Master of Business Administration (MBA) program from one of them.

You must be wondering: What about your boyfriend?

Honestly, that thought never crossed my mind. Overseas study was my decision, not considering its impact on him or our relationship. Could it be because I didn't love him? Plausible, at least not in the manner genuine affection exists when it's reciprocal, firm, and designated.

His absence from my decision-making factors reveals volumes. It doesn't mean I was cold or selfish. Beyond that, I now realize he never touched my guiding core. Perhaps I lacked words then, but my body already knew.

This is not the person I would rearrange my life for.

My instincts were protecting me, even if my conscious mind hadn't caught up. He was there, yes... even gave me gifts, attention, and a sense of status. But I didn't weave him into my future. It seems he served a temporary purpose until I gained the freedom to see the outside world.

I bought my one-way ticket for September 12, 2001. My journey was delayed because of the tragic event the day prior. However, that did not deter me from coming to the US. I eventually flew out on September 17, 2001, the minute airports reopened.

Boarding a plane towards a fresh start, the status of my relationship vanished from my thoughts, not out of cruelty or wanting to hurt him —in truth, he never held an actual place inside me. I was no longer thinking about a boyfriend; I was finally thinking about myself. That's not detachment, but survival returning to its natural rhythm. Studying abroad involved more than relocation; it represented an emergence.

I recall my mother giving me the silent treatment, and when she finally decided to speak, she said I never asked for her permission to move away... I was almost 21. Her protest was the last gasp of someone losing control, as my existence—my adulthood, independence, and future—still required her stamp of approval.

She was right that I didn't ask... I took off.

Another Guy

My first night in an unknown country and environment gave me culture shock. I slept in an empty dormitory where my roommates, whom I had yet to meet, took a weekend trip to San Francisco. Thankfully, it didn't take me long to adjust and settle in.

One week into my new surroundings, a guy pulled up in a car alongside me while I was walking back from class. He lowered his window and explained that he had been driving around for a week, hoping to see me again. I couldn't recall ever having met him.

He noticed me? Another guy showed interest? That made two.

Two individuals desired me. It seemed unbelievable because my own parents had been telling me I was ugly and they didn't even want me.

This guy had already graduated and was applying for jobs. We would then spend almost every day together outside of my classes.

I was getting a driver's license and looking to buy a car. Since I had only ever driven a manual transmission, his automatic was a first for me. I remember asking whether using the left foot for the brake was appropriate after observing his driving. That question seems naïve now, but it was genuine. I was vulnerable, uncertain, and learning.

He yelled, "You should know what to do."

My lack of common knowledge, not his temper, perplexed me.

Why am I so stupid?

His rage was unsurprising because such emotions were common-place during my childhood. It appeared to be the penalty my parents would always give me for not knowing better sooner.

He broke up with me three months later, and my cuteness was to blame. I remember asking a friend afterwards for her opinion on whether I was too cute and if I needed to tone it down.

But I eventually found out the real reason: his girlfriend, whom he had told me was an ex, returned from a long visit overseas. I was unaware that he had involved me in a cheating scheme.

Layered under that heartbreak, shock, and humiliation, I realized that my parents had been right about me: *I am a burden.*

This guy, similar to the first one, disregarded my inherent worth. He saw me as an opportunity, something convenient, a stand-in, and disposable. His leaving meant more than just a breakup; it reinforced the cruel equation my parents had always instilled in me, which would continue to hum in the background. However, what remained unknown to me then was

Attention doesn't equal care, desire doesn't equal loyalty,

and being chosen doesn't mean I'm safe.

More Guys

With that heartbreak, I returned to ICQ and even tried other messaging platforms. I ended up dating a video gamer, an aspiring day trader, a foreign exchange student, and a few fathers much older than me.

Several of those fathers were still married, and yes, I was aware. I'm not proud of that phase of my life, but my past self justified her in-volvement by believing that she could be a "better lover" because those guys would always complain to her about their spouses. It reflects that I once thought love required both chasing and winning over.

None of those relationships lasted, though, and I blamed luck.

Father-Figure

With no luck in any of the messengers, I moved on to dating websites. Despite lacking a lasting romance by that point, attracting guys posed no trouble for me. Those guys recognized something special within me, so I questioned why my parents never did.

A 39-year-old guy, almost 20 years my senior, jumped at the chance. Divorced, he had a 12-year-old son who lived with him part-time. He swept me off my feet with chocolates, roses, restaurants, and home-cooked meals.

I moved in with him and experienced what I thought was a "normal" family dynamic—something I had never known. For example, he asked his son about his preferences, including food choices, things my parents never did to me. I even experienced my first Christmas with wrapped gifts under a real tree and opened them on Christmas morning.

Love resembled a TV show, viewed but untouched. I was learning about parental love just by witnessing someone else receiving it. Regarding it as healthy, I strived to absorb it all. I found myself immersed in learning about healthy family dynamics, like stepping through a portal into a parallel universe where gentleness, inclusion, and choice were real, not imagined. Of course, I wanted to believe it; I was starving for it. It gave me both ache and softness.

But underneath it all, a part of me was still navigating blind and vulnerable to being chosen rather than choosing. I realize now that it was more than dating for me; it was my initial taste of normal. Love didn't come as punishment or silence—it came with roses and hot meals. No one beat me for having feelings or gave me the silent treatment for pursuing my future.

With only two courses remaining before graduating with an MBA, I decided to chase my dream of being a business owner. A 23-year-old running a coffee shop wasn't as glamorous as it sounds. It never made enough income to hire help, so I became the sole owner and operator.

My ignorance of self-care led me to work excessive hours, believing longer hours would equate to higher profits. The storage room soon became my bedroom, a mattress my bed, and leftovers my meals.

In retrospect, that picture had brutality and heroism. It surpassed a coffee shop; it was my first true assertion of autonomy. I wasn't trying only to make money but also to matter by building something with my name on it, for none could take it away or shame me. The part that cut the deepest was that even in my freedom, I continued living by the rules of survival. The truth is, I wasn't building a life; I was enduring one. I had internalized the belief that my worth was tied to performance, exhaustion, and self-denial. I didn't know how to rest. No one had shown me unconditional care: not parents, partners, or even myself.

Returning from getting supplies one night, I found his motorcycle parked at my coffee shop. He showed up unannounced, and I had missed no calls or texts. Upon entering, I saw him seated at the coffee bar, a large bottle of vodka in front of him. I had no concept of alcoholism at that point in my life. He glared, eyes bloodshot, then questioned my whereabouts. As I was telling him, he walked behind the bar and started throwing at me glass jars of coffee, tea, and any heavy objects within reach, as if he was trying to throw away my belief that *"this is what being wanted looks like."*

Fortunately, he didn't have good aim; dents and holes marred the walls. Someone from the gas station next door entered by breaking through a window, held him by his neck, and ordered me to dial 911.

I picked up the phone and called the police; it wouldn't go through.

I tried again: 9-9-9.

Beep-beep-beep.

My body was in panic, entrenched in survival mode; even my brain's emergency system reached for the wrong country. I was disoriented and in danger. And yet, I still kept trying.

Oh! Right! This is America! It's 911!

The call finally connected, and the police hastened to the scene. They arrested him and took statements from me and the US Marine who had rescued me. The policeman advised me to collect my belongings from his place as soon as possible, so I got into my car and started driving.

The details of that night are hazy… I recall parking, the garage door shutting, and having a fleeting thought, *"Let the engine keep running."*

That was my nervous system saying, *"I can't live like this anymore."*

Perhaps I exhausted myself after the loop of repeatedly trying to find someone who would want me. I was not suicidal, but soul-tired. What I craved was a love that wouldn't leave any bruises.

And I almost let that stick… until a friend's call saved me, like life throwing a line to a drowning person. It did more than just a phone call; it interrupted, intervened, and proved someone still noticed me. My existence had worth to someone, outside of control or usage.

Taking her advice, I filed a restraining order. Surpassing paperwork, it was the first time I had declared, *"I do not deserve this,"* and officially on a piece of paper.

That relationship seemed genuine at first, but then it hurt, echoing the previous pain. After this needless ordeal, I moved onward.

Gun Club

The exhaustion from enduring an unprofitable business pushed me to do the unthinkable: join the Marines in my late 20s. Despite having graduated with my bachelor's degree, I was enlisted because I was not yet a US citizen.

The setting of the military felt foreign. Never had I experienced daily proximity to so many males before. Some of their wives would stop by for chowtime, which seemed normal until I realized it was a pattern that began with my entry. Perhaps their distrust fueled it, or maybe it stemmed from my being the sole female spending ample time with their husbands beside them; I cannot declare which.

Many of the guys showed physical interest, and I accepted the pursuits of a lot of them. Appreciating their attention, I did not expect them to become lasting companions. That period of my life feels fuzzy now. I don't remember how many people I had dated, or even their names. The whole active-duty dating experience seemed more like a rollercoaster ride. They all gave me the sense of being stung by not returning my texts or calls. My former self would drive to their residences, knock on the doors, and get no response. She would always end up sitting in her car, waiting, sometimes even overnight.

Though one particular night stood out. One guy refused me entry, forcing me to sleep in my truck in the parking lot across from his barracks. I spoke with our mutual friend as I was setting up my truck for sleep.

I still recall her murmuring to me, "Megan, do you hear yourself? You said you're sleeping in your truck while he is in his bed." I heard my dignity whispering through her voice, but I couldn't feel it.

My brain could register the truth: *I deserve more than this.*

But my body and heart? They kept returning to the thought: *I must earn my place.*

That naïve version of me craved validation. Different guys, same uniform, and one other thing in common: I was unwanted, and I would do anything to hold on, to prove I deserved attention, even if it meant abandoning my self-respect. Because abandonment wasn't un-familiar—it had always been my baseline.

Italy

I served as a Marine Security Guard at US embassies. That assign-ment relocated me to Rome, Italy.

Arriving in Rome, I was greeted by my female supervisor, a fellow Marine, not at the airport as a welcome, but at the Marine House every evening as she was sizing me up. Despite noticing her unusual presence, I would normalize her conduct at first.

A few weeks later, she ceased visiting the House as often… maybe because she found me nonthreatening. I then verified my suspicion when Marines who had been there longer told me that her abnormally high frequency of visits was tied to her vetting of what "female type" I was.

That thought pattern is an example that shows how I was wired: my instinct sensed the truth, but I overrode it until external validation permitted me to trust what I had already known.

Amid Italian guys, male Marines lost their appeal. I was single in Italy, so why not test Italian dating?

Are they more romantic, per rumor?

I have always carried both boldness and inevitability; that's likely why I moved to a foreign country on my own at age 20. Hesitation does not color my approach to living. In pursuit of not only romance but also authenticity, I leaned into immersion. Such readiness provides strength, but it also opens up more vulnerabilities.

It didn't take long for a young, tall, and handsome Italian guy to make me feel infatuated. With him, I was swept up in the allure of cultural depth and family closeness.

On our first date, he took me home to meet his family: mom, dad, and younger sister. All four of them still lived in the same home, where their extended family members occupied other units in the same building. Though it was distinct from what I was used to, I still found it enriching.

I got to experience dating an Italian guy firsthand, as well as being dumped via messenger two years later when I was stationed in Montenegro. I had shown genuine sincerity throughout my time with him, anticipating the equivalent, leaving me defenseless when he pulled the rug from underneath me.

Having striven to move through the world with careful observation of my environment, I evaluate my experiences looking for authenticity and loyalty, and failures like this instance remind me that my wiring was tilted towards idealism. I defaulted to trust and projected forward, already picturing him transplanted into our future in the US, while missing signs that his trajectory might not have aligned with mine the whole time. It uncovered the degree I had vested and the entire imagined structural constructs I had already built. When those structures crumbled, it hit me harder because I was losing so much more than a person; I was also losing the scaffolding of possibility.

I wasn't cautious then; my wiring was expansive, and expansive visions meant expansive risks.

Excel Spreadsheet

Upon returning from my deployment, I turned to dating apps, where I found three guys to date for a couple of months until one of them informed me he had already considered me his girlfriend. He had even told his family and friends about it.

That completed my search; I became the chosen, validated by someone's desire. By the way, he never asked me; he just handed it to me like a script already in progress, unprompted. That chosen feeling remained quite potent and hopeful.

Maybe this time it's real. Perhaps true love is when someone declares you, informs their family, and brings you into their world.

This guy flaunted his career, money, fancy car, and homeownership. We frequented places that sold alcohol. He paid for everything when we first started dating, shaping the illusion of abundance: trips, gifts, and dinners.

But soon, he started sending me Excel spreadsheets detailing monthly expenses and billing me my fair share. He was kind enough to ensure I understood the proportional breakdown was based on our incomes, which made me feel lucky and indebted.

But let's be honest. That spreadsheet wasn't about money; it's about ego maintenance. He used my income to justify the cost of my presence, control posed as fairness, and condescension mimicked inclusion. He aspired to be praised for being generous without sacrifice.

Instead of a partnership, that was a business transaction dressed as intimacy. And I, having known the ache of being left out, rejected, and overlooked, told myself, *"At least I'm part of something now. At least I'm visible."*

There it was again... that familiar shape, cloaked in a different costume. Just like others before him, he used my existence to justify their poor choices. That's the deeper thread: I keep being made responsible for other people's math—financial, emotional, and moral. The cracks appeared in subtle ways. That's why it didn't set off my internal alarm.

***

Dining out on Veterans Day, the couple sitting next to us paid our bill. What gave it away was his military haircut, which was kept trimmed even outside of drill weekends of the US Coast Guard Reserve.

We thanked them, and they started asking him about his military service, all the while ignoring me. He didn't care enough to let them know I was also in the military, on active duty. I was right there, serving alongside him, even on a full-time basis, carrying my sacrifices and stories, and yet I was sidelined.

Megan in the past didn't speak up for herself, as she didn't want to boast, especially to strangers who hadn't addressed her.

I was trying to forget about it and not let it bother me, yet it wouldn't leave my mind. His unspoken connivance spoke volumes about how unseen I had felt even among my closest ties. I pondered it with him in a conversation a week later, telling him it left me feeling disrespected and unappreciated.

Puzzled by my reaction, he said I was overreacting. His dismissal wasn't just about that one incident; it reflected a deeper dynamic: he ignored my feelings, presence, and experiences. I attempted to be open and vulnerable, but my concerns were met with confusion and ignorance. That's a subtle but powerful form of disrespect. It sends the message: My feelings aren't important enough to warrant understanding.

***

His mom was the first member of his family of origin that I got to meet. The moment she discovered he had found himself a girlfriend, she invited herself to stay at his place over the summer. She asked me about my views on having children, and I confessed that it wasn't something I would ever consider for myself.

That same year, he took me to his parents' for Christmas and New Year. One of my dissertation defense sessions, which happened to be scheduled between the holidays, was a few-hour drive from their place. So we had planned a week-long post-Christmas trip by ourselves, coinciding with my school attendance, and then returning to them on New Year's Day.

We were the last to arrive at their house. His brothers, sister-in-law, and nephews had already been there since the night before. I was the only "stranger" that needed to be introduced. Walking into their home, I expected to be acknowledged as part of his life. That expectation seemed logical after one year of dating. Yet, his mom avoided and ignored me as soon as we walked in.

She took the opportunity while he went to the bathroom to tell me, in front of everyone, "Don't think I had mentioned to anyone here about you; I never did." Her words were deliberate; they flaunted the annihilation of my significance, place, and presence. She made me appear as an intruder in their narrative.

That woman erased me. And yet, somehow, I was the one navigating politeness, suppressing my discomfort, and absorbing her dismissal with grace. Not only was I being mistreated, but I was also expected to tolerate it. I, who had worked harder than anyone in that room, had already begun the journey of rebuilding myself from emotional poverty, betrayal, and the raw loneliness of being unwanted and used. It hit me at that moment that I was still not enough, no matter how hard I tried.

We slept in his childhood bedroom while he maintained the "position of attention" throughout the night. That awkward body placement was symbolic: it brought back memories of my boot camp sleep instructions and revealed he hadn't evolved past his family's control, individuated, or grown out of being a son first and a partner second. His proclaimed freedom suddenly vanished.

***

After Christmas, as we drove away for my dissertation, he informed me that my lengthy shower during our stay displeased his mom. He once entered my locked bathroom to check on me. It was, in fact, one of the most subtly violating scenes of my life. It didn't just cross a boundary; it revealed there was none—at least not one that protected me.

He revealed that his mom conceived the plan because she believed I was concealing something in the bathroom, feigning a shower. He failed to correct his mom's public erasure of me, as if he were still their boy and not my partner.

The next day, he relayed his dad's request: return to them for the new year alone or never return. His parents' ultimatum did not shock me, as I had sensed unwelcome vibes throughout my visit. I wasn't just a guest in their home; I was a suspect of disrupting their order. They didn't consider me someone to welcome but as someone to monitor, control, and eliminate.

I now recognize that even my younger self didn't crumble, scream, or chase. Although I lacked the vocabulary to explain the clarity I had amid emotional erosion, deep inside, I sensed their rejection of me wasn't necessarily personal. I assessed the situation.

I've done nothing wrong. They're being unreasonable.

Their coldness, mistrust, and refusal to welcome me stemmed from their view of me as their loss of control. I posed a danger, not from wrongdoing, but from refusal of their role; my independence terrified them. I didn't gush, submit, offer my womb, or revere.

My calmness startled him so much that he later mentioned it to his best friend, and the friend commented that I must have been someone who had high self-esteem.

He claimed he had already decided for himself not to return alone to his parents'. My judgment deemed it proper; their actions lacked reason.

What have I ever done? He is a grown man. He can make his own decisions.

***

With my PhD graduation, I accepted a job offer from a nearby city, which necessitated temporary lodging before relocation. When he found out I was looking for an Airbnb, he offered to let me stay in his home, which was very surprising to me because he had obsessive-compulsive disorder (OCD) over cosmetic imperfections on material objects. Despite that, I accepted his gracious offer.

Waking up at his place the first morning after he had already left for work, I received a phone call from him at 9 am asking me what I was doing: "drinking coffee."

The next phone call came at 10 am with the same question. This time, he asked me to help him clean the refrigerator if I had time, to which I agreed. His hourly check-ins would continue, which I found to be attentive, though unusual.

As soon as he stepped through the door after work, he emptied the fridge for inspection, scrutinizing its shelves and drawers. He shouted at me while showing me a drawer that he had pulled out, questioning if I had used the scratchy side of a sponge to clean it.

I was… shocked. Not a "thank you," but a rage over some scratches that were already there, or I could barely see. Nonetheless, I pleaded for forgiveness, but he refused to speak to me.

Despite the silent treatment, he continued to provide me with a detailed daily chore schedule for my month-long stay, emphasizing it as an exchange for free lodging.

The next morning, he called me at 9 am again, asking the same question. Rather than "drinking coffee," I mentioned my Airbnb search. That was the strongest line I said to him in the entire relationship because I finally realized that those hourly calls were surveillance. They didn't come from care but control. And when he screamed at me over some fridge scratches—after offering labor for shelter—it wasn't just about the sponge; it followed my same tired script: perform, plead, apologize, and shrink.

Instead of yielding in this instance, I grabbed my bag and headed to an Airbnb. Because in that moment, I wasn't just choosing a different roof. I was choosing myself, without drama, begging, or waiting to be chosen back. I wasn't planning on scratching another guy's standards just to be allowed to stay.

***

While it's true that he first chose me, given an ultimatum, he started yielding to his mom's pressure little by little. The relationship lingered, becoming long-distance for an additional two years before diminishing.

Even though we seemed to be a match based only on our shared child-free mindset, what didn't match were his alcoholism, spreadsheet invoices, OCD, and overbearing mom, who hated me and made him choose between me and her. In the end, I was not chosen.

CHAPTER 3: CLUTTERS

I realized now I faced rejection not from failing merit, but from defying control. I held too much inner strength to become small enough to fit inside someone else's dysfunction.

Dream Job

After my Marine Corps tenure, I started working for a law enforcement agency. This place had seemed beyond reach to my younger self; thus, it's a fulfilling dream. Only two weeks into my job, despite being brand new, I was asked to step into an acting supervisory role while my boss was on holiday.

One day, a supervisory employee from another department walked up to my desk, looking for my supervisor. I informed him she was away; he then asked me a work-related question intended for her. My inexperience led me to do extensive research.

At the time, I lacked the awareness that he already ought to have possessed the answer to his own question. He kept seeking my supervisor, posing new work questions whenever she wasn't present. When I finally mentioned it to my supervisor upon her return after a few of those similar inquiries, she wondered why he would pose such questions, those that he would already have known the answers to.

A year later, his pattern became more obvious. He started asking questions that weren't work-related, such as my plans for the weekend. That's when his intentions became clear to me.

Having explored the Marine Corps setup, this guy surfaced where norms were loose. I was no longer seen as a military rank or occupational specialty. His power didn't intimidate me, nor did I find it flattering; I don't bow down to someone simply because they are higher in the hierarchy.

Let me make one thing clear: I lacked desire for him; he was and appeared much senior. Thus, we looked mismatched. He had three daughters from two ex-wives. My previous experience with a divorced father had made me wary of dating guys with children—nothing against kids, but that lifestyle just isn't for me.

Despite all of that, I couldn't help but feel flattered by his persistence... perhaps the feeling of being wanted served as proof that I existed.

Even wise women sometimes pick feeling desired over self-enforcing principles, don't they?

Those emotions slipped past my guard and made my wisdom question my knowing: *Am I translating the attention as my value? Red flags? What red flags? Someone wants me again!*

That's my unspoken admission: watching myself soften when I didn't expect him to rankle me; offering crumbs when I was starving posed a peril. For quite a while, I had guarded myself, and then I forgot how warmth could disorient.

***

So, when he asked me about my weekend plans again, I told him I had none. My answer represented not only the open space in my schedule but also in my emotional availability.

And he filled it fast, with purpose, by consuming all my time with his constant texting, phone calls, FaceTime, and visits. He swept me off my feet with grand gestures, declarations, and sweet words I had never heard before, which made me feel special. It took him no time to claim me by informing my concierge that he was coming to see his "girlfriend."

Timing, attention, and, admittedly, loneliness that I wasn't even aware of started that relationship. I was eventually hooked, despite not having been attracted to him at first. I wish I could tell my former self that I grew dependent because he was feeding my desire; that perceived connection was infiltration.

He would often bring up his ex-wives and ex-girlfriends unprompted, painting them all as unstable, dramatic, and unfaithful, summarizing them in the "crazy" category.

Those stories resonated with me, mirroring my own experiences with partners who lacked integrity in the past, since I had been through betrayal myself. I had been wondering if any good men still existed, so when he presented himself as hurting, it forged a bond: shared failed relationships with cheating partners. I saw it as a sign that he would understand me. It never crossed my mind at the time that the shared characteristics among his past partners would be a red flag.

He invited me to spend time in his apartment, stating his intention for me to feel welcome and included within his space. Drawing me into his world was a performance shaped for women he later discarded as "crazy." I now recognize it as an illusion of intimacy, not a foundation. He was older, which I inferred to mean he was more experienced. And when he had rejected so many "crazy" women in the past, I assumed he was selective.

Many don't speak of this: it's a unique feeling to be chosen by someone discerning, so when his focus turned to me, I felt unique.

He shared his sexual fantasies early on and sent me a photograph of a woman in an attire that turned him on, suggesting I dress alike to please him in intimate moments. I had no idea that what he was doing was scripting my behavior to match his fantasies. He sought to rewrite me in his image before I established my stance. I was still gaining knowledge of what rebirth of attention entailed; he hurried to form the definition of ideal desire for me. That was manipulation disguised as a love connection.

He didn't fall in love with me; he absorbed me. And when someone absorbs me, my clarity dissolves without me even noticing. I didn't realize I had suspended my standards in the name of hope. I was finally being safe just long enough to override myself.

***

After months of almost nonstop communication and spending nearly every weekend together, his texts became infrequent, eventually reducing to a daily "good morning." He would become irritated when I asked if we were spending time the following weekend, reminding me we had already done so the weekend prior. I reached out with genuine concerns and wondered what I had done to cause his decrease in interest in me; he explained he no longer had the mental space for a relationship. When his dad passed away, he grew even more distant.

Because I loved him through my integrity, I tried to hold space, accommodate his grief, and honor his timing. When inquired concerning the duration he needed to feel ready again, he replied that he did not know, stressing that when ready, I would receive the initial call. I felt devastated but also understood his need to take care of himself. So, I didn't press. I grasped it and granted him grace… That's my nature.

***

But my care stopped once I found out the real reason: he had been seeing another woman. I confronted him about it. His excuses? Their relationship, he reasoned, had begun even before we crossed paths. To lighten the severity of the matter, he shared that she was in a "contract marriage" with a rich husband, who gave her an expensive home to raise their child. When his older daughters moved away for university, he decided to move in with her. Apparently, living free of charge in a home that his cheating girlfriend's husband bought didn't bother him.

I finally realized his previous request for space wasn't because of grief; it was a lie dressed as softness. In hindsight, it's more likely he used his dad's passing as a shield, knowing it would silence me. His dad died during that time, yes, but I wasn't sure how much of his distance came from grieving a loss versus being tired of managing a double life. He was using my emotional labor, patience, body, and trust as a stand-in until he was ready to move into her place.

***

Upon learning that he chose her, I chose myself, letting him go even before knowing every single detail of that betrayal. I didn't beg or negotiate, although deep down I questioned what I lacked compared to that woman. I kept asking friends if they saw anything that I needed to improve.

Reflecting, I see that his last words to me likely spoke more than he had meant to: "I wouldn't be jealous of her because she has to deal with me."

In hindsight, he was right—I don't envy her. Not anymore, and not when she invited home a person who lacked integrity... likely because that mirrored her own values.

I released him quickly so I could dig deeper into the details because I grieve through truth-finding. If his having a relationship with a married woman and moving into a home that her husband owned wasn't shocking enough, remember he had sent me a photo of a woman in the outfit and vibe he wanted me to replicate? That woman was her, the other woman.

Realizing she had stood there the entire time and her picture shaped me made me feel stung. What I perceived as flirtatious behavior was foreshadowing. More than betrayal; that was erasure. He didn't just cheat; he hollowed me out and filled me with someone else's silhouette. He didn't want me for who I was.

All he wanted was to mold me, reenact his obsession, and puppet someone else's presence through my body without my knowledge or consent. It's all about control. He didn't send me her photo to make me feel desired; he wanted to see if I would comply. Of course I did, because I was trusting, generous, and loyal.

***

He left me mourning for losing something that wasn't even real. I grieved our potential, a burden I bore alone. I faced rejection yet again. More accurately, I faced emotional, psychological, and symbolic betrayal.

Have you ever grieved what never was? I didn't just grieve the sweet moments we shared that would no longer repeat. I had to rewrite them, one by one, injecting the truth that I know now.

For instance, he once claimed he needed to return to his vehicle to search for his daughter's missing phone, a process that should have taken less than thirty minutes but spanned two hours because of a detour to meet at her place for lunch.

When he first pursued me, I wasn't interested at all. But because of his persistence and likely my craving for attention, I eventually showed up, believed, and tried in the end. I commit to everything I have decided on: either doing nothing or doing it with full effort. In contrast, he performed, withheld, and replaced. The truth is, he was never honest enough to be worthy of my realness, and deep down, he knew it.

I was the only real one the whole time.

Model

At a runway model casting, I needed to rush to the ladies' room as soon as I got there after a three-hour drive. Did I mention I have a small bladder? A quick "hi" was muttered from a male model bumping into me while exiting the men's. I said it back as I pushed open my door.

During my runway walk, I braced myself for silence as I attended alone, knowing no one, despite the loud cheers for other models. But I felt a pair of eyes pierce me, and to my surprise, a male voice spurred me onward. Composed, I ignored the urge to look but recognized the voice came from the guy I had just crossed paths with in front of the restrooms.

That guy inserted himself as the one who rewrote the tale, and it worked because although we ceased talking during the casting, we connected on Instagram afterwards.

***

A month of silence later, he came in hungry by flooding my inbox with messages filled with questions about my life: "Where are you from? Do you live in the area? How long have you been modeling? What do you do outside of modeling? What's your PhD in?..."

He craved total data; such focus struck my core, the part of myself that is uncommon, aware, and weary via disregard. Because so few people cared, someone noticing my doctorate and modeling career felt like magic.

He continued to shower me with attention: constant texting and phone calls. It felt nice to be cared for. "What are you up to? How was work? Any new modeling gigs coming up?"

Displaying strength for almost my whole life had consumed me; thus, someone's routine inquiry held substance: he made me feel studied, seen, and admired.

Because I had been ghosted, overlooked, or used in the past, some-one staying in touch for weeks made me think, *maybe this time, it's real.*

Because the absence of genuine connection elsewhere made even borrowed intimacy feel nourishing, I wanted to believe him even though I wasn't naïve. Until he came in like fuel, I was running on fumes. I felt wanted and valued again, associating my worth with his curiosity without my knowing.

***

Unlike the previous guy, I found this one attractive at first, except for his height, which he had lied about to be in the modeling industry. It's not a huge thing in itself, but it is symbolic: a guy lying about his height is someone whose identity is shaped by performance. He didn't just live in appearance; he led with it.

I should have caught on that he wasn't dating me; he was casting. I should have known better than to treat it as one of the early red flags, but I brushed it off because he seemed driven and goal-oriented, which were qualities I admired in a partner.

Though his physique differed from the guy before him, a similar structure existed: early intensity, grand gestures, verbal declarations of interest, three children, two ex-wives, a shared dating history with "crazy" women, and their openness about sexual fantasies.

This connection wasn't earned—it became an illusion of intimacy overnight, fast and deep. Instead of building something together, he created momentum without stability and flooded me with a closeness that didn't yet have the bones to hold actual weight. I didn't think I was being blindsided, but I wanted him to be my person so bad that I ignored the echo from the last time.

***

After a month of nonstop texting and phone calls, our first date involved meeting in a city where we both attended a runway casting. We shared a hotel room, intended as a financially sensible decision, but it quickly became a night of sexual exploration, a topic we had been discussing for weeks leading up to it. That was our first date and physical encounter, following that short restroom passing. Sadly, I failed to see it as reckless because I was ready to believe this could be different. Like before, I stepped into a script, not love.

We lived in cities four hours apart, so we would occasionally meet in a town halfway in between for quick weekend getaways when he didn't have his kids. Sometimes, he would stay at my place, but I could never stay at his, despite his claim to be divorced from his second wife, with whom he still owned a business. He said it felt wrong mixing his feelings in a home where he had once lived with her. I didn't dwell on that reasoning, so I booked a hotel room, showed up, and waited for his texts. I shrunk the size of my needs just to keep the connection intact.

***

Each morning, his call preceded my commute; each night, he was my last conversation; and in between, we would text nonstop. Perhaps you wonder what topics occupied that much time. Honestly, I don't have recollections of the specifics. It hits me now when my mind goes blank trying to recall what we were even discussing, because none of it nourished me. All I remember is how they made me feel: self-doubtful, belittled, and misunderstood.

Before my mind could catch up, though, my body had already started relying on his constant contact to survive: I would check my phone constantly to see if I had missed a text or call from him. I would even stalk his Instagram, fixating on his posts, likes, comments, and stories. Little did I know, I was becoming addicted to his interactions, even though they often left me frustrated, exhausted, and defeated.

Eventually, his texts dwindled, and the phone calls almost disappeared. My date suggestions had become irritating to him. I felt confused and diminished, even as our contact grew, and I noticed how he kept me at arm's length—not just in space, but also with his feelings, controlling the terms. His home was off-limits, his kids were a reason to compartmentalize, and his business and past were closed off.

***

One day, while dropping me off at a train station after a model casting, I saw a different side of him. He kept making wrong turns and missing the only one-way street that would lead to the drop-off area. My train was about to depart, and we were nowhere near the station. Finally, I advised him where to turn before he made another false attempt.

That revealed an aspect of him I did not expect: he fumed, accusing me of waiting until the very last minute to tell him the correct route. I felt trapped inside his car, where he unleashed his inner monster. His sudden surge of violence bewildered me.

Has it always been inside him?

The moment he lost control of his anger, I saw his true self. His rage didn't seem new; it had just been managed, contained, and filtered. I had already sensed its shadows in his irritability, uneasiness, and vanishing warmth. But that day in the car, his mask slipped.

Finally, we made it to the unloading zone. Despite the risk of missing my train, I still reached for a goodbye kiss, but he didn't reciprocate.

I then ran to catch my train, heart racing, and thinking, *maybe this is a moment he'll regret and apologize for. This is salvageable.*

***

That night, his quietness was very odd, and his usual "good morning" text didn't come through the next day. So I checked his Instagram and saw his story. The caption read "About last night…" and it was a repost of someone else's story—a photo of him, all dressed up, embracing a woman I had never met.

Her caption said, "Thank you for everything, my love."

My world shattered. That picture wasn't a coincidence—it's the ultimate act of dominance; he knew I would see it. He flaunted another woman within hours. He wasn't just done; he had already replaced me.

I'm not his person; she is.

And this reality hit me like a ton of bricks. I, yet once more, was unwanted.

Instead of confronting him, I blocked him everywhere right away: Instagram, cellphone, and email. I exited in complete silence. Although my former self kept trying to earn love, as soon as I found out that my attempt was unsuccessful, I would always retreat without chasing or begging. I believe that…

One can gain closure only through internal reckoning, not from those causing hurt in the first place.

***

Like the prior guy, he never picked me. He kept me orbiting around the illusion he sold me while he was building a life with someone else. I was holding onto a connection that only existed in my mind: one he cultivated just enough to keep me compliant but not enough to keep me secure. I gave my loyalty to someone who only gave me loops.

More than just betrayal, he mocked me by using my own nervous system against me. He trained me to crave his attention, seek his approval, and measure my safety by the next ping on my phone. He did not perceive my true self; I was conditioned by him to serve his own purpose of feeding his ego. What he did to me was an erosion— the slow, almost imperceptible decay of my clarity under the weight of constant contact, emotional ambiguity, and subtle devaluation.

He must have toiled to understand why I disappeared because he created new email addresses to demand my replies with reasons for ghosting him. He kept pressuring me to agree to remain friends so that we could talk about what had happened. I discerned his motives: he didn't want me back; he just needed to know what I had found out.

We crossed paths at a fashion show six months later, where he followed me like a puppy backstage, asking to take me out to dinner or walk me back to my hotel, but I ignored him. He deserved no more of my time or energy.

***

This heartbreak turned into an awakening. I wept not for lost love, but for lost self-worth. My prior self, valuing attention over genuine appreciation, felt undeserving. I am not someone to orbit others; I am someone to stand beside—fully, clearly, and wholly. More than physical desire, my real craving was for someone to understand me emotionally.

My body and emotions felt depleted. On the surface, I presented as someone who seemed to possess everything. But deep down, I was well aware of my struggles in sustaining a romantic relationship.

Am I too picky? But people warn against settling. I'm just trying to find someone who could match "my level."

PART III: THE CONSTANT

CHAPTER 4: COMMON DENOMINATOR

No flirting or dating apps this round. I required a break from dating to decipher a strategy before restarting. Thus, I busied myself with modeling, accepting every job offered.

Circumstances forced me to leave my rental apartment and buy my first home in a flash. Juggling everything in life costs me valuable rest.

Six months later, I would walk away from a car crash that should have taken my life.

Purpose

Because I had been given a second chance to live, I needed to know the reason for my reprieve and my continued purpose on earth.

My mindset has always been to either go big or go home. Learning to play the piano wasn't just to tick the box of having a hobby; I had to earn the highest level achievable at The Royal Schools of Music, London. To excel in academics, I had to pursue a PhD. Joining the military wasn't just a matter of; I had to become one of the few females to earn the title United States Marine. I aimed higher than just an average law enforcement agency; I sought to join the most prestigious one in the world. I consider modeling an outlet for passion, not a career. Still, I was lucky enough to be featured in Vogue magazine.

Because I had nothing left to achieve, I had been pondering my life's meaning leading up to the car crash. I didn't, however, slow down to think. I crammed my schedule, and the first chance to sleep was in the driver's seat of my car on I-95.

I was unaware of needing a wake-up call that forced me to face the repercussions of questioning my life's purpose.

Preservation of the Universe shows a task remains. The only achievement I have yet to accomplish is finding the love of my life. That has to be it!

Before the accident, my romantic failures caused me to accept my misfortune. I was doing okay, even though I never met my person. I eventually came to terms with it. My life had been fulfilling: I contributed to the world, served my country, and mentored others.

What if luck isn't the explanation? What if the timing was never right? The Universe may finally send me "my person" now. And just like other goals I have achieved, I'm sure I'll have to work for this one.

Amidst the uncertainties, this explanation felt logical until further realization. With that logical-sounding conclusion, I shifted my strategy of romantic pursuit. Instead of blaming my failure on luck, I took matters into my own hands, dissecting everything to find the root cause.

Strategy

"Why are you still single?" has to be the most common question I receive, and ironically, I couldn't comprehend it either.

Also, note that "still" always comes before "single." Society implies that there's something wrong with you if you're not partnered.

Am I too much? Or not enough?

For quite some time, that inner conflict troubled me.

To some people, owning a home, driving a nice car, and accomplishing all the goals that I have would be considered a "catch" on paper. And yet, nobody prioritized me.

Do guys feel intimidated by my success?

It might have held for certain individuals. Their inclination to see me as a decorative object or award was incomprehensible, given my logical nature. Relationships with them always ended up the same way: making me their mistress, cheating on me, or forcing me into their double lives.

If they had recognized my inner quality, they wouldn't have focused on others, correct? Is it too much to ask to be someone's number one? Their top priority? The only woman in their lives?

They left me wondering: *Why do they always end up choosing someone else? What do those women have that I'm lacking?*

Based on my track record of goal achievement, I knew I could eventually get to the bottom of it once I set it as my target.

I then reflected on my relationship patterns. My life was full of admirers. With each guy I had dated, regardless of looks, background, or how we met, the experiences remained constant.

They would always sweep me off my feet and make me feel so good at first, and I would equate that level of interest, attention, and intensity with love. Ultimately, disappointment hit because they all chose other women in the end.

Unfamiliar faces, same dynamics: a pattern I failed to recognize because I was too busy hoping the next one would be the exception.

Blame fell on luck; accountability was absent. I kept hoping for better luck next time and never imagined I would be the root cause because, on paper, I appeared desirable.

I have the total package, so maybe the next one will finally get it right or love me the way I deserve.

My younger self tried every conceivable method to manifest my person: the law of attraction, positive thinking, motivational self-talk… none of these strategies had worked.

Exes

The first guy I ever dated told me he quit his job to join an MLM company for me. It once pleased me, but I now perceive the flattery as manipulation. My decision to move to the US alone, without him, reveals how much I craved independence. It wasn't a rebellion because it had allowed me to emerge from a secluded and sheltered upbringing to see the real world. These weren't my conscious thoughts, but my body was guiding me through what I was yearning for, and I went along with it.

After moving to the US, I was soon swept up by someone who cast me as a stand-in while his girlfriend was away. I craved the attention so much that I convinced myself his raging behavior was normal, as shown by my parents, and my personality was something to be ashamed of.

Dating the older guy afterwards allowed me to gain insight into a conventional family dynamic. I'm stretching the word "normal" here because it's relative... Even a family with an alcoholic dad sharing custody of a son appeared healthier than my upbringing. At least someone inquired about the kid's preferences and offered him choices, treating him as an actual human being with his own thoughts.

I went through a period of casual dating with fellow Marines until I met the Italian guy. *That's every girl's dream!* I interpreted his early introduction of me to his family as a high level of seriousness and emotional investment in us. However, beneath all the hype and glamor lay a rug underneath my feet that would soon be pulled.

The Excel spreadsheet guy I dated after deployment never stood up for me. When the friendly couple bought our dinner as a thank-you for military service, his reaction was part of the thread that wove through many of my relationships: making me feel unseen, unheard, and unvalued even when I was right there and present.

His decision to stay with me and not return to his parents alone when they gave him the ultimatum might have seemed heroic. But I see now that it was a delay tactic: sidestepping conflict rather than confronting it. That wasn't him defending me; he just hadn't abandoned me yet. It cannot be denied that his silence, obedience to his parents, and failure to establish boundaries with them also constituted betrayal. The sting was less apparent; it stemmed from my hope, not his deeds.

I then dated two guys whose appearances and physiques were on opposite spectrums, but they each had two ex-wives and three children. Both lifted me high onto a pedestal in the beginning, only to drop me hard and fast at the end.

Those cowards had already replaced me before I could leave with dignity. They failed to perceive my worth; their ideal already occupied their thoughts before I became involved in an audition for a role I didn't intend to sign up for.

Red Flags

As I replayed all my relationships in my head, one by one, I realized I couldn't remember details about the specific moments that happened with each of them. My brain tends to erase things that cause negative feelings until I forget them.

Though unpleasant memories are hard for me to recall, I still noticed some recurring themes within my lessons. They were the same playbook under a different cover.

So I compiled a list of fifteen commonalities:

- I was more drawn to their appearance than emotional maturity in the beginning.
- They asked me many questions in the beginning.
- We shared a staggering number of things in common.
- At first, they came on strong and wouldn't give up on pursuing me; communication occupied much of my time.
- They talked a lot about themselves, especially about their sacrifices for others.
- They gave me the feeling of having butterflies in my stomach by sweeping me off my feet.
- They always talked about other people, unprovoked.
- Any refusal coming from me was unacceptable; saying no always yielded guilt.

- My request for time, not conforming to their schedule, brought guilt.
- They kept treating me like an option.
- The silent treatment was a common tactic.
- They would often reference their exes, emphasizing both their virtues and flaws, and recounting instances that pleased them. I felt compelled to be "better" than them.
- They implied or outright suggested that I should seek therapy.
- Even though I kept on pleasing them, the goalposts kept moving.
- They all left me in a state of confusion.

And … I have suppressed the rest.

My list captures not only surface behaviors but also the emotional texture of those dynamics: guilt, shifting expectations, invisibility, and the constant pressure to prove myself. To learn from my mistakes, I filed this list under the unhealthy category, labeling each bullet point as a red flag.

Awakening

The true catalyst of each instance, however, wasn't the guy. It's my longing to be wanted, chosen, and kept. They were drawn to my excellence, glow, and signal at first, but couldn't meet my depth in the end. They consumed my energy but never anchored into my truth, watched me push myself to the brink, and mistook my drive for availability.

I kept getting drawn in, not because I was weak but because I hoped someone's pursuit of me would eventually align with my ability to love with depth and loyalty. Each failure stung, but more significantly, it showed me that desire wasn't equivalent to value.

Despite it all, I kept trying since a piece of me still held faith that the subsequent attempt might finally embrace me. I wasn't wrong for hoping, but…

Let's name what I had been avoiding to in all failed relationships: I remained the only constant.

Once I saw that painful reality, it could no longer be unseen. The feeling was surreal: changing partners, hoping to end the cycle, seeing it fail again, and always being the lone presence within. And what did I do each time? I kept falling for guys with the same pattern, expecting the result would be different.

I became the textbook definition of insanity.

That's when I came to a painful but necessary awakening: luck wasn't the reason; my attraction to unhealthy patterns was. The culprit was me; I was always the one responsible.

But the good news is that it also provided me with the fortunate position of controlling the outcome, given I had the right strategy. That knowing could be the doorway to my freedom.

My relationships crumbled because the rooms I entered were incapable of embracing me, forcing me to retreat into self-reliance—in a storage room, my truck, and silence—from rage and rejection.

So I wasn't wrong in thinking that my life was spared because my story wasn't done: I had yet to experience sharing my life with "my person." I needed to understand how to choose better, instead of hoping for luck.

The person I was, relying upon desire, reward, or selection, perished with the wreckage of my car, which shifted my aim. This new version of me is here to live as if my existence doesn't require external justification: no more sacrificing sleep for the sake of conquering achievements or asking what I must do to be someone's number one.

Choosing Better

How do I choose better, though?

If I kept being sucked into unhealthy relationships, maybe I had the idea of love all wrong to begin with. Just because I made a list of red flags for identifying unhealthy partners doesn't mean I would be able to feel loved when given with sincerity.

It's hard because no one ever showed me what genuine love looked like or gave me a blueprint of healthy relationships, so I had to develop my own.

Recognizing feelings and reviewing unhealthy relationships within my experience is my best approach at this time… a decent beginning, at minimum.

My anxiety used to be a suffocating weight, far beyond simple worry. No matter the guy, I always felt unsafe when they didn't text, call, or see me. *Are they cheating on me? Did they forget about me? What's going on?*

I know now that's my body and mind reacting to patterns carved so deep they feel like survival. It signaled to me that having a roller-coaster-ride feeling in a relationship was unhealthy.

I also wondered if love was transactional; if so, my subconscious efforts to earn affection should have garnered a life partner. I thought that was me giving love and expecting the other party to reciprocate and show me their love.

The Origin

Almost every time after a heartbreak, my friends often asked if I recognized my value. I had always considered it an odd question, and my reflex would declare, "Of course, I know my worth!"

But not until after surviving my car crash did I give it some serious thought that it deserved.

If I know my worth, why would I keep running from guy to guy, trying to please each one by fitting into a role they cast me in, hoping that eventually one of them would love me?

This mismatch in timing between my body and mind highlighted my nervous system's craving for the emotional chaos I had experienced in childhood and mistaking it for love.

This profound insight was a powerful breakthrough because it gave me hope that I could finally find my person... all I needed to do was to rewire my nervous system. It's like relearning the language of love, teaching my body and heart to trust consistent care instead of unpredictable highs and lows. I framed it as the next life goal to achieve.

Disappointment followed each new guy; building trust felt like a genuine challenge; I was resolute, however. My initial task was to trust myself, believing I could select a better man in the future. I understood that avoiding familiarity was crucial, as I had to venture forward into the unknown.

CHAPTER 5: CHILDHOOD

S omehow, despite being used, yelled at, or discarded, I didn't crumble or shut down. I kept learning and growing.

This resilience mirrored what my mother told me when I was little: I insisted on surviving even though she tried to abort me when I was in her womb.

Suppression

I realized that if I wanted my nervous system to recognize and "tolerate" healthy relationship dynamics, I must first identify what familiarity looked like so I could avoid it.

This chapter is, indeed, the hardest one to write about, as I struggle to recall my childhood. I learned to suppress unpleasant memories, likely because of my body's natural coping mechanism.

Similar to my dating experience, I have forgotten many of my childhood moments, so I'll do my best to share the bits and pieces I still recall.

However, there's one thing I vividly remember about my younger years: I was never enough, and that's my core belief.

Flower

One of my oldest memories is of being interviewed for kindergarten admission. That's right. At age four, I underwent an assessment to determine my eligibility for entering an esteemed kindergarten.

My mother accompanied me inside the interview room, seated behind me, to prevent any influence upon my performance. The interviewer, a teacher, inquired whether I would select a bloom to bring home from a lovely garden. I told her "yes" without hesitation. The interviewer looked over me straight at my mother, and even though I was young, I could tell that her facial expressions said I had given the wrong answer.

We then met with my father, who was waiting outside, as she told him what had happened. They then told me I should have answered "no" because now I had lost my chance to get into that kindergarten.

Instead of thinking, *"Okay, I will from now on,"* little Megan instinctively thought, *"Why would I say no when yes is the answer?"*

Accident

Another one of my earliest memories is from around age six, when my mother told me I was an accident, in these exact words and straight to my face. She stated that before my existence, she had carried a boy but caused her miscarriage by tumbling down the stairs on purpose. According to her, her attempt to do the same to me was unsuccessful—I insisted on being born. My father was present when she shared those stories, and it was also his first time hearing them.

Since then, I would tell myself that I am the "extra person" on earth.

Offspring

I remember sitting at a table with my mother, eating breakfast at a restaurant before she dropped me off at school when I was seven. Ultimately, I inquired about her thoughts on procreation, something that had been occupying my mind: "Why do people have kids?"

She gazed at me, unshaken, but she did not possess a solid answer, as she uttered, "I guess that's what people do."

Her answer didn't give me the relief I was hoping for; even a partial reason would have helped me stop pondering that topic. Henceforth, the logic behind humankind's ceaseless habit would remain my query:

creating more individuals to accomplish their goals because previous generations had progeny before achieving theirs.

Hangers

After moving to the US, I needed to shop for supplies for my new room off campus. Intending to purchase hangers, I drove to the store. I remember walking in and strolling down the aisle where hangers were displayed. My body froze as I stared at them. That encounter became the first instance when I understood I held a longstanding fear of hangers... They served as the weapon of choice for my parents' punishments of me, especially my father, the stronger of the two. I left empty-handed because I could not overcome the trauma that the simple objects meant to hang clothes brought me. Instead, I decided to fold and arrange my clothes in stacks in my closet.

You're likely wondering, "Why would they beat you? Were you a disobedient kid?"

Honestly, I can't recall the specifics, but I doubt I was a trouble-maker if I can't remember the events that caused my parents to snatch up a specific wire hanger just to hit me with.

Though one incident from when I was ten still burns in my recollection today. My parents and I were sitting on the top deck of a double-decker. I was confused why they still hadn't hit me with a hanger that day, and it was already late afternoon. So I asked them why... and they told me to wait until we were home.

I then endured physical punishment delivered with a wire hanger after we got home, simply because I posed that question.

Number One

Growing up, I believed I needed to be the best pupil in my school so my parents would be proud of me and hence, love me. Annually, 160 students attended, and grade reports positioned us amongst our peers. I worked hard to be number one, and while I succeeded most of the time, sometimes I fell short, landing second or third. In those moments, I knew my parents wouldn't love me.

I'm not the best kid in school—why would they?

But let's be honest, even when my report card said "Ranked 1/160," they would still tell me someone else's child was better than me. I was perplexed; I didn't understand what I was missing or needed to do to improve so they would love me.

I kept hoping that maybe, just once, instead of hearing "I hate you" or "I wish you were never born," I would hear "I'm proud of you" or even "I love you."

Cake

My parents wouldn't let me eat sweets growing up. While I spotted an ice cream cake in a TV commercial that looked delectable, I knew asking for it would be futile.

I discovered it during one supermarket trip with my mother. So, I made her a deal: if I ranked number one at the end of that school year, she would reward me with that cake. To my surprise, she agreed.

But what didn't surprise me was her breaking the promise when I earned the top place in school.

Seclusion

During my upbringing, my parents isolated me. My only interactions with children my age were at school, during recess, and on the occasional phone calls they allowed me to make for homework-related topics. Outings and sleepovers were, of course, off-limits.

Communication with my parents wasn't open; they were authoritative figures, not friends. They made me feel ashamed for having crushes on boys, so it was something that I kept to myself.

How dare I prioritize boys over my studies?

A single boy-related thought, spoken or unspoken, meant a hanger-beating session from my parents.

I had no friends. Teachers noticed I didn't hang out with other kids outside of school. Every school year would end with a teacher-parent meeting, where parents convened with the teachers to collect our report cards. When I was 14, ranking in the top three out of 160 peers, my teacher told my parents that I deserved to hang out with my classmates because I had done so well in school. My parents smiled and nodded. I left that meeting thinking the situation would finally change. But as the days passed, confusion mounted about why they had already forgotten what my teacher had suggested.

Piano

When my music teacher introduced us to the piano during my first year of primary school, I was captivated by the elegance she exuded while playing and the beautiful tones of the instrument; I had wanted to learn how to play. It took three years of begging my parents to allow me to take lessons. They then kept every payment receipt, displaying them on the wall that was always in my line of sight. Binding them together was a heavy-duty clip that kept opening up wider with each new one. It's their attempt to show me their monetary investment in something that I wanted to learn.

When it came time to buy my first piano so I wouldn't have to keep commuting to my music school for practice, my parents told me they had to empty my mother's lifelong savings account to get me one. I was around 11 years old. Maybe that's why I rushed to earn the highest-level achievable at only age 14. It's unheard of for someone that young to get qualified at that level of piano performance, but I got there as soon as possible so I wouldn't waste any more of my parents' money.

Schools

I attended Christian schools during primary and secondary education, as they were the ones that provided free schooling where I grew up. And with free education sponsored by churches came mandatory Bible lessons. At age 12, I raised contradictions among Bible verses until my Bible teachers stopped answering my questions and told me that they would have to be God to know the answer.

It's an early sign that I don't just absorb or believe in anything without questioning first.

Lego

One Christmas stands out in my memory. My father's colleague knocked on our door, holding an enormous box of Battleship Lego, telling my father it was a Christmas gift for me. I didn't go to the door, but I observed from afar and overheard my father turning him away.

A few days later, my father came home with that same box of Lego and told me his colleague had insisted that I would have it. All I remember was the guilt trip my mother gave each of us afterwards.

I hurried to build that battleship, and his friend prompted me to question my prior conviction: *I never considered myself worthy. Why did he get me this gift?*

Silent Treatment

The silent treatment was the norm in my childhood. My parents would often stonewall each other, a behavior that also involved me. They would go silent for days or weeks owing to conflict or disagreement. I would then become the messenger between them to relay messages: "Tell your mom..." or "Tell your dad...."

After they hit me with a hanger, they often would ignore me also and didn't speak with me until at least a few days had passed, or after my begging on my knees for forgiveness.

I recall one morning when I was 15, my father tasked me with delivering a message to my mother during the silent treatment. I finally refused and said to him, "Tell me, are you not going to talk to each other ever again? If so, why don't you just end it right now? If you are, then what are you doing?"

His response to me was complete silence. He then waited for her to come by and started speaking.

Commute

At 16, I lost my father to stage four lung cancer. That surprised everyone who knew him: he never smoked, even competed in swimming, and tried out for the Olympics. Having him as my coach, I have become a strong swimmer since I was little.

My mother, who had never shown much affection for me until that point, instantly shifted her reliance from my father onto me, making me her surrogate spouse.

My academic success helped me get into my first school of choice, a prestigious university that many envied, including her. After learning about the acceptance, not only did she not congratulate me, but she also responded with the silent treatment. Her intimidation through guilt tripping kept me living at home with her instead of in a dorm; I had to endure a daily three-hour commute between home and school.

Business

I told my mother about my business venture—that I would open up my coffee shop. I admit it might seem too young at 23, but I wasn't stealing or doing anything illegal. Could I have predicted the lack of profit? Of course not. But do I regret that decision? No, because that experience proved crucial in shaping my current self. The lessons I learned during that time—whether it was about running a business or handling customers and logistics—taught me things about myself that I would not have known unless I went through that stage of my life exactly the way I did.

When I informed my mother about my coffee shop during the planning stage, she asked, "Why don't you just find a job like everyone else does?" By that point, not having her encouragement or support on anything I did in life was already the norm, and therefore, I proceeded without considering her words.

Eyesight

Being secluded also meant that I had no outside source to fact-check what my parents wanted me to believe.

It was not until my mid-twenties that I comprehended the body hair removal practices, including those of females. As a youth, I often puzzled over limb hairlessness, and my mother would relate that those individuals were born without body hair. I couldn't help but feel unfortunate.

I recall many hanger-beating sessions resulted from positioning my writing and reading materials off-center to the right. According to my parents, it was my fault that I had poor eyesight in my left eye because of my improper placement of stationery. I had blamed myself for my disability until an optometry visit when I was in my mid-thirties.

Without disclosing the mistake I had made in my childhood that caused my poor eyesight, the optometrist said to me, "It wasn't your fault, Megan. You were born with this condition, and that's why you unconsciously adjusted the way you read and wrote. There was nothing you could have done to 'correct' your eyesight."

Tears immediately started pouring.

How did she read my mind?

Megan in that exam chair suddenly collapsed into her five-year-old self, hearing for the first time that the guilt she had held since childhood was never hers.

Birthday

Instead of an annual celebration, my birthday had always been a yearly memorial of my mother's sacrifice in giving birth to me. No, she didn't die in labor, but that was her exact description of my birthdays growing up, instead of celebrating my growth with cakes or presents.

At some point, I outgrew that tradition. My 40th birthday marked my resolution to embrace life, having endured another year as "the extra person on earth."

I recall visiting the nearest Starbucks from my office during lunchtime to claim my birthday coffee. Busting through the door, I announced, "It's my birthday!" I witnessed many smiles and a smattering of laughter. As I waited for my order, a man in worn and dirty clothes emerged from the restroom and inquired, "Which girl claimed it's her birthday?" I identified myself to him. He handed me a dollar bill and wished me a happy birthday. He described his lack of possessions, saying that dollar bill comprised almost everything he owned.

I was overflowing with gratitude. Even a stranger celebrated my birthday with almost all that he had. I have kept that dollar bill to this day, calling it my "lucky dollar."

Quietness

My silence offered me safety, influencing my perceived quietude growing up. When I neared age three, my parents brought me to a physician because of my absence of speech... Perhaps infant Megan had already calculated her initial utterance to gain acceptance from those who gave her life.

My world had been confusing since the day I was born, or likely sooner. Without the ability to articulate, I sensed that I was unwelcome. Having grown up in environments where my emotions were ignored or punished, I had to learn that my voice would be minimized even when I spoke up. My survival instincts told me to avoid conflict, keep the peace, and not rock the boat—especially when the world was already hard enough.

Honestly, all I remember about my childhood is that I had tried different ways to be the best daughter, hoping to deserve their love, and one day they would be proud of me. Maybe when the day came that they finally loved me, they would stop hitting me with a hanger. Maybe one day, my mother wouldn't resent me for insisting on surviving even though she tried to have a miscarriage by rolling down the stairs. I had to succeed in everything they wanted me to, hoping to prove to them that even someone who was an accident would still turn out to be worthy of their love.

Without conscious awareness, I desired their approval. They had conditioned my nervous system to need it for survival. I never expected my parents would love me as I was, or just for existing by doing nothing.

My parents raised me to carry the shame that belonged to them. Love that didn't come with tests, terms, or conditions was baffling. I didn't fail them as a daughter—they failed me as my caretakers.

Mirror

My nervous system craved the sensation of emotional rollercoaster rides because my parents set me up for them growing up, and I mistook those experiences as love throughout infancy, childhood, and early adulthood, prompting my misguided search for love in adulthood.

Because I was never reflected in my childhood by people capable of showing me my worth, I looked for mirrors in the worst places as an adult: the emotionally unavailable, the already taken, and the ones with flowers and pretty words. My upbringing taught me to survive under restriction, shame, and obedience, so when someone choosing me offered even the bare minimum of attention, it could feel like a revolution, like oxygen after years underwater.

When the first guy I dated told me he had spent his life savings to join the MLM company for me, I felt part flattered, part bewildered, and part silent. Growing up, my world taught me that challenging adult choices brought penalties, importance held obligations, and influence presented peril, not strength. At that point, I was still figuring out how to be a person outside my mother's shadow. So when he turned his financial instability into my responsibility, my instinct was confusion.

I now see why I never flinched at my decision to move abroad alone. I had lived a life dictated by survival and control. So when I saw a window of opportunity to build something that was mine—not for my mother, the guy I was dating, or anyone else—I seized it with certainty. I didn't hesitate because my freedom had always been theoretical and now had a chance to materialize.

For the first time, I was choosing myself without apology or permission. Although I lacked the awareness of my motivation then, my body knew and went along with the motions.

After years of restriction, shame, silent treatments, beatings for being human, and being forced into the role of caretaker and emotional surrogate for those who were supposed to be grown-ups, I finally crossed a border physically and, more importantly, psychologically.

I departed, leaving two individuals treating my being as something they could control or exploit. I didn't look back. Although I didn't realize it, this might have been the first authentic instance of affection I experienced since my existence, not between me and someone else, but between me and myself.

That guy who circled my university campus for one week to locate me—for that brief instant, it appeared the Universe had revised the tale my parents had taught me.

Maybe I am wanted. I may be worth pursuing…

That hunger in my younger self was deeply human. After being denied affection, agency, and even basic validation from my parents, I would take that guy's attention as proof that maybe it wasn't me after all.

See! I'm lovable. Someone saw me and sought me out.

But when I pleaded for his guidance on how to drive an automatic, he didn't say, "It's okay," or that he would help me. Instead, he shouted, just like my mother would. He made me feel stupid and small in the same way my parents did, like love was conditional again.

I'm only worthy if I already have it all figured out.

That belief unfolded not because of my naivety nor my brokenness, but owing to my having been forced to learn love backwards.

Opening my coffee shop at 23 was no easy feat, but I did it anyway. If I could, I would tell my younger self that I am so proud of her: she started something from nothing—that coffee shop symbolized her willpower, independence, and refusal to play small. But it also mirrored her childhood: she was the adult before her time, carrying the full weight alone, serving others without being served in return.

The mattress in the storage space wasn't a failure; it stood as a mirror. It revealed the depth to which my survival mechanisms had formed my reality: return on investment would always be higher by putting in more effort.

If I keep going, it'll be worth it.

I strived to win the recognition and acknowledgment I had deserved from the beginning.

My experience with the guy imprisoned for hurling heavy objects at me proved to be a terrible relationship in the end. This was the violent culmination of a pattern that had been building since childhood: be chosen, be useful, endure, minimize, and survive. All he did was replace hangers with glass jars.

I will never sleep in my vehicle to wait for a guy again. I'm now looking back and asking, "Why did I stay? Why did I try so hard?"

And then there was the "Excel Spreadsheet guy," who was quantifying my worth as a line item… as if I were a cost to be balanced out.

What I have described isn't just pain—it's a haunting portrait of what happens when a child grows up unwanted and spends adulthood trying to reverse that verdict.

Beneath everything, I was drained, beyond toil. I was tired from proving my worth in a world that treated my brilliance, independence, and ambition as currency, not care.

Blueprint

And you know what? Luck wasn't to blame for all my failed relationships. I was conditioned by a childhood emotional blueprint that shaped what I sought, how I sought it, and how I felt love had to be earned. My body confused familiarity with love, drawing me to the only dynamic I knew.

I was raised and taught to be functional, impressive, or independent just by constantly striving to achieve the next goal, hoping my parents would finally see me. But those things didn't bring me love. In adulthood, they might have brought admiration, envy, and even praise. But none of those was the care I craved.

My system adapted to chaos, and anything gentler than chaos felt like love, even if it's not. That's not my fault. That's the emotional math I was taught to solve.

I recognize now that I was never clingy; I was starved and raised in an emotional desert, where affection was withheld or weaponized. So when someone showed a flicker of interest, my entire system lit up— not because I was needy, but because my survival wiring had never been met with care.

But here's the hidden heartbreak: I wasn't shown how to recognize healthy love—only how to survive without it. I wasn't yet able to tell the difference between "stable" and "just not abusive," or between "healthy" and "temporarily soothing." How could I have known the difference between love and possession, or attention and care, when my blueprint was so warped by parents who punished connection and replaced affection with obligation?

I didn't know how to vet someone's intentions, because my earliest training was about obeying, not evaluating. It embodies a complex childhood logic where fondness and hurt intertwine. I gave my loyalty to pain, not because of the craving for suffering, but because it always wore the mask of love in my narrative.

Rewiring

At last, I view my past self's desperation and clinginess as a cry for love and a plea against being exploited. Battling for love defined my entire existence before the car crash: the love that granted the right to exist, to matter, to avoid erasure, or self-punishment. It had involved a lengthy, flawed process of striving towards self-discovery following eras of being used yet remaining unseen.

Because I finally realized that I was the common denominator of all my failed relationships, I knew I was in control of my relationship outcome. That was a pivotal turning point from reaction to intention: I was evolving from surviving to choosing.

The concepts or experiences of love should have been modeled to me during my childhood, but they weren't, and that's why I had to step into the parenting role for myself, for my heart. It's difficult because I started this rewiring journey much later than ideal, but that didn't diminish the importance or the strength it took to do.

Although I could identify a few characteristics of emotionally unhealthy relationships based on my experience and label them "red flags" as a warning to stay away, I was aware I still lacked an understanding of healthy relational dynamics. I also had an insightful reflection:

> **Just as familiarity doesn't equate to healthy, the missing**
>
> **red flags also don't imply a healthy relationship.**

So I needed to learn from scratch, train, and acclimate my nervous system to recognize and become accustomed to healthy relationship behaviors that represented unconditional love: the type that I didn't have to earn.

I treated it as the next project to tackle: I started listening to podcasts and audiobooks, reading books, and absorbing knowledge of signs of healthy partnerships. After all, learning is one of my strongest suits. And the more I studied, the more eye-opening it became.

You mean being swept off my feet is not emotionally healthy? But it feels so good. That was love, right? What do they mean by "taking it slow"? How slow is "slow"? No one ever taught me that before.

One main takeaway I had was that love shouldn't be transactional: it shouldn't be a prize to be won through achievement or fixing others. This space should allow me to exist—complete and valuable, without conditions. But that shift required unlearning what I was taught and relearning how to feel safe without constant positive feedback or external validation.

I didn't just survive an accident—it symbolized a rebirth: I'm finally unbound. I wasn't confused anymore. My life was spared to finish what I hadn't: to live in unconditional love.

Ready

Having spent months studying healthy relationships, I felt ready to enact them because I understood that my growing knowledge would remain only concepts until it was put into practice. I rationalized that it would take two people to be in a relationship, and so, realistically, the involved partner would be required to partake in the "experiment."

I told myself that I had prepared well enough to recognize an emotionally unhealthy partner when one were to be presented. Also, I knew that to choose better, I needed someone "on my level." Why? Many acquaintances, believing they knew me, offered that advice. Therefore, besides the list of fifteen red flags that I had put together, I also made a list of the ten elements that my ideal partner would need to embody. It looked something like this:

- Taller than I (which wasn't easy, since I'm 5'9")
- Not a criminal or a registered sex offender

- Doesn't have kids and doesn't want kids
- Doesn't need to sign a contract, aka get married
- Good-looking
- Fit (because I am), not the bodybuilder type, but he needs to be active, whatever that means for him.
- Has an advanced college degree (doesn't have to be a PhD, but ideally at least a master's degree)
- His income exceeded mine, not because I aspired to be reliant, but because I didn't want him to be dependent on me.
- His car rivals or surpasses mine; it must be a stick shift (my love of cars and owning a nice car mean I'm not keen on riding in lesser vehicles on dates, nor do I want to always be the driver)
- Doesn't have unhealthy habits that I don't do myself, such as smoking, doing drugs, or excessive drinking.

And… that's about it.

This list captured deal breakers and personal preferences that mattered to my identity and lifestyle, reflected practical criteria, and revealed an understanding of what environment I needed to thrive with feelings and intellect.

Armed with those two lists—red flags and ideal partner—I was ready to try dating apps again. I viewed it as a solid first step in my new journey: defining clear boundaries and standards based on what I wouldn't accept and what I desired. I was no longer just hoping for luck to manifest but taking control with intention. It felt like a strategic move informed by experience rather than blind hope.

Meeting my standards was a prerequisite; I aimed to learn about others before revealing anything personal because I had learned from former partners that people can fabricate chemistry by studying my likes and dislikes. Those experiences led me to control myself, evaluating others' worthiness for my emotional space. I was committed to selecting with mental vigilance and refused to lower my standards. Drawing boundaries helped me avoid wasting time on those who didn't share my values. Seeing their soul map was necessary before I let them near my real self.

I'm not looking for someone to complete me, as I'm already the whole cake myself. However, a cherry on top would be nice, but not necessary.

PART IV: THE EXPERIMENT

CHAPTER 6: CONTROL

In this borrowed time, I was seeking an equal partner. I was committed to learning from the past, evolving standards, and   reclaiming agency.

This time around, I was armored.

Transmission

A month passed before I swiped right on five guys; interestingly, they all reciprocated. Two passed the vehicle test: one drove a Jeep, and the other, a Tesla. You're thinking Teslas aren't stick shifts; I know... I talked myself into it. I had lived in the US long enough to notice that most people here lack stick-shift driving skills.

An automatic guy? As long as it's a Tesla.

I know you must be laughing at my logic right now. It's okay... I am too. It shows how symbolic my criteria were. As a car enthusiast, I have always felt that a person's car choice goes deeper than just the mode of transportation; it reveals their energy and what they perceive to be important in life.

Interrogation

Responding to me with longer paragraphs, the Tesla guy caught my attention. I approached this possibility as a battle-tested strategist. Instead of casual conversation, I proceeded with methodical interrogation.

Despite my caution, this felt exhilarating and precarious: connecting with a reflection who might understand me, even though its endurance remained questionable. I had been burned before, so I refused to repeat the same mistake.

I first inquired about the most obvious questions: location, family, career, relationship history, whether he had kids, etc. Afterwards, I queried him regarding behavior, like his feelings towards individuals engrossed in their phones instead of those present right in front of them. He thought their actions lacked niceness.

My top priority was resolving my number one non-negotiable deal-breaker: children. I inquired whether he desired any. He told me he would let his partner decide. That response did not sit right with me, so I doubled down, conveying I possessed no offspring, desired none then nor in the future, and my decision would remain fixed.

Being the only child was our shared experience. And knowing family dynamics shape everything, I wanted transparency about his relationship with his parents. He said he had a close relationship with his mom and that the one with his dad had gotten "better." They divorced when he was two, and his maternal grandparents raised him. Inquiring about his opinion on holidays, I still remember his response: holidays were between him and his partner, and even if he were to visit his mom or dad, the company of his partner wouldn't be mandatory.

I was upfront with him by warning, "I'm someone who calls out bullshit as I see it. If you have a problem with that, it won't work."

That made up my boundary.

He highlighted a point I support: "individuals should be whole before entering into a partnership." A guy verbalizing my philosophy, unprompted, which was music to my ear.

Potential

I asked him to rank his ways of receiving love. He preferred using quality time and physical touch.

How does he know that these are my preferences, too?

He then confessed he saw a therapist regularly, which started a few months prior, when he had to process the grief of losing his maternal grandma and his ex's announcement of divorcing him on the same day.

I value individuals who prioritize mental health; seeking therapy shows this, so his openness about this made an impression on me, which scored him bonus points. It amazed me how much his insights resonated before I opened up to him.

The fact that we had the same preferences in ways of receiving love and that he was attending therapy and talked about achieving wholeness before partnership—these weren't just points on a checklist for me. They were signs he was in a similar mental space, maybe even the partner who could meet my level.

Before the car crash, I had learned that:

Being alone beats feeling lonely in a relationship.

Given one more chance to live made connections feel high-stakes. So I gave him one final question that would determine whether I would continue conversing with him: "Convince me with one logical reason I should open my life up to include another person."

He conveyed that my potential had limits being alone. By joining forces with the "male version of me," we could achieve a higher potential, something neither of us could reach on our own.

That insight enlightened me because of my desire for a partner who would contribute equally to construct something grander.

I had been carrying the weight of being on borrowed time, which shaped my perspective of everything, including love. Settling for less than the truth was never my aim, even in solitude. I was fierce in what I allowed to touch my life.

September 27

Finally, when I had exhausted my meticulously prepared questions, I circled back to the information that he had provided on his profile: his zodiac sign and birthday. Seeing that he said he was a Libra, I asked him when his birthday was.

He said, "September 27."

"No way, you're lying," I said. That answer floored me.

He then fell silent for about two hours, the first such instance since we started chatting. It felt like more than a casual glitch, but I couldn't pinpoint its significance then. He then apologized and said he was at the hotel gym, claiming working out for hours was a daily ritual of his.

He then sent a photo of his passport card proving his birthday and asked me when mine was.

"September 27," I said.

"Fate!!! Lol," he exclaimed.

I had an obsession with birthdays that started in my early 20s. Watching an interview of Taylor Swift… she was talking about how accurate she found the Book of Birthdays to be. I searched for it on my next bookstore visit, eager to see my page. Turned out, it described me to a T.

That book came home with me, and since then, whenever I met someone new, I would first ask for their birthdates and consult that book before getting to know them. Though appearing childish, my obsession became a ritual, a tool I used to decipher emotional data before engaging.

It hit me hard: sharing that rare synchronicity felt like validation. It's an undeniable sign that I was still worthy of a connection that felt alive. I still remember how I felt when my guarded self allowed a crack for something worthy to shine through.

He's my person! I'm lucky, finally! Crossing paths with him was destiny! That's the reason I'm on borrowed time!

I expressed gratitude to the Universe for letting me walk away from the car accident unharmed to experience the rare gift I hadn't yet had—a real-life love story.

Tempo

He ended our conversation that night by providing his cell number and informing me of his departure flight time the next morning. He was a commuter, splitting time between my city and his. I texted to wish him safe travels the next day when he was at the airport. He told me he could still change his flight to stay in town. That reply appeared... odd. I was uncertain about it then, as our communication had just started.

What's the rush?

I don't believe I addressed his comment because I was still assessing the situation.

Since then, we had constantly exchanged texts, discussing various topics. He once called without warning, letting us hear each other's voices for the first time. The more we chatted, the more I realized how magically similar we were. I labeled him the "male version of me," which I had thought never existed, let alone meeting one.

That kind of rare mirroring might have softened my skepticism, but I still noticed details that made me cautious.

He claimed LinkedIn to be his only social media presence, so we connected there. I noted his frequent job changes of not staying with the same company for longer than two years, at age 36. Yet I reserved judgment.

There must be a cause. In time, either he'll tell me, or I'll find out.

I noticed the minor details others might miss. But I didn't see them as red flags... not yet. All I did was to catalogue them... in case I had to weigh them when the time came.

Baggage Claim

He was returning one week later for work, so we scheduled our first date. By that point, I had already felt a deep but strange familiarity, as if I had known him forever, and my mind had already labeled him my soulmate. Despite my caution, this felt exhilarating and precarious:

connecting with a reflection who might understand me, even though its endurance remained questionable.

Returning home late from a runway job at night, I took a quick nap before heading to the airport to surprise him when he was due to land at 5 am.

Upon arrival, I phoned him to inquire about his location. He told me he had just landed, but when I pressed on where in the airport he was, he responded, "You're here?" before we got disconnected.

I redialed, but nobody picked up.

That's strange.

Another attempt yielded nothing.

I eventually walked to baggage claim, and there he was, waiting for his bag. He saw me approaching from afar. I walked up to him and gave him a long hug. That moment of connection was like me reaching for possibility even amidst all the uncertainties. He released me after a while and took my hand instead.

Soulmates

I went with him to his car rental pickup and hotel check-in. He pulled out a Starbucks destination tumbler and handed it to me. That gesture surprised me, for I didn't grasp its importance. I had frequented many Starbucks geographically but never felt compelled to possess a tumbler from that particular location. (But espresso mugs? Yes!)

Nonetheless, I smiled and accepted it, stating, "You didn't have to."

He mentioned a brief visit for business and didn't want me to think I was forgotten. It seemed like he enjoyed using gifts to express care, which wasn't how I received love, as we had discussed previously.

Maybe he forgot.

In his hotel room, we shared our first kiss following his shower.

"Argh, we had our first kiss here, which means we gotta come back to this hotel on this day every year and kiss," he said. "I'm sentimental like this."

A smile was my only response because I was speechless... I told myself that I had to get used to dating someone so romantic.

We then spent the entire day together. First, we went on a scenic drive in my convertible. Our stops along the way were for capturing photos of the scenery, framed by our hands forming heart shapes.

We then visited an annual street fair near my place. As we were walking, I looked over at him and thought, *"This is my person; how did I get so lucky?"*

I was once reaching for my phone and realized that it wasn't with me. I wasn't sure whether I had lost it or just left it at home, but he said he would buy me a new one if it was the former. Hearing that offer, my emotions became mixed with confusion and flattery. Confused, because he would spend a thousand dollars on me already; flattered, because finally I experienced what it felt like to be with my person—things were floating with ease.

That week, we spent time daily after work—dinner and movies—and eventually, I invited him to my home. His bedroom performance felt theatrical; his focus seemed less on the act itself and more on using words to enthrall me. But doubts didn't linger, as I wouldn't let them.

I met my person — the male version of me — after all.

One week passed. Indeed, it was the best week of my life. Everything seemed to be so effortless.

We had to part ways—he had to fly back home while I had a runway job to attend. That separation pained me; I still remember how my tears wouldn't stop pouring. It had been a long time since I had sobbed; it's not pretty. I even had problems breathing—it was a raw exposure of how much I let myself feel despite all the armor.

As soon as I was driving away, he called and spoke with me throughout my two-hour drive to my destination, comforting me that he would return in a week. Finding consolation in his voice, I finally stopped crying.

I have always valued emotional precision over comfort. So, I did my best to prevent myself from wasting time on surface-level fluff. Knowing what I wouldn't tolerate, I tried to guard my boundaries. I craved a partner who mirrored my depth and allowed that craving to overpower the glimpses of moments that I should have questioned.

Checklist

During his plane ride, he texted me a screenshot of an ideal partner checklist titled "My Partner: What I'm looking for" and said he thought it would be interesting for me to read. Interesting was an understatement... It was unbelievable. The timestamp on that note was about six months before we met, yet every bullet point described me to a T. That's not just a coincidence; it's almost uncanny. I accepted that fate had decided it.

However, I did not identify with one bullet point: "Disney or Disney Parks lover." Growing up not exposed to typical things children usually experience, I had never grasped Disney. Of course, I had heard of it and had explored many Disney Parks worldwide.

I recognized that reality isn't flawless; even in something almost scripted for me, I noted that deviation because I value truth. I didn't buy the "perfect match" story boundlessly.

This shows a pattern I was developing, looking for love after being given a second chance to live: I started noticing minor details and testing ideas against reality; I made sure not to settle for narratives—even those that felt like destiny. I constantly held the tension between wanting something miraculous to be real and aligned with who I was.

The following week without him was the longest week it had ever been. Our connection blazed into near-constant contact via texts and phone calls, where he opened and ended my daily communication. We yearned for our reunion, this time in Canada.

He even suggested that we share GPS locations on our phones because he wanted to ensure my safety.

That's very thoughtful of him! How can I refuse such clear care?

Canada

Have I mentioned that I'm well-traveled within my country and abroad? Often alone because I'm uninterested in waiting for others' availability to live my life. Before meeting him, I had booked two international trips: Canada and Europe, both for modeling jobs. He tagged along, especially because he had never set foot in Europe. He shared that he had planned to go until his former partner canceled. I blurted out, "Why didn't you go alone if it's already paid for?" He didn't answer me. That silence alone created a sharp contrast between us. His lack of response confirmed that I had exposed him as having a passive streak, a dependency on others' momentum to decide for himself.

He entered my domain, riding in one that had already been designed before him, seeing me in action on the runway in Canada. The power dynamic was already skewed. I was the architect; he was the visitor.

Blind Spot

Unrelated to our surroundings in Canada, the topic of his therapy sessions surfaced again. I welcomed it because I gravitate towards conversing about deeper aspects—that's how I have always been, and it has become instinctive. He told me he went to therapy alone, as his mom refused to join him because of her pride.

This was a red flag I had overlooked: he pathologized others while presenting himself as superior. Although I seek to understand things on a deeper level, I don't pry into others' personal lives because I have never been nosy enough to. I operate on the assumption that individuals share when they feel at ease, without prompting.

He expressed that he didn't understand why she kept asking him for gifts, like an iPad, but she never used them and kept asking for more. It seemed like he was sharing a lot with me, but he didn't offer depth. Instead, he gave me scattered fragments of complaints, but my surgical insight still pierced through the noise to reach the psychological root.

I shared that the material objects were not the point; it's about his action of gifting itself on her cue… It's all about control. He met my response with complete silence, which meant either he hadn't considered it that way, or he had, and my naming it made it too real. I might have confronted the limit of his emotional insight and maybe even his tolerance of mine because it created tension that stripped away his ability to curate… He was uncomfortable being seen.

In hindsight, this was a pivotal juncture in our evolving relationship: I had emotional precision; he had fragments but receded when I brought sharp focus.

Home Base

A week later, it's his week to be in town for work again. He skipped hotel reservations this time. His choice of staying at my place seemed intimate on the surface but displayed his integration into my existence. Though I allowed it, my rituals remained: weekly ballet, pole dancing, and handstand practice. They were nonnegotiable. I didn't realize it then, but that alone reinforced who held the ground in that dynamic: me.

That week, he brought up a brilliant idea: why wouldn't he make my city his home base since he divided his time fifty-fifty anyway? It sounded logical, but my instinct detected the mismatch: it changed nothing in practice because his job still demanded equal time in both places.

What's the point of pushing this?

I pondered his suggestion, noting that he could make independent decisions about his life.

He started mentioning that idea more often, cloaking it in romantic terms: strengthening our bond. But it's vague, loaded with emotions, and framed in intimacy. Though I couldn't name it then, my body sensed that his suggestion was emotional dependency masquerading as romance.

At long last, I inquired about his decision. At first, he resisted answering, but then faltered and framed the matter using practicality.

"You possessed a home with space, so why not?" He reasoned.

I didn't like that he failed to account for my internal foundation: I had lived alone. Owning my home after renting for so many years gave me an unexpected sense of contentment because it's like I had built my independence brick by brick.

My home wasn't just my hard-earned property—it was the proof of my autonomy. Letting someone else in, even him, meant surrendering part of what made me feel clearest in myself. That clarity revealed the strength of my internal compass, even when every external marker looked like love.

Having held my ground, I refused him with no leniency. That was new: it's the first time I held my stance since we had met, and he slammed into an unyielding wall.

Europe

The following month, we went to London and Milan, marking his first time visiting Europe. He wasn't just accompanying me on vacation; he was exposed to my world. I was walking in runway shows; he was watching me operate in my craft.

He was exploring alone all day in London while I was backstage getting ready for the show. Meeting up with him afterwards, I could sense the annoyance he was carrying. I inquired whether anything was bothering him. That innocent question was met with rage about his feet hurting.

"Do you have any idea how long I had to be standing to watch you?" He fumed.

Didn't we talk about how alike we are regarding physical endurance?

I was taken aback by his irritation. It cracked the illusion of sameness; I had seen him as my twin flame. I bet that exhaustion played zero role. Rather, the issue originated from entitlement alongside irritability, exhibited by someone expecting the experience to center on him.

This wasn't the behavior of someone synced with me, yet I didn't allow the doubt to linger. Instead, I employed my usual strategy, redirecting the attention back to his discomfort, offering consolation by telling him I was sorry to have put him through it and remarking that those shoes perhaps weren't intended for extended walking or standing.

Earrings

We then went to Milan, stopping in Brussels for two nights. No one was there to check us into the hotel I had booked when we arrived, so we were forced to find somewhere else to stay until the next day. We each hunted for vacancies on our phones, and I was discouraged by the unaffordable last-minute options.

"I secured a five-star hotel down the street," he declared suddenly, "and I don't want to hear any complaints about the cost."

I had no prior experience dating someone wealthy; therefore, I reminded myself not to question the cost.

It's his money after all.

In Milan, he again explored alone before my show. This time, his approach shifted: no rage... Perhaps he had learned his lesson. Instead, he gave me another birthday present, although he had already gotten me one before we left for the trip. He got me earrings, which aligned with my secret obsession that he knew about.

I also noticed that he had on a new pair of shoes from the same fashion house. I pointed them out, and he said the store happened to have his size while looking for my earrings. He emphasized buying my birthday present, not his shoes, as the primary reason for walking a lengthy distance there. Regardless of his primary intention, I would still have cherished his generosity.

My earrings were a surprise, though not random; they were a targeted generosity. That framing often signals impression manage-ment: he aspired to be seen as selfless, even while being self-serving. That oddness didn't go unnoticed; it revealed that I was operating on multiple channels: one still took part in the relationship as it appeared, and the more incisive one registered the minor fractures between image and substance.

This Euro trip exposed that he didn't know how to witness me in my element without folding himself into the spotlight. Irritation in London and calculated generosity in Belgium and Milan: all returned to him. I saw everything but hadn't yet decided what it all meant. I didn't name them red flags because my former self gave him the benefit of the doubt. Though my clarity never left, I noticed and filed it.

Walt Disney

Turns out he was a huge Disney fan. When I say huge, I'm referring to the fact that he would speak Disney quotes to me. He sent me the song "I See The Light" from a Disney movie, saying it reminded him of us.

Unfamiliar with the song, I researched its lyrics: they framed me as the one who clarified his world. I wept... he knew how to make mean-ing feel sacred. And I, having lived my life alone on my own terms, had long been immune to superficial gestures.

But this was composed with precision. It disarmed even me. He chose that song to curate a vision, as if he cast me in resolving his disorientation. The rawness of my tears showed how effectively the performance worked.

A few months before we met, he had already bought two tickets to the Halloween special event at Disney California because he had hoped to meet his person before his birthday.

I'm not a Disney person, so he checked whether I desired a Disneyland visit for my birthday celebration. Ironically, what I wanted to do on my birthday was to honor his dream; I let myself be pulled into his sacred place. To allow for a compromise, I stepped out of my frame.

If I can go to Disneyland for free to fulfill his dream, although I'm not a huge fan, why not?

I wasn't just someone he liked—I was cast as the answer to a long-held hope. This moved the narrative into mythic territory: I was destined for you, and you showed up.

He called it "fate." That "fate" in his narrative, however, was something he constructed. He retrofitted past actions into a destiny arc. It provoked feelings, though it lacked truth.

I didn't believe in fantasy for fantasy's sake—but when the story seemed to align, I opened my heart. I offered myself with full clarity, which made it beautiful—and costly—because an imbalance existed within the flawless scene. I sensed that discrepancy, but I let myself believe, because the belief itself was healing for a moment.

That's how we spent our birthdays that year. He said spending his birthday in his favorite place on earth, with his person, was the fairy tale he was hoping for, and perhaps mine too, because I had met my person.

This trip marked an illusion of fate wrapped in his childhood nostalgia and romantic scripting. Disneyland was an identity for him. Bringing me there—especially on our shared birthday—was the ultimate convergence of fantasy and reality. He got to live the story he had always wanted, with a co-star who matched his birthdate.

That may have felt harmonious, but looking back, the asymmetry was clear: I brought structure, while he brought enchantment that required sustained effort rather than intrinsic nature throughout the progression.

Canceled Flight

Despite knowing him for only two months, he felt like a lifelong friend. His presence felt familiar, and that familiarity lulled my defenses by inching forward as if my instincts were allowing room for possibility. Perhaps that's why I warmed to his idea of moving in, so we chose a few days on our calendar for me to fly to him and road trip back with his belongings to my place. I could not pinpoint it then, but it's clear now: I relented because a semblance of emotional security held just long enough to seem deserving.

He wanted me to meet his mom and grandpa before he moved away, but I had the emotional foresight to oppose that idea. The romanticism of introductions before leaving didn't appeal to me. I imagined what that moment would feel like for his mom, what it symbolized. I asked him to put himself in her shoes to think about how he would feel meeting the woman who was taking her son away.

He didn't push back on my refusal, and the flight change resulting from the airline's issues also nullified that idea, so I had to snatch a ticket with another airline to fly to the closest airport. He promised reimbursement for flight substitution, yet it has not occurred.

Relocation

I was meeting him at a parking lot where his stuffed Tesla was, with all the belongings that he couldn't live without—Disney clothes dominated. His wardrobe revealed he hadn't matured: that external identity fused with a childhood brand stood out in contrast because I'm self-built; I had done the hard work of individuation.

We bought his grandpa a jersey of the local football team, a ritual he said he had, which reminded me of the Starbucks tumbler gifting gesture he had done for me months earlier.

He also started referring to his car as "our Tesla" without prompting, which felt like a subtle boundary overreach. I was still deliberating, but he was already collapsing the distinction between mine and ours. He gave me one of his keys and later installed the app on my phone so that I could use keyless entry. He insisted I would drive his car whenever he wasn't using it because, he claimed, it's safer than my convertible, and he could ensure my safety when he monitored my movements on his phone. I read it as attentiveness, influenced by my near-death driving fatigue not long ago.

Why didn't I see it as surveillance dressed as protection and disguised as care? I don't know.

That drive consumed the entire day. It was past 9 pm when we arrived back at my place, right before a workday... my workday. His work-from-home situation meant he did not need to wake up early and dress for a commute the next morning.

I can't help him unload the next day.

Therefore, I insisted on unpacking that night so he wouldn't need to do it alone. His annoyance met my offer, a crack he didn't mask. But I didn't confront him either; I ignored both his facial expression and my feelings. Back then, I prioritized harmony, even if it meant suppressing my feelings.

I went to work the following morning; it's an unfamiliar feeling to leave my home while someone else remained inside because I had never shared my sovereign space. I had always built my world to orbit me; allowing someone into that orbit marked a monumental shift.

Though I did not phone him hourly to ask what he was doing. Unlike my ex, who did that to me, I didn't feel the need to micromanage.

Integration

My life had been built on discipline. I let him in because he seemed to be aligned, intentional, and rare, perhaps. I adapted to our new life, no longer just me, but also with the "male version of me."

The first shift was external: my space began to absorb someone else's things. My busy schedule caused me to spend at least a month reorganizing my home to assimilate his belongings because, instead of helping, he let organizing become my task.

Without an obvious reason, his temper worsened, blaming the unease of settling in a different city and residence. I blamed his irritation on the unwelcoming working-from-home environment I had created for him.

But he assured me by saying, "Home is where you are."

That line was romantic yet manipulative because it glossed over my pacing. My former self failed to see his shortcut to emotional entitlement. He was turning his discomfort into my emotional burden and his disorganization into my responsibility, and when I didn't move fast enough, he became irritable.

The second shift was internal: he demanded closeness as if it were the metric for love. He emphasized the desire for maximum time together outside of work commitments. With that expectation, I felt my brain and practical routines readjust as I integrated a long-term life partner, when I had been pursuing my own thing, having no one else accountable for me in my former life.

He needed to be everywhere. I would inform him about my work schedule, weekly workout sessions, and upcoming modeling jobs so he would accompany me. What he framed as devotion became low-grade surveillance.

He drove me to my pole dancing class and waited for me outside. He would do the same to my handstand practice until my coach invited him in to do a tandem lesson. Outside my ballet school, he would wait. He came with me to my runway shows or photoshoots and took on the "Instagram boyfriend" responsibilities of capturing content.

His way of framing his support by inserting himself into every corner of my routine made it difficult to push back without sounding ungrateful. But it's symptomatic—an encroachment cloaked in availability. What he was doing was saturating my field under the guise of love. I was still handling the weight of my high-functioning life. Meanwhile, he provided proximity as proof of devotion. He believed that being near me was the same as being compatible with me. I had lived a life of sovereignty, and this guy blurred the distinction between my space and his control.

The third shift was financial. The kitchen remained unusable until it received the assembly of the kitchenware he had brought, so we dined out every evening. It's his idea because money was not an issue... he always reminded me he had plenty. But dining out broke my happy hour ritual.

Why spend extra for the identical item when you can pay less?

He expressed annoyance the moment I chose cheaper items on the menu. Now I realize that it revealed that his generosity was performative. You see, he didn't want a partner who was wise about money; he wanted someone who would spend his way and mirror his consumption as proof of compatibility. My frugality became an irritant to him because it reminded him I didn't need him.

These shifts unveiled the version of him that courted me with thoughtfulness to be a projection. The need for structure arose upon our return to reality; his unraveling stemmed from my adult existence failing to meet his desires.

Cohabitation

He didn't just enter my life; he displaced me from it, bit by bit, always occurring under the claim of support and framed as love. When I hesitated, he would offer little, passive-aggressive cues suggesting I was mistaken. He wanted me to mirror his image of abundance, splurging because he equated compatibility with conformity. I had to match his idea of "us." So, I would adjust, piece by piece, and chip away at the structures that had kept me whole. Whenever I questioned the imbalance, he would offer just enough narrative of "us" as sentiment to pull me back from my clarity. He didn't care about my joy. It's about control, just like his mom.

I thought I was creating a life with the "male version of me," but in fact, I had invited someone into my life who wanted access to my independent creations without the desire to calibrate. My intuition processed everything before my awareness was able to label it.

Straw

It's finally time for me to enter the world that made him: his family home, where his mom and 100-year-old grandpa still lived. He would fly there to spend Thanksgiving Day with them, and I would join them on Black Friday and the weekend that followed.

Are you tracking the contradiction? He had told me holidays were for him and his partner. But when it came time to enact that belief, he reverted. Or, perhaps, he was playing with technicality. I didn't join them on Thanksgiving day, nor did he force me to.

This is an isolated incident, right? If this is the real deal, there's going to be time for him to prove to me he's a "man of his word."

That was me thinking ahead while he performed moment by moment. I gave him the benefit of the doubt. Though he made principled declarations in the abstract, he defaulted to comfort zones when tested in reality. I rationalized that discrepancy away because I was still seeing this through the lens of long-term clarity.

He picked me up from the airport in his mom's car, which he had bought for her. I requested a straw for the beverage I had gotten, anticipating nothing. To my surprise, he gestured towards the glove compartment.

"That's the only thing you have in common with my mom—collecting straws," he stated.

His innocent comments revealed his mom was embedded. He referred to her quirks compared to mine. And what did he choose? A peculiar triviality: collecting straws. He inserted me into a frame that belonged to her. Perhaps without realizing it, he had to ensure that I wouldn't take her place.

He booked a hotel room for us because, he claimed, her mom's house lacked space. At the time, it didn't cross my consciousness that the hotel was vital for his mental barrier between the two female roles: the caretaker and the romantic interest. Keeping me out of the house could have been how he maintained the hierarchy. He portrayed it as if it were for me.

As usual, everything was for me.

But me? The one who survived the Marine Corps—comfort isn't one of my necessities.

I never requested a hotel. And yet he insisted on it. Why? Money was never an issue, remember? He needed the optics of generosity while managing a deeper truth he couldn't articulate: he couldn't integrate his mom and me in the same space. That's the real story here. He was constructing a dual-track reality: one where I received curated treatment, and one where his pre-existing loyalties remained unchallenged. He had performed from the start, masking who he was, and I was already beginning to feel the gap.

Hoarding

A female and an elderly male greeted us upon arrival at their residence. I sat near the front door; the sofa offered the only unoccupied spot amongst the clutter. Somebody must have cleared a path so I could reach the restroom. His bed overflowed, forcing him to clear a space big enough for his body to rest on. Then, I understood his hotel booking.

Oh, right! Disney! It made so much sense now about his Disney obsession. From the instant I walked inside, that place presented itself as a Disney museum. That home did not facilitate adult life; it was a shrine to nostalgia, specifically to his childhood and her need to preserve it. A 37-year-old's unwavering obsession still puzzled me.

I helped clear items off the floor, preventing Grandpa's stumble during his journey towards the bathroom.

Poor Grandpa has to maneuver in his wheelchair around these objects at his age. What happens when I'm not here?

All the clutter reflected that emotional chaos had never been confronted. The very space where he was raised had never evolved, and neither had he. Despite his curated adult identity, the emotional center of his upbringing remained unchanged. That's why his obsession with Disney was more regressive than quirky. It's a refusal to outgrow the comfort narrative handed to him by his environment: fantasy over function, decoration over depth.

My comfort wasn't the only purpose of the hotel, to be frank. It's also a preservation of his illusion: he couldn't bring me into his life without confronting what shaped him. Objects took up space where intimacy should have lived. That house symbolized the woman who kept him stagnant, and I represented the primary threat to that gravity.

Intrusion

We would get takeout from an expensive restaurant that his mom wanted to try.

Ah, I see. Even his mom knows that money isn't an issue for him.

They asked me about my favorite movies. The truth is, I'm not into movies. I value my two hours—I have more productive activities. His mom then asked about our home viewing selection on TV, believing we did nothing else. Interesting assumption indeed.

They seemed to be interested in listening to my Marine Corps stories, though… I suppose because his grandpa was a WWII veteran. Otherwise, my time there comprised staring at a TV screen that was playing movies, or more precisely, Disney movies.

His mom took one golden opportunity while he was in the bathroom to say to me, "If I were you, I wouldn't have come." That was the real matriarchal verdict: I did not belong. She was telling me I was an intrusion. I represented the forward motion—everything that their dynamic couldn't metabolize.

Their environment clashed with my presence—a female veteran who forged her existence and chose structure. My visit was a collision of systems: mine, which ran on intentionality and efficiency, versus theirs, which ran on sentimentality and clutter. I didn't visit just his childhood home; I visited the emotional origin of his limitations. It saw me—and rejected me.

He didn't let us linger in his childhood home—he sensed my discomfort… but he would never explore it with me. That's telling: he wasn't interested in resolution but in maintaining his dual-system existence.

Centurion

We stopped in an airport lounge on our way back home. He recounted something he had shared before: I could use an add-on card for entry devoid of traveling alongside him. I never requested it, but he kept dangling it as a symbol of status. It means his offer was a script he needed to perform, with me being the audience.

His repeated, unsolicited offers frustrated my logic, prompting me to ask why he kept offering words instead of actions. He was crafting himself into the thoughtful, giving partner, while my innocent question triggered his frustration because it punctured the illusion.

He ordered me an add-on card on the mobile app right then and there. His defensive response was about protecting the image he was curating: he was a guy who took care of his partner with shared luxury. That's transactional posturing and has nothing to do with love.

My astute awareness detected the inconsistency: he presented something that conferred heroism until I revealed the disparity between speech and deed. Before my mind had this deeper insight, my body was already asking for congruence and holding him to his own standard without fanfare. People who live in curated versions of themselves don't react well when asked to align their narratives with reality. He needed me to be impressed, but I didn't play along.

Christmas

We would spend time with his mom and grandpa again over Christmas. He planned to fly there ahead of me to decorate. I would then show up again, repeating the same logistics we had for Thanksgiving.

Gifts awaited unwrapping, including some for me. Many bore labels showing the gifters as his mom, even his grandpa, who was incapable of shopping. I opened up the first one from her, thanked her, and hugged her. Unpacking more gifts revealed that their labels were being misattributed to them.

It's his generosity, not theirs.

I brushed my odd feelings aside, thinking he was making up for his mom's rejection of me during Thanksgiving. He attempted to manufacture the illusion of family acceptance for me, much like the way someone would curate a social media post. He created a feeling he wanted me to have: you are loved and welcomed by my family. You're one of us.

Rather than allowing me to forge a connection with his mom and grandpa, a process that would require mutual effort, he fabricated one, which was brutal despite its generous appearance. He saw that there was no closeness between us because we had nothing in common—a narrative that didn't suit his fantasy—so he rewrote it by filling in emotional gaps with artifice. He needed the optics of family cohesion more than the reality of it, and I was being used to completing that image, both his and mine. His self-serving motive robbed me of my reality: I was the only one on the stage who didn't know I was in a play of a scene where he appeared like a doting son and thoughtful partner, where he planted false origin stories on gifts. I gave genuine hugs to fake connections with people who appeared to be thrilled to have me as a new addition to their family.

I felt two things at once: gratitude, since my parents never offered presents, and disorientation, because it mimicked closeness while bypassing truth.

Debt

One night, he exploded with anger about the time it took me to integrate his belongings into the kitchen, asking if I knew how much money he had been spending on our restaurant dining. I was confused because of all his early declarations that money wasn't an issue. After apologizing, I explained to him that I was unaware of his distress. I let him know I wish he had said something sooner so that I could sense the urgency to put the kitchen together.

He then added that he had just paid off a chunk of his credit card debt that he had been reluctant to: the extravagant wedding ceremony with his ex. He claimed that made him examine his spending and realize how much we had spent on eating out.

Irritation built from a pressure he hadn't disclosed. Then he shifted the burden of his unspoken resentment onto me, pretending his frustration was logistical when it was emotional.

That's another red flag I had missed: he withheld the real score and then punished me for not guessing it. He presented himself as a generous partner who wanted to care for me, but with the daily realities of sustained intimacy, he seemed to unravel. He professed readiness for a home, but in actuality, he was enamored with domesticity's presentation more than its obligations.

Cooking

As the fixer that I was, I then ensured we cooked at home during the week and dined out only on weekends.

He boasted, "My cooking is the best perk of dating me, which you have yet to experience."

His comment left me perplexed because of his choice of words: "dating." I had opened my home to him—after he insisted—and yet he referred to our relationship as "dating," as if my act of profound trust was casual. It felt strange to me because he still saw himself as trying to win me over, rather than build something reciprocal.

Because he insisted, I allowed him to impress me with his cooking. He, in fact, remained home often, claiming executive job flexibility equaled freedom. I cannot tell you what kind of legitimate work he performed because I witnessed plenty of teleconferences that looked more like chit-chatting than productivity.

Oh, right! I can't forget that he also said he spent two hours at the gym daily!

But this vital daily practice never manifested itself in action... at least, not in front of me.

I was surrounded by inconsistencies, patterns that didn't match his narratives. He spoke of success, though the proof offered minimal substance. Despite that, I took responsibility like I always did. I shifted my routines, rearranged my home, managed shared meals, and gave him space to lead where he said he would. He treated it like a stage rather than honoring it as a sacred act.

He continued his monthly visits to Mom and Grandpa while my nervous system chose other pursuits—anything but a shallow simulation of connection in a Disney-cluttered home. What I saw but couldn't yet name was the widening split: My body chose alignment with my actions without justification; he chose escape, cloaked in familial duty.

Tag

I noticed that the tag was expiring on his car soon and presumed he had forgotten. Knowing I was in a car with an expired tag went against my internal code, and I didn't want him to commit any illegal acts, not even a traffic violation. I also refused to manage his basic adult tasks because caring for a grown man is never my role. When I brought up my concern, he got irritated with me and told me he would never get pulled over. He reminded me that, unlike me, he wasn't working in law enforcement, so obeying the law wasn't his top priority.

After his tag expired, I had to plan a fun day trip to a driving range, embedding an auto-tag service appointment so it would be more appealing for him to take part in. Without my intervention, he might have continued neglecting the expired tag indefinitely. This minor episode encapsulated the larger pattern of his resistance to adult responsibility and my role as the one who had to anchor reality, even when I didn't want to.

It's a fundamental mismatch in values: my striving for order against his asserting autonomy in a way that relied on me to hold the system in place. He leaned into convenience and risk, while I held to rules and consequences. I failed to recognize then that I had taken on the "mothering" role even though I resisted it.

Cloak

He used to have an annual pass to Disneyland until he moved in with me; we started contemplating the idea of getting our annual passes to Disney World.

But have you noticed my penny-pinching nature? I wasn't willing to leap into expensive commitments without careful consideration; I proposed that we would explore other parks in the area before committing to the costlier passes. I often navigate decisions with a sense of equity.

We then visited Orlando... never would I have expected to like Universal so much; I even got myself a Gryffindor cloak embroidered with my name, "Dr. Megan." That meant I was committed to revisiting the parks, more precisely, the Wizarding World of Harry Potter.

So, I upgraded our three-day tickets to annual passes. Yes, I did... because remember? He liked Disney, not Universal, and he was going to get us the more expensive Disney passes. So, I thought it was only a fair gesture on my part to upgrade our Universal ones. That was me balancing the relationship's give-and-take on my terms. I accepted his plan and made a parallel gesture, showing that I expected mutual investment.

He gave me his word: he would never be the one who said "no" when I put our Universal trips on the calendar. I took it at face value with my self-reliant nature. Rather than waiting for his follow-through, I exercised my strategic planning, turning his verbal offer into a concrete plan and scheduling monthly Universal trips in advance for the six months that followed.

New Normalcy

Three months since he moved in, a routine had set in. It looked like we had created a structure. He worked from home during the week, which mainly consisted of showing up for virtual meetings.

My work, however, took me away from home. I exercised each evening; thus, upon arrival home, cooking would prove impossible. Without him, I would have prepared meals for the week on the weekend, like I used to do.

His work-from-home setup allowed him a flexibility that looked like contribution—preparing dinner before I arrived home, for instance—but this gesture, though thoughtful on the surface, carried an implicit imbalance. He then frequented his local office more often, although the nature of his job was remote. He informed me of a new hire requiring hands-on training. His explanation was validated through GPS data, yet I couldn't comprehend his activity when unobserved, solely based on the location of his phone.

While incorporating him into my life, I kept my routines without disruption. My discipline showed my internal steadiness. Learning from my failed relationships before the car crash, I carried a kind of high-functioning solitude within this relationship.

I can let someone in, but only if they don't interfere with my rhythm.

What resembled harmony on the outside was a hidden partition that revealed asymmetries in effort. I lived forward; he hovered between; I was committed; he was adjacent.

Enmeshment

Our weekends continued to reflect my initiative: whether Universal trips or modeling gigs, they were set by my calendar. If nothing was pre-planned, he would fly back to stay with his mom and grandpa. He split his time between two worlds—my home and his childhood one, following either my lead or his mom's, planting his roots in both places. It clarified that, despite living together, he did not share an existence with me. It showed that his emotional migration hadn't kept up with the physical one. His monthly returns to his family of origin blurred the lines of commitment.

By now, I had also noticed something different about him from people I had dated: he and his mom communicated at an unnatural volume… all day, every day, via texts, phone calls, and FaceTime. He was an only child, after all.

What do I know? Maybe that's normal; I have never experienced a normal family dynamic.

I saw her as the needy one, but what I wasn't able to name was his emotional attunement to her. While I softened into trust, she remained his primary attachment. My mind circled back to something he told me when we first met: when he told me he had a close relationship with her… but it's closer than that—it's enmeshment. That suspicion was my inner compass noticing something being off, even if I couldn't decode it yet.

The One

Because he constantly showed up wherever I was, I became reliant on his presence without realizing it. As much as I tried holding onto my internal structure that was built from fierce autonomy, I softened in the presence of someone who seemed to meet me in rhythm. I had been the architect of my survival for so long, and when he offered the appearance of co-piloting, a presence that followed me everywhere and cooked dinner, my shift was subtle, yet human.

I remember thinking, *"This is so easy. Is this what people mean by saying you'll know when you've found 'the one'?"*

I felt joy experiencing borrowed time, relishing something others crave, but I failed to see that I was the one who created that ease because of my readiness to welcome someone in, not because he proved himself worthy of that welcome. That's what made it dangerous, because my earned hope was not durable but fueled my belief in this relationship's validity.

Valentine's Day

Around Valentine's Day, his mom sent him a card, saying, "I wish you were taking me out to dinner on Valentine's Day, but you're just too far away now. P.S. The flowers you bought me have died."

WHAT??? Which mother would send these words to her son, knowing he has a woman in his life, and send them to her address?

What she wrote was a veiled claim: I should be your Valentine, not her.

That's not nurturing.

And that P.S. was another needle: a reminder of his ongoing obligations to her, laced with guilt, as if the death of those flowers reflected his failure to nurture her. She didn't just miss her son but wanted to position herself as the woman most deserving of his attention. Her mailing of the card to my address symbolized, "This is the life you've built without me, and I refuse to be displaced." The card revealed that boundaries were never set between them.

I spoke to him with honesty, communicating that I had read her words and how they wounded me. My lucid approach was met with a silence that spoke louder than any justification he could have given. It shielded her position and avoided choosing me. In that avoidance, he revealed the central truth: I was his present, but she was his default.

The card brought forward what I had feared: she was the primary emotional figure in his life, and I was not given the position of true partner. His emotional loyalty remained bound to the woman who still made emotional demands on him as though she were his partner, not his parent. I had made space for him. She refused to make space for me, and he never required her to.

New Job

He accepted a remote position at a local company that removed his need to travel back to his hometown. I know… like you, I'm noticing this trend too: he preferred jobs that didn't require him to go into the office and gave him freedom without responsibility. Perhaps "remote" wasn't just about physical distance from an office; it mirrored his emotional stance: engaged but noncommittal. He curated situations where he could say, "I'm here," without ever having to stay in the deeper sense. Working from home also meant I was under the illusion of constant proximity, while he remained distant.

He claimed he changed jobs to spend more time with me because it didn't require frequent travel, which made me feel good. On the surface, his actions presented devotion, but his statement was designed to make me feel chosen. Seeing it through a wider lens, this fit a behavioral script he had followed for years: his avoidance of accountability. This transition resembled his LinkedIn job experience I had   observed: the frequent on-and-off boarding meant he integrated nowhere.

And over time, it became clear: he structured his life to appear present while always preserving the exit routes. He didn't grow roots; he just shifted pots. He was always in transition, and the appearance of availability masked his emotional inaccessibility. I could sense it, even though I couldn't label it.

Grandpa

One day, he told me his mom had called to tell him to fly home because Grandpa needed to go to the hospital. Her dramatic tendency to exaggerate made me doubt the urgency.

I then asked the most basic, grounding question, "What happened?"

To my surprise, he said his mom was "useless" and that he would have to speak with the doctor himself the following day. His response revealed more than he realized: he both resented her and remained tethered to her, trapped in a dynamic where contempt and obedience coexisted.

While at work the next morning, I received a screenshot of his one-way flight itinerary to their city. Examining the departure time, I understood it involved a last-minute booking.

I guess he must have spoken directly to the doctor.

So I replied to wish him safe travels and hope that things would go well.

He texted me as soon as he landed, "I think he didn't make it. I was so close. I'm almost there."

"Wait, what? You mean he passed?" I asked.

He said he didn't know, and I asked whether he had talked to his mom.

He then phoned me to explain that he had spoken with her on the phone, but all she said was, "Oh my God! Oh my God! Oh my God!" before cutting off, and she never answered again when he called back.

Without knowing Grandpa's exact state, I responded, "Okay, we don't know yet at this point. You'll find out soon when you get there. If he did pass, just remember that he was proud of you. But something in my gut says he pulled it off."

"This was not what I called you for. What you said is not helpful." He then hung up.

His lashing out shocked me. What I failed to recognize then was that he wasn't looking for support; he was looking for an accomplice in his mom's manufactured crisis. And when I didn't play along, he turned cold. I had no awareness that my body saw through the scene before my consciousness did, and that's why I didn't feed into his emotional performance.

Turns out my instinct was right: Grandpa was fine. I had never understood why my body could always sense what was coming. No, I'm not a psychic, but now I understand that my nervous system has learned to recognize patterns. I had seen enough to know that his mom's operating method involved manipulation, using crisis as a mask for dependence. That's why my instinct knew she would use that opportunity to "get her son back." My body had read the truth before my mind could fully name it: she had created a false urgency to summon him home, and he had complied without verifying the facts.

His decisions were a product of a lifetime of enmeshment, with her emotional turmoil dictating his responses and inciting reactive action rather than logic.

Despite Grandpa's recovery, she still relied on him to stay to organize and make decisions on everything. Regardless of all his talk of moving in, changing jobs, and building a life with me, he was still her emotional son-husband, slipping back into her gravity the moment she called.

Tugs-Of-Need

I kept internalizing: If he had never switched his home base to my city, he wouldn't have to worry about the long commute when they needed him so much. I also regretted not standing my ground when he was insisting that he would move in with me. Had I maintained my boundaries, he would have avoided emergency returns.

I questioned my place in his life, and here's the core truth: *I'm just a girl he had met online months ago. They need him more; I need not be selfish.*

My text message then told him, "They need you more than I do; I was independent before knowing you," as I stepped aside with care. "I feel bad that you live here for me when you're so far away from them. Your mom would be happy if you moved back there. Our dating can continue unchanged, regardless. It would ease my mind greatly to know that I'm not preventing you from being with your family during their time of need."

His immediate response, "Don't tell me what to do!" surprised me, since I hadn't considered dictating his actions. I was doing the very opposite of what he was accusing me of doing—striving to lighten his plate—and he met my selfless gesture with hostility, as if my autonomy challenged his narrative. His outburst concealed a defense, for my clarity demanded that he confront his faltering decision.

He, more in anger than empathy, reminded me that he had moved for love. Desiring to uphold that image, though still serving as a son reachable when summoned. But those roles were incompatible, and my offer made that tension undeniable.

Offering him an exit made him feel exposed, not relieved, since I did what manipulators shun: I offered him a graceful exit instead of framing it as abandonment. His anger revealed what his charm had concealed: he had never wanted full ownership of his decisions. His wish involved offering devotion, not bearing responsibility for conse-quences.

When he returned weeks later, the vibe changed. I blamed it on his stressful circumstances then, but examining the past, I experience the pang of truth: my personal strength conflicted with his desire for ease, and he resented my offering of distance he struggled to manage.

Now I see it: his sense of self was reactive, defined by whoever needed him most. First his mom, then me, then again his mom. And when no one pulled hard enough, he drifted.

Hospital Bed

Since then, he would dedicate half his time to them, visiting every other week. I kept pressing him to consider moving back, but he kept resisting me because staying tethered to both worlds let him evade committing to either.

That was my blindness: his existence structured around access, not intimacy. Instead of an equal, he positioned me as his sanctuary: he explained he had to pour everything out of his cup to them, so he needed to come back to me to recharge.

Relationships are about compromise... he needs me during this time; I can fill his cup if that's what he needs for his well-being. Why not?

Except, it wasn't a shared compromise: before I knew it, I had already become the emotional pit stop after every trip back from the chaotic gravitational pull of his mom's world. His cup analogy seemed logical: framing me as a recovery resource, though he did not perceive my needs.

During one of those visits, he purchased everything necessary to set up his mom's home to accommodate a hospital bed and equipment for his grandpa. In a hoarded home, that's no simple task.

He called me that night to unload, starting by saying, "If you were wondering what I did all day..." and gave me the details of each object that he had to either move or discard.

I can't say that I didn't see it coming—a thought I refrained from vocalizing.

Stations

The following day, he texted to inform me that upon his return, he was going to rent an apartment across the street, but we would stay together. His suggestion sounded like a compromise that functioned as a deflection of responsibility from his living contradictions. He didn't want a home base to root; all he wanted were stations to recharge, just like his Tesla.

That confused me because my point was not that I didn't want him to live with me; it was for him to move back in with his mom so he could take care of the elderly. A matter of this significance warranted direct conversation, so I didn't text back. In contrast, he delivered this plan via text because it gave him control over tone, thus avoiding vocal accountability. He was trying to manage optics and access at once: close enough to access my stability, but far enough to preserve his freedom to leave. He desired to appear partnered while preserving parts of existence that remained enmeshed in reliance and evasion.

But upon returning, where presence requires congruence, it slipped away like every other future promise that relied on distance to feel real. The lack of follow-through after his return didn't shock me. His text was sent to appear decisive, which had already served its purpose at the moment.

And deep down, I hoped he was no longer contemplating because my former self was not ready to give up on my "person."

The Cayman Islands

We had a Cayman Islands trip coming up—yet another overseas vacation that I had planned to coincide with my modeling gig. We had already scheduled and booked it months ahead. However, because of his new, self-arranged fifty-fifty living situation, the trip fell on his

"Mom & Grandpa week." I explained that his family took precedence; skipping my modeling gig would be fine. He insisted we wouldn't cancel and positioned the trip as his recovery, saying he needed a vacation to get away from everything. Similar to our trips to Canada and Europe, he, once again, robbed it of its original meaning by centering himself in the attention.

So we booked everything, and by "we," I mean he funded it, and I handled the logistics. He had no financial concerns, and I think even you, by now, are annoyed with this frequent reminder. I viewed us as the perfect team then: he put in money, while I was contributing to planning. What I had failed to see was that the role-splitting between his physical presence and my emotional labor was imbalanced.

Roaming

Even though I traveled around the world often, I never purchased extra global cellphone plans because I faced no accountability regarding my whereabouts. There's never "I'll let you know when I get there safely" with anyone. And this trip was no exception.

As we landed, I asked him to let me tether to his phone so that I could make a quick call to the fashion show producer to come pick us up, as instructed by her. I didn't know that my innocent request would provoke anger in him. He asked how many times he had told me to get a global plan, and I wouldn't budge, even when he said he would pay for it. I was shaken by the rage he displayed while standing in line at the airport customs. I asked for a slight point of reliance, and he snapped. But that was the dynamic he had often relied on me for seamless adaptability. He was fine being the provider, so long as I remained the self-sufficient partner. The moment I flipped the equation, his discomfort surfaced. So I connected to the airport Wi-Fi to place the call instead.

Fashion Show

He came to my fashion show, and, for once, I remained with him, audience-side, until backstage preparations demanded my presence.

While waiting for my turn, he said, "Now you know what I have to go through just to wait for your turn to walk at every show."

Early on, he revealed to me that since my modeling endeavors encroached upon his valuable schedule, I should exercise discretion regarding engagements. I first perceived it as support... but now I know that his comment was a soft scolding in love and humor. What he meant was that my passions were an inconvenience if they didn't include him. He needed to be in everything I do, or else he felt irrelevant. What he wanted was mutual centrality, but my independence chipped away at the illusion that I needed him.

The Kiss

Our flight home included the Disney film featuring our song through in-flight entertainment. As tears streamed from my eyes while watching, I glanced his way and kissed him because I felt touched.

The compelling moments I experienced were real, but the depth of that emotional response was one-sided: I was kissing the ideal version of him that seemed to reflect my soul. However, in reality, I held that ideal alone the entire journey; he only ever held it when it was easy.

That trip wasn't just a vacation; it was a chance for my nervous system to observe the full architecture of our relationship. Though things appeared balanced, my body perceived the cracks. What was new was my growing ability to name them.

The following day, he had a confession to share. He informed me he had been testing me for two weeks, which started before we even left for the Cayman Islands.

I couldn't believe what I heard.

Testing? How?

He explained he avoided kissing my lips to see if I would initiate one on my own. Then he delivered the test results: according to him, since I didn't initiate, it was proof that I didn't want him, and that's why I kept telling him to move back to his mom's.

PARDON ME???

"I'm sorry, but did you completely forget about what happened just yesterday on our plane ride back??? I leaned over and kissed you because our movie and song reminded me of our fate," I exclaimed.

His answer? Absolute silence—what he always offered when I brought up reality, because confrontation with the truth would have unraveled his illusion of moral superiority. The facts contradicted his accusation, so he couldn't engage.

His so-called "test" wasn't just immature; it was a form of emotional sabotage disguised as logic. It's not a measure of love; it was a tool to induce doubt in me again. What he meant was he didn't feel in control of my affection, so he created a scenario where my failure would let him reclaim emotional power. And when he followed that by tying it to my suggestion of his move back home, it revealed the manufactured trap he designed to validate a script he had already written: I was the reason he felt unloved, and I, not him, was the one breaking us. He needed me to fail because if I did, he could rewrite history and place the blame for his growing detachment onto me. He omitted the prior day's vulnerability because it didn't fit the outcome he wanted. But my nervous system saw it: my kiss came from truth, while his test came from control.

Fifty-Fifty

Life went on as he resumed his fifty-fifty living with his family and me. I had built a home founded on earned structure, surpassing material existence. And he tried to retrofit my life into his chaos, asking me to reshape everything for a version of love that offered him shelter while causing live-in weather. I had repeatedly contorted my life to make space for him: I adjusted when he moved in and again when he kept half his life elsewhere.

He finally brought up face-to-face the idea of his moving out. It crystallized a truth my nervous system had been circling for months: the emotional contract between us had become circumstantial. I failed to name it then, but it's his sleight of hand: trying to redefine "together" without having to say out loud that his commitment was retracting. His request wasn't about needing space; it's about keeping access while shedding responsibility. He wanted the illusion of a part-nership without the commitment of presence. And now he wanted to move out but still stay tethered on his terms.

"If you leave my door, you're never allowed back in again," my body responded before my mind could catch up with the fact that I had just issued an ultimatum.

My nervous system was drawing the line for me between shared life and part-time performance by naming the truth: a person who opts out of the shared center cannot still lay claim to its intimacy. So he backed off after meeting my firm truth because, deep down, he knew I was right.

Scratches

One day, he inspected the scratches on his black car. As his face turned red, he swore those scratches were new after moving to my city. Though he never blamed me outright, I felt horrible not only because I had driven his car but also because of his constant reminder of moving to my city for me. His simmering anger at how immaculate the car was in the past communicated a silent accusation that I couldn't quite shake off.

My instinct was to take responsibility—even without clear evidence—because I sought to defuse tension.

I apologized, "It must have been me."

He became even more enraged. "Why do you always take everything I say so personally? I didn't say it was you!"

My intellect was trying to fix the situation. I questioned his need for a black car, given his concern over scratches. He didn't have a straight answer for me.

His rage made me feel so horrible that I no longer wanted to drive his car. I devised a way for him to understand my emotions without direct communication by leaving my car key in his drawer for him to discover for himself. It's also a way for me to set a boundary.

I refuse to keep taking on blame that's not mine, especially when the conditions of that blame are vague.

When he found the key, he texted me to inquire, and I responded with the reason that I didn't want him to drive my car, so it's only fair that I shouldn't drive his. He stopped pressing, but I could sense his unspoken tension behind that acceptance.

Since then, he would always park his car at the airport instead of needing my pickup and drop-off. Airport parking fees wouldn't burden him, of course.

New York City

We went to NYC for my annual hotel stay using my credit card rewards. We watched a Broadway show, and upon exiting the theater, he received a text from his mom asking about the show.

Your mom knew we were at a show? She isn't here with us, is she? Is she watching my every move?

I felt violated. He kept his mom abreast of every move throughout the day, every day; it's like we had an invisible third wheel. Instead of feeling like a couple exploring the city, I was part of a triad I never agreed to. It desecrated the private space I valued in our relationship. Her text felt like a piercing reminder that we weren't alone on that trip; there's always an unseen observer hovering over our moments together. Their constant communication was an intrusion that made it impossible for me to feel connected to him. It undermined the intimacy of my time and chipped away at the trust I needed.

That trip appeared to possess considerable promise—a chance for us to take a respite from the norm. Yet, the shadow of his mom's constant presence kept intruding into that space and was impossible to ignore. Wherever we went, whatever we experienced, we were never alone—a feeling that can erode the foundation of any partnership.

Seashell

Spring had just arrived, and the blue skies visible from my floor-to-ceiling office window fueled my envy of those outdoors in lighter clothing. His phone's GPS showed he was at the shore, a place I had yet to be despite having moved there much earlier. The contrast was laid bare: the isolation experienced while trapped in duty, with the individual I admitted enjoying freedom outside my crafted existence.

This wasn't unexpected, though. During the preceding week, he described to me a male former coworker who was divorcing and had been requesting his company for outings. He told me he had been turning him down because he wanted to experience new things and places with me first. He finally gave in and accepted his invitation to the beach because I had failed to fill his cup, so he needed to find other ways.

That's fair.

My schedule had kept me busy, and I felt relieved that he would recharge without me. But his explanation was an accusation cloaked in faux emotional maturity: he turned his unmet needs into a ledger, and I became the shortfall. The context he created implied that my structured, full life was something to blame. I was present, though not within his codependent upbringing. So he punished me in secret for not playing that role.

He placed the seashell that he had found on the shelves in "his bathroom," my guest bathroom that he had claimed as his sanctuary, where he would spend time with the fan humming, which created a silent boundary I couldn't cross. That seashell served as a trophy that confirmed his existence, irrespective of me.

Quality Time

I was getting adjusted to his fifty-fifty living arrangement by telling myself that it wasn't a big deal because I was alone before he came into my life. As I had always assumed the planner role since we met, I would plan activities for us when he was in town, but I started receiving pushback. He wanted time to go golfing with his friends on the weekends instead, and sometimes even during office hours. To compensate for the lost work time, he started working on his laptop in bed and told me to avoid deep conversations. This routine became a symbol of the shadowy distance between me and the guy I let into my bed. His time restriction on deep conversation was a strategy to limit when and how I could reach him on an emotional level. I wasn't even allowed to talk anymore; his refusal was absolute.

When I expressed disappointment in not spending time together on the weekends, he told me the feeling was mutual because I wouldn't spend time with him during the week. That comparison confused me because we both possess weekday full-time jobs.

I still aimed to reconcile, since quality interactions were our preferred way to receive love—a commonality we discovered when we first met.

Compromise

So, I gave up a workout class that I usually attended once a week to make it "our night." But he said that date wouldn't work weekly because he would rather socialize with his former colleagues. I questioned if that's the only day of the week they were available, and yet he answered my question with a question of his own: "Would you rather I hang out with them on the weekend instead?"

My brain was going to explode because his logic didn't line up. Each time I asked a fair question, he would sidestep it by twisting my inquiry into an ultimatum. It's his way of reducing complex emotional realities to false either-or choices, forcing me to abandon my valid desires or risk appearing controlling—that's manipulation under the guise of self-preservation. And to top it off, it's passed the "talking curfew" he had imposed upon me, so I couldn't bring up any concerns. I was living in a fog that was getting denser and denser.

That pattern continued for a couple of months: he would go see his family for a week, leaving me to contemplate how to replenish his energy upon his return enough to sustain him the following week when he would pour himself out for others again. During the half he lived with me, he was frequently away from my home, either going into the office for a "remote" job or spending time with friends to recharge. And his late-night laptop habit forbade deep conversations.

I rationalized away my needs, justified his fragmented availability, and stitched it into a new belief: love means tolerating inconsistency.

It's healthy for him to have a life outside of me.

He knew my strength would keep seeking internal coherence. But while I was extending grace, he receded further rather than stepping towards me, using every allowance I gave him to build a compartmentalized life—until I became a side task on his calendar. As I kept trying to make space for him, he was dividing me out of the equation.

Depth

My body registered the distance, attributing it to our infrequent in-person encounters. But whenever I attempted to talk, I sensed walls rising between us. Curiosity drove me to explore his emotional vulnerability: I asked him what he would usually talk about with his mom and grandpa. That was me extending an invitation.

Let me see the inner world you have let no one touch.

Judging from his facial expression, the question surprised him. He replied with uncertainty: their neighbors, football, or TV shows—no inner realm existed among them. I had a suspicion he hadn't grown up with in-depth conversations; what he called closeness was just maintenance. Emotional oxygen was missing between us because emotional muscle had never been built in his childhood. And the mother-son bond that ran so thick was proof of enmeshment. They had a relationship built on dependence: constant contact as a proxy for genuine connection.

I then asked him to tell me the deepest conversation he had ever had with anyone. It took a lengthy pause before he told me it was when he and his ex were talking about where they would house their parents when they got older. I questioned why he would even consider that to be his deepest conversation because it concerned logistics, not souls. His answer solidified what my body knew all along: I had been speaking with someone who had never learned how to hold depth. He had only ever skimmed the surface of emotional connection and called it love.

I then presumed that his deepest conversations would happen with me in the future. While that's determination, it's also heartbreak waiting to happen. My former self kept dating someone's potential instead of what was shown right in front of me.

I was raised on emotional survival; he, on avoidance—it's silly of me to believe we could still build a bond worth preserving.

GPS

One day, his GPS location stopped at a parking spot in an apartment community that we had never visited, nor had he mentioned before.

Before making any assumptions, I texted, "Would you mind telling me where you are and what you're doing?"

He explained that the divorcing male friend had invited him to tour his niece's apartment on short notice. He then blew up my phone, saying I had violated his privacy. And when I apologized, he assured me he wasn't angry, just disappointed. He even asked me which cheesecake I wanted him to bring home because they were dining at The Cheesecake Factory next to the apartment. He remembered our shared love for that restaurant, something that solidified our twin flames' status when we first met. His gracious offer reset the emotional mood before I went home.

However, no one welcomed me upon my return; my nervous system already knew: I walked into a room where presence didn't match intention. The shift from "I'm not angry" to the silent treatment hit me as I was entering the living room, observing him sitting with a furious expression. Though he returned home, his thoughts lingered on the performance, uncertain how he would preserve his wronged facade without revealing his actions.

I let him know that I believed him when he told me earlier he wasn't angry. I felt it was unfair when he spoke one thing and acted another. Frankly, guessing someone's alternative motives has always been exhausting to me.

He claimed I should have told him the details of what I saw instead of an unbiased inquiry. Once more, I experienced emotional depletion; his statement held minimal meaning. That darkened emotional fog came from my tug-of-war: I knew I wasn't doing anything wrong, but I also felt a tremendous amount of guilt for causing him upset.

He emphasized I should have accused him more directly because he was used to people spiraling—the opposite of my character, and that unsettled him. I overlooked the cause of his distress: my calmness made the behavior he had displayed after being caught with mismatched moments of his words and location stand out. My self-control left him with no clear emotional advantage.

His unexpected defensiveness was, in fact, a control mechanism: a reframe of events that turned my reasonable question into an unforgivable offense. He wasn't clarifying my tone; he was rewriting the narrative to make himself the victim. That allowed him to maintain the illusion of moral high ground: his secrecy and control weren't the problem; my truth-seeking baseline was.

He then removed the GPS tracking while I was sobbing into the night.

Letter

My crying continued through the following day. With pen and paper in hand, I wrote him a heartfelt letter, describing my lack of appreciation for his love. I was so eager to give it to him when he got home; I missed him so much.

That eagerness led me to track his whereabouts using the Tesla app: from a restaurant to IKEA, a place we bonded over when we first met. Hoping to ask him to bring home some meatballs, I phoned him, but he didn't answer.

Upon his return, he volunteered to tell me he didn't want to seem rude and pick up the phone when I call. He drove that same male friend to IKEA for some household items because of his larger vehicle.

You mean the same friend who you had told me owned a pickup truck?

I kept that thought to myself, pressing no further. I was just thankful he—the love of my life—finally came home. Plus, he was transparent with me about his whereabouts this time, even unprompted. I saw it as a step in the right direction.

I then folded into an apology, handed him the letter, sobbed, and told him I had been ungrateful. Taking the letter from my hands, he confessed that it was the sweetest thing anyone had ever done for him. He read it in front of me as I kept apologizing, asking for his forgiveness.

I'm not proud of that behavior anymore, but I also didn't know the feeling I had stemmed from emotional starvation. I wasn't the misleading one, but why was I the one begging for connection?

Embracing me, he whispered, "What would I be if I gave up on us so easily?" He continued, "You don't know who you're dealing with because you have no prior experience of true love."

How did he know? That's precisely a problem I had been facing.

But what he meant really was, "You don't recognize love when it's manipulative, and I need you to accept it regardless."

This makeup didn't restore us to where we were, though. Despite sharing my bed with him half the time, logistical constraints prevented us from having meaningful conversations. I couldn't put my finger on what the block between us was, but it's clear with his lack of sharing of what's happening in his life regularly. And he would get irritated every time I stumbled upon a truth before he was ready to package it. He offered timed doses of affection, yet the core of deep connection—real-time transparency—was withheld. He was living beside me, but not with me.

He allowed me to receive the curated version of events after they had already happened once he sanitized them. In contrast, I felt comfortable enough to think aloud to him. I explained to him that his refusal to reciprocate my openness made me feel excluded, and he responded that my desire for closeness was too demanding because his thoughts were "dark."

But isn't he my soulmate?

Burrito

Our shared Chipotle enthusiasm increased the frequency of my visits. I always order from their mobile app, even when I am already in the store, because I receive a smaller portion size otherwise.

Whenever I'm in a cafeteria setting where I'm required to point at my selections to the staff, they always give me less than others. I am not imagining this—it's my lived experience, including chow halls in the Marine Corps. I had years of data stretching across contexts, and all of it led to one clear, embodied truth: my appetite is underestimated based on how I appear.

The first time we drove there, I had already started ordering our items on the mobile app. But he didn't like it, so I explained my past stories to him. I was asking him to trust me and hoping he would say, "I've never noticed that, but I believe you."

But he told me it was just "all in my head." His comment was a direct rejection of my right to interpret my life.

Why claim my experience is wrong if you weren't there? As if you're implying that my feelings are invalid.

We returned on another occasion; this time, we ordered at the counter. The smaller size of my burrito, although we ordered the same one, proved my point. But I chose silence because I already knew he wouldn't validate me, even with the real-world evidence landed right in front of him.

The deeper violation was his undermining my right to name my experience by positioning himself as the authority on my experience with my perception. He edited reality and expected me to adjust.

This marked my emotional turning point because this was the first time his dismissive behavior struck me.

Mind-Reader

One day, he told me he could no longer look me in the eye and say that I was his "person." I felt devastated.

Where did this even come from? What did I do? All I did was love him.

He then gave me a presentation by drawing a diagram. A circle surrounded his name, which was in the center. Outside of the circle, he scattered x's representing family and acquaintances.

Pointing to the circle's center with the marker in his hand, he said, "That's where you used to be."

Then he wrote my name on the outside of the circle, among those x's, and stated, "That's where you are now."

I asked him what I had done wrong for him to demote me. He reminded me of our phone conversation as he was traveling to the hospital for his grandpa, stating that's the moment he realized he didn't need someone "special." According to him, all he wanted was for me to say, "I'm so sorry to hear." Instead, I had responded with calm reasoning. He claimed I didn't know how to comfort him since I was unlike anyone "normal." My love for him, he claimed, would have been clear if I had known what he wanted me to say. I then blamed my abnormal upbringing for my inability to predict his wishes.

In his eyes, love meant perfect predictability, and I was inadequate. I see now that he framed it as an emotional failure on my part, but he shifted the goalposts to something I could never reach. The disappointment he felt stemmed from his own inability to accept love unless it matched his specific vision.

He judged my response after the fact by an invisible standard and punished me for not knowing it. What I failed to perceive then: he had stopped trying, and instead of taking accountability for it, he made it about my failure to expect an unspoken script... one that I was never handed. He expected me to be a mind-reader. But I cannot read minds, regardless of effort; it would require a superpower that I don't have.

I surrender.

Depression

Then he finally revealed something he had hidden from me for months—his therapist diagnosed him with depression. That's the first time I learned that he had started seeing her again after his grandpa got admitted to the hospital.

I felt like a terrible partner, because it's not his fault that his depression caused him to withdraw, and yet I still demanded things from him. He shouldn't have needed to fulfill my needs while depressed.

How can I better support him now?

I have always appreciated alone time when I can do deep thinking without distractions. His week to spend with his family coincided right then, so I used that opportunity to study how to support a depressed partner. I consulted guidance from books, podcasts, and even YouTube videos.

I then wrote an extensive list of bullet points in the I-statement format. Psychology 101 taught me that starting a sentence with "I" can lessen the defensiveness of the receiver.

I believed emotional fluency was the key to his happiness and waited all week for him to come back just to get it resolved. I figured the most straightforward way to support him would be for him to tell me.

He tells me what he needs from me. I do those things. Simple!

His answer, however, was not simple: "I don't know what I want."

That response overwhelmed me. He handed me a void and called it truth. He couldn't define his needs because he preferred vague discomfort to the vulnerable clarity of asking for what he needed. I was ready to do anything he wanted me to, but his helplessness passed the emotional labor back to me, and, in turn, I felt helpless.

If I could, I would tell my former self that she wasn't a terrible partner—she was the only partner doing it all for both.

Children

He then also shared his inner thoughts with me and told me he had been thinking about having kids. It stunned me.

The only deal-breaker that I had, and we agreed on before I allowed you into my home… You just changed your mind on me?

I had made my boundaries clear, which he agreed to as a condition of entering my life.

I inquired about the source of his changed mind. He explained that his grandpa told him he had never found a life purpose until he came into his life. I understood his grandpa's sentiment, though I questioned its relevance to his decision regarding offspring. He was afraid that he would later regret not finding life meaning at an old age if he were childless.

Each of us interpreted Grandpa's words differently. I saw it as gratitude; he was self-focused in seeking a shortcut to feeling significant. Instead of facing his inner emptiness, he assigned future children the burden of giving his life meaning; that's avoidance disguised through sentimentality.

I felt devastated—the Universe led me to "my person," only to reveal that even he could be just as unreliable as my past partners. I concede people change, yet it's beyond belief that the "male version of me" could be persuaded regarding a fundamental value. His change revealed that he was never my equal. Upon reflection, it became clear that the Universe delivered an image: a flavor of existence with someone mimicking patterns while lacking essence. And that realization was the real devastation.

Couples Therapy

This felt pivotal, impacting both our relationship and my life, prompting my suggestion that we seek couples therapy. He beamed, sharing that he was pleased I initiated the suggestion, given he also intended to propose the idea yet hesitated, uncertain of my reaction. He suggested that he would find a therapist and have our first session before leaving for his mom and grandpa again.

His eagerness suggested the crack in the wall wasn't just my imagination, but his willingness to try felt like a real thread of hope: that the distance between us could be bridged through guided conversation. Therapy signified an act of courage on both our parts, especially given how complicated our dynamic had become.

I kissed him goodbye and went to work. As soon as I got to my office, he had already texted me a few options of therapists for me to choose from. We selected the one who could provide the soonest appointment availability, which was on the day before his next departure to his family. That timing appeared to be an attempt to untangle the threads of unspoken feelings before they got buried under more weeks of physical separation.

Friends

He had always been glued to his phone. Recall our initial chat before dating; I specifically brought up this topic, and he told me those who did so were impolite.

I would stop talking mid-sentence until he looked up at me—it's something that annoyed him, but his neglect was something that annoyed me.

He regularly reasoned: he was always present, so how could I expect him to set aside his phone, especially when the people he was talking to lived in other time zones? It sounded reasonable to me then, so I agreed with him.

I also used this opportunity to let him know that I wished I had heard about his friends sooner. He blamed me and said that I had shown no interest in meeting them. I was confused.

WHAT did you just say??? Where did that even come from?

His response was defensive, like he was turning my reasonable desire for inclusion into a blame game, flipping the script to make me seem disinterested, when in reality I was striving to be involved. Of the one friend that he had in my city, I insisted on having brunch with him so that we could meet. His refusal to acknowledge my efforts made me feel unseen. That kind of response isn't just hurtful; it creates an emotional distance that's hard to bridge. I sought a shared existence, yet encountered evasion. It's telling that something as simple as sharing friendships, which in healthy relationships fosters closeness, became a source of tension.

Distance

The day before our therapy appointment, we visited the driving range after work. It's my idea—I made myself more available during the week ever since he commented on feeling neglected when I kept myself so busy. I canceled my normal workout class that day to play golf with him because it's something he loved. He agreed, though, if he could work upon our return to offset the lost hours.

Following golf, he treated me to an unfamiliar restaurant, one he had discovered with that one male friend, believing I would enjoy it.

His distant parking puzzled me, yet I refrained from interfering. He finished texting, then left his phone in the car—unusual behavior, especially when he would always use his phone to unlock the door. His extreme measures to avoid having his phone in the restaurant confused me. Therefore, I inquired whether he was certain regarding that decision. His answer was sweet; he wanted to give me his full attention. For months, I had longed for his emotional resonance. Finally, he endeavored to connect, honoring my request.

I'm someone who doesn't just notice behavior—I register energy shifts. That's why his response made me feel both validated and suspicious at once. I also noticed the details: the unusual parking spot and the decision to leave his phone despite its usual proximity. These discrepancies didn't disappear just because his gesture was sweet.

Rubber Duck

We got two seats at the bar. It's about fifteen minutes too early for happy hour, and if you have been paying attention, you should already know how important happy hour deals are to me. Like you, he also understood that it mattered to me, but he coached me to order off the regular menu anyway, and I went along.

He highlighted the restaurant's colorful sliders, a featured item that included a souvenir rubber duck. His suggestion to order it stemmed from his prior visit with his friend. I mocked the fact that two grown men were sharing some rainbow-themed sliders with a free toy, but he didn't find it amusing.

I asked, "What happened to that rubber duck? You didn't take it home for me."

That was my nervous system wanting to know whether he was aware enough to do something that would have made me smile. He explained his friend took it back to his daughter. Recollection told me she was a college graduate, living elsewhere. I bet he didn't expect me to remember those details, but I didn't want to push further because I already sensed the cost of doing so.

We then sat there in complete silence.

But he said he wanted to give me his full attention… Isn't that why he left his phone in the car?

Jacket

He once more acted out of character, asking if I was cold. No, the sun was shining through the windows onto our seats. He told me he needed to grab his jacket from the car.

But he's never cold; he would usually take his jacket off and let me wear it.

I kept my thoughts to myself because my gut sensed it: he was stepping out to check his phone and into a version of his life he couldn't bring into the restaurant with me. His excuse didn't track, and I knew it, even if I didn't call it out.

Fifteen minutes passed as happy hour began.

His return was elusive, but food appeared. I waited for him. My meager food portion fueled my hunger, prompting a happy hour order.

Yay! Just the way I wanted!

He finally walked back in, wearing his jacket, and saw the food sitting on the table, untouched.

"You should have started eating instead of waiting for me," he said.

His body language told me he didn't enjoy the time with me and wanted to leave, although he insisted he had left his phone behind to pay full attention to me. The dissonance between his words and actions baffled me. But I digress.

I let him know I had ordered more food off the happy hour menu while he stepped away. His irritation became more visible concerning additional food arriving. I could sense that people nearby picked up on the tension between us, and the staff left us alone. I scarfed down my meal as the food appeared, aiming to leave soon.

Our interactions captured the illusion of closeness clashing with the reality of emotional distance, his performative gestures at odds with my sharp read of incongruent behavior. He said he wanted to give me all of his attention, but then he vanished for twenty minutes over a jacket he didn't need. He claimed money wasn't an issue, yet criticized my choices in a way that implied my behavior was inconvenient. Every detail was a contradiction.

This is what I couldn't name then: those details were about him being the one who set the pace, defined the rules, and framed my needs as excessive when they diverged from his plan.

I canceled a workout to prioritize spending time with him and attempted to craft something lovely from the evening. He brought me there after all... I let myself hope that leaving the phone in the car might finally mean emotional access. However, his actions reiterated: not really.

Done

He gave me the silent treatment on the car ride home while I was processing the entire instance in my head, trying to link those dots until they unveiled an alternate reality.

Despite seeing him as the "male version of me," our personalities differed in how we approached communication: I preferred to reflect before speaking; he would retreat and hope that we would never discuss the same topic again.

I broke our silence and informed him I had started to walk on eggshells. I apologized for having reached that point. He interrupted me to tell me that the feeling was mutual.

He said he had told me he had to work that evening. Yet, I remained at the restaurant for eternity. But his lack of urgency regarding his return home for work perplexed me.

"If I were in a hurry, I would have brought it up," I said.

"If you truly love me, you wouldn't have needed a reminder," he asserted.

Sitting at a traffic light, I shouted, "I'm done! I'm done! I'm done!"

My body sprang into action before my conscious consideration, a rarity, since I often reflect before I vocalize. That scream was the release of months of his silent restraint: all my swallowed concerns, recalibrated needs, unanswered questions, and contradictions erupted from my chest because no other choice remained. I had tried to meet him with compassion and even tried to support him, but he had only met me with tests designed for me to fail.

The breaking of my character stunned him; he had never seen me behave that way. I had always been the composed one. But the moment I screamed, the roles reversed: he saw someone no longer willing to carry both our emotional loads, finally placing her own signal above the noise of his inconsistency. So, his demeanor softened.

What he couldn't say was, "I hear you now, because I can no longer un-hear you."

I said the words he didn't aspire to say first; my scream gave him the exit he had long been rehearsing in his head.

And me—I was finally hearing myself.

That ride home revealed our core rupture: I believed love meant staying engaged even through discomfort; he believed it meant never needing to ask, because in his fantasy version of love, my needs would align with his without discussion. That fantasy dissolved the moment I stopped suppressing myself to keep the peace.

I-Statements

He then told me I was self-centered, ran upstairs, and came back down with papers in his hand—the bullet points of I-statements I had given him weeks ago, which he treated as a keepsake. He handed it to me, requesting that I examine the initial word of each sentence.

They all started with the word "I." I used those statements because I internalized the emotional labor and expressed my feelings in a way designed to make him feel safe. It's my attempt to include him in my emotional process—the inverse of self-centered. I was trying to bring him closer. But to him, it's evidence that everything was about me. He held that page like proof of my flaw to build a case against me.

Feeling misunderstood, I told him about what I learned in psychology and expressed my regret that it didn't work for him.

He told me, "That sounds like sarcasm."

He had already decided that my intentions couldn't be trusted; he couldn't accept love from me unless it came in the exact packaging he had imagined, delivered without error. Anything else—even empathy—was reframed as ego.

That emotional inversion had become the norm in our relationship: I extended emotional responsibility, and he weaponized it. The problem wasn't that page of I-statements, but his inability to feel with me.

First Session

We had our first couples' therapy session the following day. The therapist asked us about our goals. We both agreed that we needed help with communication because neither of us felt heard. For me, I had to extra-polish my choice of words, living in layers of thinking and rethinking before speaking. In contrast, he lived in withdrawal, saying little until he blurted out everything with just enough polish to seem reasonable.

He began conferring with the therapist. It's typical; I allow others to speak for the evaluation of different viewpoints before my contribution. Plus, I'm not the type who needs to be heard out loud. That's why I'm always mistaken for being quiet.

He told the therapist his version of the story about the previous day, about how I screamed, "I was done," framing it as a singular, jarring event rather than the inevitable breaking point after months of circular conversations that never landed. He emphasized that he had never raised his voice at me.

Our therapist asked me if I meant it, but before I even opened my mouth, he interjected and told her I didn't. He didn't even give me the dignity of answering for myself, but I didn't correct him because, honestly, I was still digesting the gravity of what my body had already expressed: exhaustion so deep it bypassed words. My body jolted, though my thoughts lingered.

It's too early to tell, especially with his attempt at therapy to resolve this.

Finally, it's my turn to speak: I told her that couples therapy was my idea because we had an unresolved issue that would determine our fate: children. I let her know about our child-free agreement in the beginning, and that's one of the many reasons we considered each other our "person." And his sudden change of heart shocked me.

The therapist realized I am a straightforward, communicative problem-solver, whereas he was the internal withholder, who only became expressive in controlled environments. That therapy session let him present his thoughts in a curated monologue, with my pain contained by the therapist's interventions.

The first session flew by. Before our departure, though, the therapist gave us homework: she asked that I refrain from asking him questions past a certain time into the night and that he try to articulate to me his thoughts as soon as they go through his mind. On the surface, it appeared balanced: one involved suppression from me, while the other required initiative from him. The truth is, one of us had already been used to carrying that kind of load.

One last request from her: stop referring to each other as "my person."

What does she mean? But he is my person.

This request was the most jarring, and I was reluctant to comply because the phrase had anchored our entire bond with the spiritual promise we built the future around. My former self had yet to realize that the phrase had long been hollow on his end; it's apparent to our therapist that "my person" hadn't been showing up as one, and what I had been investing in was a symbol, not the lived reality.

She then asked about the frequency of upcoming sessions.

He answered on our behalf, "As often as it'd take for us to communicate better. So, weekly?"

That rapid dedication functioned as an appearance of collaboration.

I entered therapy seeking clarity, but instead left with more fog. Departing for the airport unbothered, he left me burdened with unspoken sentiments. The initial session revealed the stifling dynamic: I was seeking my partner; he was looking for relief.

Debrief

We had a brief text exchange to follow up with the session before he boarded the plane. I told him that the topic of children was the core motivation for me to suggest couples therapy, but his ambiguity about that topic during the session concerned me. To me, if only one of us wanted kids, there was no amount of "good communication" that could reconcile the issue.

So, I texted him a binary question: Do you or do you not want children?

I wasn't asking for complex nuances. Instead, he drowned it in just enough plausible deniability to keep me spinning: he said I wasn't listening to what he and the therapist were trying to tell me. My head hurt again.

What does that even mean???

I promise I'm not a stupid person, but he sure made me feel that way just by... saying a lot and meaning almost nothing. He cast himself and the therapist as a united front, positioning me as the one who misunderstood both of them, when in truth, I was the only one naming the actual core rupture. He made me question my intelligence because I understood too well, and he had no intention of matching me in truth. What he did was sidestep the actual issue—children—and instead turn the focus onto my supposed failure to comprehend, keeping me on the defensive.

He wanted my confusion because it let him remain noncommittal while blaming me for the fallout. I was still operating in good faith, assuming that mutual love implied mutual effort towards a shared future. Yet, he was trying to maintain control over the narrative while keeping me attached and off-balance.

Chores

He returned after one week, harboring fresh discontent.

According to him, I ignored his contribution in housework—bathroom cleaning and cooking, and never showed gratitude. Knowing my preferred way to feel loved was quality time together and not   receiving acts of service, he explained he performed them while I was away so that he could prioritize time spent with me when we were both home.

That makes sense, I guess.

What made little sense was that he said I didn't show appreciation, but I did; it's in my nature. Though my kind of appreciation wasn't constant enough to satisfy his need to feel indispensable. His complaint had nothing to do with my actual behavior; he wanted to position himself as the martyr while I "overlooked" it all. That role allowed him to withhold affection while demanding mine.

I went into solution-searching mode and asked him to list the chores he did daily so I wouldn't miss thanking him for any task completion. Reviewing the lengthy list, I noted many redundancies and tasks I could manage. So I sent back a shorter, simpler list. I didn't just listen; I solved the puzzle by offering a path forward. By that action, I revealed the self-imposed nature of many of his proclaimed burdens. And that rational revelation undermined his entire narrative because his request for gratitude was a manufactured grievance meant to keep me small. What he sought was the moral high ground.

He exploited my sense of fairness, knowing I would respond with accountability. But no act of service on his part could match the real emotional labor I was doing. I was tending to the architecture of the relationship itself, while he polished surfaces and waited for applause.

Fog

Early therapy sessions emphasized communication improvement rather than his concerns about fatherhood. Admittedly, it was an assumption on my part that he had dropped the idea of having kids.

Perhaps our lack of communication caused him to consider having children as a straightforward solution to finding someone else?

He then dropped the bombshell: he told the therapist that I didn't like his family, and the feeling was mutual because they didn't like me either.

You can't just twist my words right in front of me like I'm not here.

I interjected and said, "By family, you just mean your mom, right? Even then, I never said I didn't like her. I just don't care for her because she hasn't earned my respect, and there is a vast difference." I lost it. He twisted my legitimate boundaries into sweeping accusations. In framing my emotional discernment as hostility, he became the misunderstood victim.

Home situations outside weekly couples' therapy sessions stagnated. And I consider those therapy sessions unproductive: they always began with him discussing himself and his life, while I listened because the therapist instructed me to be a better listener and offer comforting words, not solutions. He now even possessed the therapist's support, saying I was not heeding what both sought to impart.

So I would retreat into my head, where someone's word still meant what they said.

What are they telling me I don't grasp? Why am I like this? Everyone gets it, except for me.

Looking back, what I walked into was a performance where he could reframe his grievances as facts and recruit the therapist's authority to chip away at my clarity until I questioned my comprehension. He turned therapy into a triangulation under the guise of growth and was erasing me from the narrative while sitting right there in the therapist's office.

It's not that I didn't understand; it's that I refused to pretend that their version of events made sense. And when I spoke up for myself, he cloaked it all in therapeutic language, laced with just enough jargon to make me doubt my intelligence. My listening had exceeded any reasonable limit: I sought clarity, adjusted my responses, restrained my instincts to solve problems, practiced I-statements, and somehow it's still never enough.

Signs

My depressed partner was a volatile project that demanded maintenance. Not only did I rationalize his behavior, but I also sacrificed my clarity to protect his instability. I told myself he was my person, so I stayed rooted in the belief that if I could just be more supportive, I would earn back what had eroded.

Sometimes, I would make a casual comment about the altered passenger seat settings in his car; he would look at me, surprised, likely because he didn't think that I would have noticed, and claimed that he was cleaning the car or giving a coworker a ride.

I knew that my life before him was simpler. Then he came in with tracking of crumbs to piece together a reality he couldn't hide. I was placed in a permanent state of adjusting. Details that triggered my intuition must diminish for peace. But the peace never came, because it wasn't mine to create; it's his to withhold.

His mom alone brought a level of drama I never wanted. But I always rationalized it away.

I'm here now; we are here now. He is my person; we'll resolve this.

Or, more accurately, I could resolve this.

Despite two months of weekly couples therapy and his fifty-fifty life split, his depression and our dynamic hadn't improved. Therapy, a potential aid, became another site of self-regulation. It served as a stage for him to perform like someone trying, while I carried the actual cost. He never rose to meet me. If I could share with my past self, I would tell her that betterment wasn't crucial; she just needed to be free from the illusion that love must be earned through endurance.

That wasn't a connection; it represented emotional duty, appearing like love, with me bearing the entire burden. My body had the awareness, but my mind just kept hoping that effort would equal reciprocity, and I still wasn't ready to admit that he wasn't "my person."

His Dad

We went on the last Universal trip that we had in our books. He showed relief because all the planned trips in the past had made him feel stuck. This time, we added SeaWorld so that his dad and his girl-friend could tag along, using my Veterans Appreciation free admissions. I had met them once before; they liked me... or at least, that's what it seemed.

He once mentioned to me he perceived himself as a parent to his dad, painting him to be the most stubborn person, especially with his ego. I noticed his attempt to amend their father-son relationship, as he pointed out, "This is the first time you have come to a theme park with me since I was born."

That devastating comment was his attempt at vulnerability: childhood pain peeking through as a joke that went unnoticed.

His dad seemed surprised, saying, "Really?"

Their dynamic explained the cycle he came from: being bypassed in an emotional sense.

Megan back then was devoted to generosity. She failed to see what was happening in reality: he was trying to rewrite a father-son story that never existed, and she was the backdrop while he wrestled with ghosts.

But to be fair, I don't think he was aware of it.

I was the one offering a future that could hold meaning, but he couldn't hold it because he hadn't resolved his own emotional fractures from the past, and instead of healing alongside me, he retreated. And in that retreat, he made me feel responsible for his discomfort.

That trip made me realize something crucial: I wasn't the problem; his existing life was. I planned an experience that blended fun, family, and generosity, offering space for healing within his family dynamic. And instead of feeling grateful, he felt relieved because it marked the finality of his commitment to me.

Accountability

Having no further trips planned, I offered him an invitation to Universal several months down the road. To my surprise, he agreed, so I booked the flights and hotels as usual. I also reassured him it's no pressure if he'd rather spend time with friends instead. I just wanted him to do what's best for him. He thanked me and said he would refund me if he decided not to go.

By the way, he told me several times about refunding my money in the past. But he never reimbursed me as he had promised. His repeated phrase about it became a linguistic placeholder for something he never intended to do. Those were temporary comfort words, not promises meant to be honored. Demanding has never been in my nature. I usually just take the loss and make a mental note about the person who deceived me instead of making emotional scenes, which would require more energy. I'd rather gather evidence of character in silence instead of bargaining for scraps.

Therefore, I acknowledged his statement, yet I wouldn't pursue him concerning the funds, considering I indeed had not. The recollection revealed his culpability, leaving him vulnerable. His complexion flushed; he wondered why I had started a conversation so late into the night, explaining that his lack of mental energy prevented a proper response; he feared misspeaking. But it's well before the conversation curfew that he had imposed upon me. Unresolved problems bother me, and when I finally voiced them without blame, he panicked because I didn't leave him room to feel like the "good guy."

To me, it wasn't about money. The fact of the matter was that if he couldn't keep his word, please don't offer it in the beginning. I was tracking his patterns, not reimbursement. Day after day, he used the softness of my approach to continue slipping away from the version of himself I tried to believe in. And he was right: money had never been the issue; his accountability was.

Words

That brought up another concern we had discussed: my literal interpretation of his words annoyed him, and his annoyance baffled me.

If you don't mean your words, why did you let them come out of your mouth in the first place?

With him, everything was ambiguous, but:

Ambiguity brings out anxiety, and anxiety prevents peace.

I had also mentioned to him that I put more weight on people's actions than their words. I still remember his face showing confusion before he opined that words and actions were equally important.

We shared a precise clash of internal operating systems: I had a structure; he had a fog. And the more I tried to find a stable footing inside that fog, the more I blamed myself for not adapting to its shifting shape.

To me, language is a contract: if I say it, I mean it. If I offer it, I deliver. If I promise, I follow through. Anything less is destabilizing, which creates emotional risk. In contrast, he treated language as impressionistic. He spoke to manage moods, not to convey commitments. That's why when I took his words at face value, he felt trapped, as if I was holding what he had spoken aloud to a standard he hadn't consented to.

I listened to a guy unwilling to take responsibility for their words. And that's the paradox that drained me: being seen as a problem for hearing him. I wasn't too literal; he was just too slippery, and I kept trying to stand upright on a surface that was never meant to hold weight.

Staying In

Since the Fourth of July weekend was getting closer, it was my tradition to vacation then. My suggestion of a trip angered him; he replied he had not been present in town for the Fourth.

"Why are we always going somewhere else?" he asked.

He proposed that we stay home and watch the fireworks. My person, the "male version of me," who once said travel was a shared joy, now announced his fatigue. I internalized his words and absorbed the dissonance between his current self and the self who once mirrored my values.

That's true; he has never spent the Fourth in our city before. I'm not fond of fireworks, but he has never witnessed them here. Ugh, fine. I'll stay, even though it's not what I had wished for.

The emotional cost of choosing to stay was to suppress my rhythms in the name of accommodating someone whose center kept shifting while demanding that I stay still. Again, I didn't just hear what he said —I absorbed it, reasoned with it, and adjusted around it. That's the work of someone who lives in constant attunement to another's changing needs. But that work became invisible because it's expected of me. I set aside my default and deferred to his momentary frustration, just to preserve the relationship's equilibrium.

Breaking News

He had become more open with me, especially about his depression. One morning, upon arriving at my office, I received a text from him that began with, "I do love you..."

My entire being signaled anticipation. He was still typing when I was looking at the open tab. What followed was his telling me he needed to go live on his own to "find himself," which he had lost somewhere along our relationship because he kept giving to me. He said I was the reason he stopped going to the gym, playing golf, or hanging out with friends, which caused his depression, according to his therapist. Also, living with me influenced his decision about wanting kids or not. He said his therapist had told him to be selfish for once.

Umm... I just saw you in person this morning. Why wait until we are apart to text me something so important?

Because what he declared was an emotional bluff disguised as therapeutic insight. Confused, I vowed to support his healing journey, even if he had to move out.

"Even if it means you'll wait for me to come back?" He asked.

"Right, you mean move back? I'm hopeful that you'll find yourself again and move back soon." I responded.

"Thanks! Love you."

By the way, he had dropped the "I" from the "I love you" since he started the self-imposed fifty-fifty life split.

He then reassured me I was his partner and that I had shown him "the difference between a partner and a girlfriend/wife"... whatever that meant.

I have longed for the ambiguity to end. If living on his own is the solution, according to his therapist, then please get started soon.

Thus, following further consideration, I messaged him in the afternoon, instructing him to secure his own place as soon as possible.

Backfire

That night, he questioned why I constantly spoiled positive situations and explained that I had been very supportive that morning... even made him feel loved. Yet, in the afternoon, he became upset at my request for his timely departure.

Wait, what?

My attempt at supportive guidance backfired; a definitive deadline turned me into the villain. He explained that my follow-up text in the afternoon was why he had stayed at the office, searching for apartments, arranging viewings, and even touring one on his way home.

He desired my gentle gaze to fix on him, but when I gave him what he claimed to need—a green light to begin—it dismantled the illusion. I guess he didn't expect to be met with follow-through. That's the deeper pattern: my boundaries disrupted his control. He framed my message as rejection, and once I moved from emotional availability to logistical clarity, he lost the upper hand.

Again, my body felt confused, and this time, so did my brain. I couldn't understand his logic, but did he even have any? That contradiction allowed him to be the wounded hero, as if he were saying, "I must leave, yet how audacious of you to command my departure."

So, when did he plan on executing his plan if I didn't give him a timeline? The truth I failed to see then: he never planned on executing it. What he desired was to keep me orbiting his indecision.

Will he stay? Will he come back? Will he find himself and return as the man I once knew?

But the moment I called the question, his deferral of accountability was exposed—a way to leave me holding the weight of his confusion while he got credit for "doing the work." So, no, he never planned a timeline. There was only a script, and my clarity disrupted it.

Independence Day

His July Fourth weekend plan changed: he worked the holiday and then golfed with friends the subsequent days. I thought we had made a deal that we would stay in town for him, so I had already given up on the trip idea.

He promised he would come back for the fireworks display. But I don't give a flying fuck about fireworks, and he knew it! And he mentioned them as a placeholder gesture: something performative that required no effort.

He proposed covering for my trip should I change my mind about traveling—leaving me home was something he regretted, he claimed. I thanked him for his offer and told him I would like to stay home the entire weekend. I kept from him my plan: productive home research on supporting a depressed partner's journey of self-discovery. As usual, my internal frustration did not sit with me for long until I redirected my focus back on him.

My intellect made that plan, but my physical body wanted to grieve first. My tears followed as soon as he walked out the door for work on Independence Day. I grieved the vanishing of a future, one that hadn't met its end but had escaped my grasp already.

Even then, I desired to learn how I might aid him. I didn't know I was still trying to love someone who had already exited the bond. I grieved alone while trying to become more valuable to someone who never once studied how to stay.

Even as he receded, I still tried to be a good student, researcher, listener, and partner. The divergence between my continued immersion and his begun withdrawal caused my torment. My intellect understood it when he framed his departure as a journey of self-discovery, but my body's response revealed he had already discovered who he was when things got hard—someone who flees instead of roots.

Objects

He kept objects that had meaning for him, like the plastic bunny that his mom had sent him along with that Valentine's Day card. Occasionally, I would use his bathroom and see the seashell he had discovered at the beach still sitting on his shelves.

There's nothing special on the outside. What does this seashell represent?

This curiosity became obscured, eclipsed by several other matters of concern.

According to the diagram he had drawn, I was replaced, reclassified, and pushed to the outside of the circle. Yet he didn't harbor any expectations regarding the seashell or argue with the bunny; those objects occupied space in his world because they didn't demand reciprocation. They just existed—something I couldn't settle into without lying to myself.

He kept simple symbols, while I reflected depth. That seashell stood in contrast to what I offered: structure with meaning, and that meaning is threatening for someone not ready to live in it. He evaded me and preserved the objects on his shelves because they didn't challenge him to grow.

Fireworks

Five minutes before the scheduled fireworks display, he invited me to walk outside to watch; I declined. With that, he told me he was headed to the gym to "pop his back," a new habit he started coinciding with his fifty-fifty life split.

But I changed my mind as soon as the door slammed shut.

What the heck, it's an annual thing, and I hadn't watched the fireworks with him. It's right outside, only ten minutes of my time.

Thus, I donned footwear, searching for him at the gym.

The gym precedes the pool, which opens onto the deck, where I noticed his presence, using video chat to show fireworks from cities across the river, not those in front of us. My unexpected appearance forced a brief disruption in his performance. I assumed that was his mom and apologized for interrupting.

He concluded the call, put on a smile, and said, "You're my partner—the most important thing in my life. Others can wait."

We then found a spot to watch the fireworks. His body was next to mine during the display, but his mind was somewhere else. I picked up on his vibe and asked if he meant to watch with his mom via FaceTime instead. He reassured me I had not interrupted while pulling out his phone to snap and text photos of the fireworks.

He wasn't choosing me anymore, and he wasn't ready for that truth to be seen. I read him correctly, like I always did.

Once concluded, I inquired whether his mom enjoyed those photos. He said he hadn't texted his mom. That confused me.

To whom, then, if not his mom?

Our return path led past the gym; he desired entry, so I went in with him.

He just needed to pop his back, right? This should be quick!

But he halted and said he would be returning to our condo soon. That gesture meant he wanted space and my understanding without responsibility. I took the hint and walked home by myself.

In hindsight, the gym wasn't meant to fix his back. It functioned as an excuse, an escape from connection, giving an impression of consideration during his priority: the video call. Even in moments where intimacy could have existed, he chose control over the terms of closeness.

He didn't strive to stay, though he wasn't prepared to leave. The intimacy had hollowed out. And the person who once called me the center of his circle had already moved his emotional core elsewhere— even if his body hadn't departed yet.

Hypothetical

He claimed he only had to work the following morning, but he didn't return home until late evening. I wasn't pleased about it. He picked up on it and asked me what was wrong. I told him I had desired more time together before his move, especially since he was soon leaving for his golf weekend.

He then revealed a secret withheld from that morning: he had planned a garden visit as a surprise, but he perceived my sadness upon waking, scrapped the plans, went to his job, and then shopped, wishing to avoid witnessing my tears upon returning home.

I was confused.

Did he mention the plan before, and I didn't hear him? Or was it something he decided after waking up this morning?

I resented my mood because otherwise, we would have visited the garden. Had he informed me beforehand, I would have set my alarm and risen early.

But what if that surprise involved rewriting the past to justify his actions? Had tears not fallen, perhaps he would have offered the garden as proof of effort... or not. So it remained a hypothetical kindness, a non-event he could weaponize.

And if he indeed planned the surprise, it would reveal a deeper issue: his avoidance of my sadness was about his discomfort with intimacy. He desired to become the person performing kind gestures, provided I remained joyous enough to welcome them, devoid of back-story. I wasn't allowed to react to the reality he created with emotions, because my visible grief disrupted his narrative: that he was making me happy. He didn't want me to be sad about his move because it made him feel guilty. I see now that what happened here encapsulated the dissonance that plagued our entire relationship: he withheld information, then punished me for not responding to what he never shared.

Golf

During his drive to the golf course the following morning, he texted the news of the rental apartment acceptance, also adding that he felt weird telling me about it, but he aspired to be transparent with me.

To carry him through the void that he claimed to be facing, I spent the rest of that long weekend creating something tangible to leave him with: a book, just for him, filled with page after page of motivational words for him to flip through when he felt hopelessness living alone.

I felt that isolation was a strange suggestion by his therapist to heal his depression, but what would I know? I'm not a licensed therapist.

I had already done all the crying that was needed during his absence so that I could focus on becoming a better partner for someone dealing with depression upon his return. Hearing the doorknob turn, I raced to greet him with an enormous hug and kisses. Right. Plural. I had learned my lesson from his prior test.

He said, "Haha, you're cute."

Leading him to the living room, I seated him and handed him my book. That's me giving him my whole heart in the form I know best.

Scanning its thickness, he declared, "That's the nicest thing anyone has done for me."

I was grieving the loss of my shared home, fighting for clarity, and aching with confusion, and what I received in return was casual amusement.

His response was hollow, and that emptiness made me feel invisible again. He didn't sit with me under the weight of what that book symbolized: I was still trying, loving, and anchoring both of us in something real while he prepared to detach. He failed to treat the book with reverence during that devoted instant, which I only realized following his departure.

My instinct was to pivot the conversation back to him and ask him to tell me all about his golf weekend because, after all, he had given up his hobbies for me. Using a map on my phone, he showed me the golf courses and restaurants they visited. He shared that he was eye candy on the golf course because everyone was admiring his golf skills. I felt relieved hearing that he had enjoyed his trip; it marked a promising beginning to his self-discovery.

He kept showing me who he was—someone who felt more comfortable with admiration from a distance than engagement up close.

Did denial blind me, or did I not perceive it?

More Therapy

He asked whether lodging with me for several additional days was permissible before moving out. That inquiry felt weighty, concealing implied strain, as it strove to ease unavoidable parting. He requested space to ease his transition, a query that conveyed a fear regarding his departure. I, despite everything, provided space for it, agreeing to his request. It's an act of grace amid the growing distance, a fragile pause, and a brief extension of the life we once shared, even as the reality of change pressed in.

A therapy session occurred during those last days, when we first revealed the news to our therapist. She questioned whether we would take a break, go our separate ways, or stay together.

Per usual, I let him talk first. He gazed at me, then turned to the therapist and told her it would hurt him if I met someone else, but he would also understand it if I did. His words contrasted my stance; though they demonstrated a mix of vulnerability and fear, they also revealed a detachment that left me feeling lost.

Then it was my turn to speak. I explained to them that I believed our altered living situation had a minimal impact on our bond. Further couples therapy wouldn't prove useful if our relationship had already ended, as he had declared.

That session laid bare the gulf between our realities and hopes. He framed moving out as a necessary step for his own healing—even if it meant drifting apart—while I still clung to the hope of navigating this shift together, reimagining the relationship rather than ending it.

Our therapist then challenged him to think about how, in isolation, he would know he had "found himself" when no one was there to mirror him back. Her question cut deep; an unspoken tension hung in the room.

Our homework was to resolve our differences before the next session: staying together with a different living arrangement? Or is this goodbye permanent?

Upon the conclusion of the session, he sought that conversation... He had never been so keen to discuss anything. He exclaimed my position wasn't what we had agreed on, and I reminded him we never agreed on anything because we had never discussed it. He emphasized he could never "find himself" if staying in our relationship.

So then I asked, "What's the point of couples therapy if we will not be a couple?"

He reasoned he couldn't just quit cold turkey and continued to press, "I still want to date you. You mean if I asked you out to dinner, you wouldn't say yes?"

How does this make any sense? Why is he making everything so complicated?

My confusion stemmed not only from the emotional complexity involved in clinging to departing circumstances while respecting his wish to withdraw. His desire to still take me out on dates blurred boundaries further, making the breakup feel like a limbo.

Hopes

I helped him pack up and load his belongings into his car and inquired whether he wanted me to ride along and help with unloading.

He blurted out a practiced script, "I hear what you want. I don't want to have the memory of you being in my new place. And that's what I want."

Despite my disappointment, his answer impressed me. It felt like a stark contrast to the confusion and uncertainty he had shown for months. He, who once declared indecision, denied me a visit to his new apartment. It revealed how much therapy and time had shaped his responses, perhaps making him more certain of his boundaries but also more distant.

I thanked him, "I appreciate that you're being open with me about what you thought was best for you. I'm proud of you."

Even as I navigated my heartbreak, I let my strength and compassion show through by acknowledging his openness and effort in my message.

He thanked me and told me it wasn't easy, but he was trying. His message hinted at his struggle beneath the surface, a vulnerability that maybe wasn't always visible before.

He wanted to show me a video of his apartment on his phone. Asking if I was ready to see it because it was for me. My thoughts focused on his words.

Of course it's for me. Who else?

That question mirrored the one I had when he said he didn't text his mom the photos of fireworks.

If not her, then who?

Our dating anniversary was approaching, and I explained that the gift I had gotten for him had yet to arrive. He claimed he had already bought one for me, planning to leave it behind. But since I had brought up the topic, he intended to exchange them at a later time instead.

Isolation

I inquired whether his isolation included just me or everyone else. My question was about emotional boundaries, especially with his mom, whom I saw as the core issue.

He reported conveying to her the necessity for personal space owing to his depression. She then stopped texting that day... and resumed the very next day, asking if he had felt any better.

While his admission to her suggested a step towards setting boundaries, which was a hopeful sign, it baffled me that she was expecting a depressed person to heal over a night of sleep. Although I kept my opinions to myself, my surprise must have shown on my face because he asked, "What? You expect her not to care?"

He then pulled out his phone and showed it to me. His unresponsiveness for several dates, a change, proved surprising. The absence of an immediate reply offered a crack in the cycle of his emotional entanglement with her, and maybe, a space where he could start defining himself on his own terms.

Moving Out

A prior modeling commitment forced my early departure on his move-out day. That busy morning became our last in-person encounter before the upcoming therapy session.

He walked me to my car and hugged me goodbye. I told him to please keep the keys to my place because that's our home. I assured him he would be welcomed back whenever he was ready. Those last words were genuine, though I failed to grasp that his departure involved avoidance cloaked in self-exploration, a method to withdraw without naming it for what it represented: desertion presented as righteousness.

His phone rang as we were letting go of our hug. I believe he hit the answer button by accident.

"Hello?" a female voice asked on the line.

He hung up without responding, and I assumed it was a colleague looking for him.

I drove off and received a text from him: "Drive safe. Let me know when you get there. I love you."

The "I" reappeared in the "I love you" as an echo that softened the rupture he had already planned.

Upon my return home, my emotions hit harder seeing empty spaces where his belongings used to be. He left behind his dry-erase board, the one that he had used to draw the diagram to illustrate my downgraded significance in his life.

This time, he wrote a note: "I have to go do this. I tried finding myself while living with you, but it didn't work. I need to be selfish for once. Remember, like my therapist said, we have love for each other; we'll figure it out."

After scanning it once, I wiped the board clean before fully understanding its content. My body was keeping the score: it understood what my mind couldn't yet name and moved before I could think—just like that moment in the car when I kept screaming, "I'm done." It recalled each instance I felt ungrateful for seeking understanding behind his words. What seemed like an impulse was clarity coming from somewhere deeper than logic.

He also left behind a residue of dangling promises. He framed his leaving as courageous, but in reality, the courage lay in me, the one who kept giving even while unraveling, and the healing began the moment my hands wiped the board clean. I didn't just erase his words; I reclaimed my space.

Aftermath

My first night alone was spent in tears. Perhaps I was grieving, but it wasn't an official goodbye to me. We never came to terms with our status as a unit. I didn't want to pressure someone suffocating in pain to do anything. That's why I left it undiscussed on purpose; my restraint was intentional.

Things are going to unfold by themselves.

My refusal to chase stemmed from my firm belief that love cannot be coerced. Instead, I tracked his actions, which led me in circles.

He messaged me the next day saying, "I was thinking about you last night. Just wanted you to know."

His apparent attempt to connect represented communication maintenance: it kept the link alive, yet never closed the gap.

I didn't talk to him for a few days until he texted me the first weekend we were apart. He communicated that he had exercised at the gym for two hours, which marked his initial workout session since relocating to my city. He emphasized that I was right in saying that physical exercise could improve mental health. I didn't recall ever using those exact words, but it sounded like a sentiment I do believe.

That day, I walked the runway in a Disney princess look. I sent him a backstage photo, and he responded, saying I was a real princess. That's emotional bread-crumbing—a compliment meant to soothe without restoring.

Ranting

He contacted me at the end of another silent week, cloaking his return in self-discovery. His rhythm emerged: he reached out just enough to signal presence, never enough to stand still beside me.

He typed self-focused paragraphs at length over the weekend, timed right before our upcoming therapy session: he had been homeless (his word, not mine) following his first night alone because of a roach infestation in his apartment, for which he needed to seek legal counsel. Complaining to me, he couldn't understand why, despite his high executive salary, they had given him an apartment that was unlivable. He emphasized that he hadn't returned to my condo even though he needed a place to stay and claimed he wouldn't return until he found himself because he loved me.

I thanked him for opening up. While I conveyed my understanding of his perspective, I clarified that I would have welcomed his return. Likewise, turning away wouldn't be something that I do to someone I loved.

He then ended the call with a rushed conclusion, stating he was unsure why the Universe had tested him or what lessons he was supposed to learn, but he gained significant self-knowledge. His reference to the Universe was to manipulate me with tenderness because he knew that's my spiritual anchoring.

He performed his openness when it was aligned with the external structure, making him appear like he was trying. But it's always about him: his apartment, injustice, and homelessness. Explanations for his absence made up the entire text exchange, lacking inquiry concerning my well-being.

I wasn't invited into his healing process but kept as a container for dropping his narratives into so they didn't spill over. He would never inquire regarding its impact, since that action demanded consideration of others.

I thought I was grieving his departure, but I now realize that I was mothering the emotional truth alone, even in his leaving. I offered him my participation in continued couples therapy as a middle path, believing in shared commitment, but he treated it like a scheduled purge, not a bridge back to me.

On My Way

The next communication I received from him was before our couples therapy session, saying, "On my way."

That message provided a lifeline; relief mingled with happy tears washed over me.

I had spent a month learning to support a depressed partner. As soon as I saw him, I gave him a long, unrelenting hug and wouldn't let go, because "my person" was in my arms again; I had longed for him. That hug was my whole body saying what my words had been forced to hold in: I missed you. I am still here. I am still trying.

He got us coffee, which was ritualistic, but he didn't ask me what I had gone through in his absence, which was no longer surprising.

What I wouldn't have expected was that he grew facial hair. From the start of our relationship, I had let him know that I chose him because he didn't have facial hair. It was a joke, but I meant it sincerely. Facial hair was a turnoff for me, and perhaps I'm in the minority. So, showing up to therapy in a version of himself he knew I wasn't attracted to meant he no longer wanted to impress me. It represented dissent through subdued detachment.

It's like him saying, "I no longer shape myself with you in mind."

Continued Therapy

Our therapist asked about our communication. Unlike my habit of letting him talk first, I rushed to answer without hesitation.

"What communication? We hardly talked." I said.

I wasn't angry, just honest, which was a quirk that he claimed he had wanted but then resented me for embodying it.

He then took over the space and filled it with himself, recounting his homelessness, a reminder that he was the protagonist of an ongoing crisis. And at 37, he told us that living alone was a first.

Our therapist vocalized my thought: "Welcome to the club."

Her light sarcasm landed where it needed to. Indeed, I live alone, embrace silence, and confront myself—acts he lacked the courage for.

He told the therapist that the hiccups he encountered delayed the start of his journey because he couldn't start doing the things he planned to. I was still absorbing every drop of information he gave, even when it was recycled. The therapist asked whether he meant his self-discovery journey was going to take longer than expected.

Thank you — my thought exactly!

But his answer, "No, I'm just stating that I couldn't start my plan," wasn't helpful.

He kept using the language of healing… but when pressed, he couldn't explain what that journey entailed, how long it would take, or how he would know when it's done because her question revealed the truth: there's no real journey.

Graduate School

He also said that he was looking into attending classes again for an MBA, emphasizing he had tried to begin it about six times in the past but never went through with it because previous partners stopped him from pursuing further education.

That reminded me of an interesting moment the morning of his move-out day: he pointed at my PhD regalia displayed on my wall and said he was proud of me, unprompted.

He was queried by the therapist whether he had planned to begin it during the upcoming school term, fall.

Smiling, he responded, "I'm thinking more like spring."

Let's do the math.

Fall.

Winter.

Spring.

Ah. I see. Three more seasons!

That's sufficient duration to delay responsibility while keeping tomorrow beyond grasp. I didn't say it aloud—but I saw through it.

When I had my turn to talk, I thanked him for coming. He chuckled, then inquired if I had assumed he wouldn't show up, to which I didn't respond.

Instead, I told the truth of what it had cost me by stating that it had been twenty-eight days since he moved out, and I had been crying through every one of them. Grief felt endless; unlike normal breakups, this situation lacked finality. I remained trapped in uncertainty, permitted neither progress nor granted release.

Announcement

Before the session ended, the therapist asked me if I had anything to add, likely because he had used the entire session talking about himself.

Frankly, I didn't mind because I centered on his pain with intention: my goal was to become a better partner for someone dealing with depression. I was adjusting to listening, hoping devotion would serve its purpose: his return.

He interjected with a proclamation: he told his parents they must look after themselves because he refused to be their financial and emotional support. He added he hadn't visited his mom and grandpa since our new living arrangement, which meant he dropped the fifty-fifty life split completely. He emphasized he wanted me to know about those improvements before the end of our session, anticipating that I would feel relief or maybe even hopeful.

Good for him. I'm impressed. I have faith that he's on the right path to self-discovery.

However, I couldn't help but notice he held it up like some prize, a badge of growth, as if he wanted credit from me for finally doing what I had long known he needed to do.

Agreement

Then, the therapist asked us both to agree on communication frequency. I explained why I refused to initiate; chasing would erase my dignity because he was the one who departed. He became concerned, expressing that he would cherish my communication to gauge his presence within my thoughts. That comment sounded ridiculous, so I responded by telling him I had never stopped thinking about him or us. So, did he want me to be constantly texting him?

But what he really meant was, "Carry the burden for me. Make this easier for me. Even now, I need you to reach for me first."

I had tried to stay supportive. But I wasn't confused anymore, not really. I knew his quest for self-discovery would always mean my loss. Perhaps this always served his plan: to vanish, evading responsibility with a subtle touch, while leaving an opening to return should solitude prove unfulfilling.

And me... I finally let the silence speak for itself.

I wanted a definition; he offered a delay.

I wanted connection; he offered recounting.

I wanted the relationship; he wanted the spotlight.

This session didn't reunite us. If anything, it reminded me he had already left. Even when he was there, his center of gravity was always himself.

Another Letter

I walked him to his car after the session and left him with a seven-page letter I had handwritten for him. Yes, I do like writing letters, and this one contained a reflection of our year together because the next therapy session would have passed our anniversary. He responded by saying he wasn't aware we were exchanging gifts that day, so he had left mine in his apartment. What seemed like humility was, in fact, his holding onto ambiguity. I still tried to show up, even in grief.

I never received the gift that he said he had already gotten for me, nor did I do the follow-up, because my body already knew the answer: I was done chasing meaning in the empty spaces where it should have been. The gift itself wasn't the point; his lack of follow-through was. I had already learned that confronting him would only lead to more confusion, so he dragged me through under the guise of finding himself. And my gut was telling me he had never gotten me a gift to begin with.

What he called depression was real, but what he did with it, how he used it to obscure, was damaging to my internal compass because he was evasive, even with himself... Actually, especially with himself.

Mindset

His nonexistent contact that showed he didn't want a relationship with me somehow brought me ease. I started seeing how he would take my attendance at our monthly therapy session as a cushion, a soft place to land if he needed proximity without commitment. I refused to be a safety net: I was there to witness closure, not to keep the door propped open for someone who stayed halfway in.

I deserve someone who chooses me, day after day.

That's a revelation I had. Instead of trying to make him see me, I began seeing myself. This clarity accompanied me into the next therapy session: it's no longer about him.

Because I had a TV modeling job that morning, I asked about his availability to reschedule our appointment, providing no details. Previously, he had instructed me to notify him of my TV appearances because he claimed he wished to view them. Given the worsening circumstances, compliance felt unnecessary.

So I showed up at the session, looking all "model-like."

Upon first seeing me, his expression brightened, stating, "You look nice."

Whatever. Just words.

Finally, not only did my body feel it, but my intellect also saw through his performance disguised as connection. His words lacked importance, since inquiring about rescheduling would have revealed it sooner.

This version of me walked into that therapy office no longer hoping to be chosen. I had already realized that I deserved someone who chose me on their own, with no need to figure themselves out first at my emotional expense.

One More Session

The therapist asked how we were doing.

He alone answered, "It's nice to see Megan looking healthier."

Then, he repeated most things that he had already told us during the earlier sessions.

Before that session concluded, and it was then that I could talk, I declared:

Everyone deserves to have someone who chooses them, again and again.

"I'm not talking about just me like I'm special; I'm talking about anyone, even those whom you bump into on the street," I added.

He didn't respond or even seem moved. My offering was a universal truth, yet it was met with silence.

Our therapist suggested that we increase the frequency of our sessions if the only communication we would ever have was in her presence.

I know... It's an irony I've already seen ever since he stopped communicating with me after he moved out.

As she was walking us out, she gazed at both of us, focusing on me, and asked us to contemplate whether our relationship met each of our needs. She witnessed the disparity: me arriving more self-aware each month, while facing this individual repeating the same story without progression.

She caught me shaking my head and called it out, telling me that meeting our partner's needs is crucial in a relationship. I didn't even realize that my head was moving on impulse when my body was already ahead of my brain again. I was neglecting myself while serving someone who did not pick me. My nervous system was screaming for me to return to myself with the devotion given to him. So my head shook, and that was my answer.

Worry

He offered me a ride home afterwards, but I was walking to meet "someone" for happy hour down the street.

He seemed surprised and said, "Oh... I think... I think it is good that you're meeting someone for dinner."

It caught him off guard because I was no longer showing up to play the emotional caretaker role he had expected.

As soon as I got to the restaurant, I received a text from him: "Are these conversations hitting a dead end if I do not meet your needs?"

Conversations? What conversations? We don't talk anymore.

Confusion reigned; not until later did I realize that what he posed was not a question. Instead of asking what he could do differently to show up better, it was a manipulative bid for control disguised as curiosity. The wording placed the obligation upon me, as though my needs generated difficulty for him.

The following day, I informed him I was departing for the airport that afternoon. Should he desire discussion, I could create space. He replied right away by asking where I was headed. I didn't respond to his inquiry because I didn't owe him my itinerary after his lack of effort in communicating with me. I was drawing a boundary without realizing it.

My silence prompted another text from him, which let me know that his boss was nearby, preventing him from stepping away. He inquired regarding my return. Again, I didn't owe him my whereabouts. He relinquished entry into intimacy when he vanished following his move.

He was the one who changed the relationship. All I did was to honor that shift, keeping the clarity he evaded.

I was no longer operating under his rules, where he got to disappear for weeks and then drop breadcrumbs, expecting me to follow. I had already spent months offering effort while he delivered self-preservation cloaked as healing. He no longer knew how to locate me. Because for once, I was no longer holding space for his uncertainty.

Going Solo

Once I got settled in Universal, my heart softened, likely because the memory of being there with him was still fresh. So I texted him a photo of it and told him that the following Monday I would be available to talk.

He didn't reply until Monday, when we were supposed to talk, and relayed that he had opted to golf instead. It was a passive dismissal. He showed me yet again that when faced with the chance to step towards me, he would rather preserve his comfort.

I didn't respond and instead stopped texting him altogether because I finally saw that he wasn't sincere in wanting to talk to me.

Despite my continuous silence, he texted again, "I've been reflecting on how enjoyable Universal must've been for you. I don't know if I can go there without you yet. I'm so proud of you."

On the surface, his message was a safe, sentimental gesture designed to evoke warmth. He was trying to maintain emotional relevance without doing the work of being present or stepping into real accountability.

But look closer, and you'll see that it was he saying, "How dare you go there without me so soon as if I never happened in your life."

I waited until the next day to respond: "It was definitely different, but certainly a lot of fun. Thank you!"

My reply was poised without reopening the door: I confirmed my experience, but not in his story anymore. He strove to keep me connected, yet never offered tangible commitment. But I stopped grasping for coherence in his ambiguity and finally chose myself without apology. Unintentionally, I confirmed his biggest fear: she doesn't need me.

Mail

A day later, he requested to come by to pick up his mail. That's right. He never changed his address with the post office.

As I was going to let him know that I would leave them with the concierge, he added, "Plus, it'd be nice to see you again."

So I told him to come by the next day during lunchtime.

Before his expected arrival, he texted to say he still planned to collect his mail but needed to hurry back to the office to attend a meeting. I saw through him. I knew it was his way of telling me he wouldn't stay long, not that I wanted him to either, though.

He phoned me upon his arrival to announce that he had just parked and inquired whether he ought to visit my apartment.

How dare he think he's still allowed into my space!

I rejected his request and told him to wait downstairs.

He saw me approaching from afar, as he put a big grin on his face, which I did not return. He embraced me and wouldn't let go, but my face couldn't lie: I was over it.

I gave him his mail, together with his birthday present, which only arrived after he had moved out. He told me he wasn't made aware that we were exchanging birthday gifts, or he would have brought mine with him, mirroring his speech about the anniversary gift that I had never received.

He added that he also wanted to do something "extravagant" for my birthday and even allowed me to choose between a gift and an experience. His statement confused me because he said he had gotten me a gift already, which he didn't bring.

So why let me choose an experience?

Anyway, I answered by asking if it must be either/or. He assured me we would further discuss it at a later time.

He then presented his phone and declared, "This is me being vulnerable with you," something I had always desired.

He then showed me a photo of his grandpa's chopped-off toes. I flinched and told him I didn't want to see it. He stowed his phone away and commented that he would delete that photo. That moment reminded me of the time when he had told me that discussing with his ex the logistics of relocating their aging parents was the deepest conversation he had ever had. And this time, a gruesome photo equated vulnerability.

He added that he preferred regular communication to prevent me from withholding details, similar to the recent Universal solo-trip situation. I didn't respond because I lacked the understanding of why he always had to announce his actions when he could have simply executed them.

Instead, I let him know I no longer saw the point of wasting time on attending couples therapy when we didn't even talk. He stated we would converse further, his specialty being forecasting discussion, yet it never transpired. I then cancelled the upcoming appointments without consulting him again.

Before leaving for the meeting that he didn't seem to have to rush back for anymore, he asked if I wanted to grab breakfast together the following week without setting an actual date. Yet another announcement of hypothetical future actions. Confusion set in, and we hadn't even met for ten minutes by this point. His consistent pattern involved prominent pronouncements replacing genuine deeds. He deployed pledges to occupy space, just long enough to stop me from leaving, without committing to the labor involved in staying.

My nervous system had finally memorized the pattern: big words, vague plans, no follow-through, and a kind smile to mask his withdrawal.

I had been trained in inconsistency to doubt my perception. But now, I had stepped out of the fog. This time, my silence said, "I'm done," with dignity. And so, he shifted tactics: layered on possibilities, hoping I would anchor to one.

Caretaking

He texted me and claimed, once again, that he wanted to do something extravagant for my birthday. He was even so kind as to give me three choices. They are Show A, Show B, or Show C of the NYC Broadway ticket.

Wait, so is he sending me there on my own, or is he coming?

A thought that I eventually asked him, and he dodged my question by saying that he would get me "my ticket."

You have got to be kidding. I never suggested a Broadway trip for my birthday.

Again, I wasn't interested in a texting war, so I told him to call me to discuss. He called me and mentioned the convenience of talking on the phone during his drive home from work. That in itself sounded confusing to me...

What's wrong with calling me after getting home?

I struggled to understand him with the audio quality in his car. He started by asking if I had decided which show I wanted to see. I announced that going to NYC for a Broadway show alone wasn't something I had in mind for my birthday. I then asked him about his birthday plan.

Beep-beep-beep...

Sounds like we got disconnected.

He called back and answered my question with a defensive attitude that I could sense even over the phone. He shared plans to spend it with his mom and grandpa; this occasion harks back to his high school years.

Beep-beep-beep.

Sounds like we got disconnected again.

After calling back, he urged me to reconsider his offer. He emphasized that he wanted to "take good care of me" while he was on his self-discovery journey and claimed it was his responsibility to ensure my birthday was decent.

And this time, the connection remained active. He just hung up on me before I could respond.

Then I understood that the previous disconnections weren't technical glitches of cellphone connection; they were glimpses of his mask slipping. When the conversation became real, he would find ways to exit, literally and figuratively. Hanging up mid-conversation wasn't just rude; it was a refusal to engage vulnerably.

Those phone calls were a perfect microcosm of everything that had been unfolding between us. The extravagance he promised felt like an attempt to control the narrative: "I did something grand, so don't question me." I was left with an empty gesture. The gift he claimed to want to give was about preserving his own emotional distance, wrapped in a showy package. His behavior, however, spoke louder than any words: his inability to stay connected even in small moments revealed how fractured the relationship was in real time.

Gift

The next day, I received an alert from an online retailer saying two Harry Potter books were being shipped to my address, followed by his text telling me he had just sent some pre-birthday gifts my way.

I couldn't believe it. Those were the same books he had bought for me for Valentine's Day. It almost felt like a gesture on autopilot, lacking consideration. It was a sign of how little attention he had paid to our history together. His saying that he already got my birthday gift before also caused my confusion. I recalled him telling me he had it but left it in his apartment, which mirrored what he had told me about the anniversary gift, too.

He must have received notification of those returns because he texted to ask if I already had them. His question was almost absurd given the context, highlighting his detachment. He didn't remember getting them for me seven months ago. I kept my thoughts to myself, though, without replying. It showed a striking disconnect between his awareness and my reality.

By that point, I had ignored every single one of his text messages since he had hung up on me the previous week. He transitioned from sending zero texts to sending at least one daily. When he saw me disengage, he ramped up the volume, but without the substance needed to reconnect. I had already transcended to a place where his words and actions no longer carried weight. This was the point where I started protecting my peace. It was a boundary silently drawn, even if he didn't fully register it.

Birthday

Our birthday came. I avoided greeting him.

In contrast, he waited until late afternoon to text me, "Happy Birthday, 9/27. Even though we're spending this day apart, it doesn't change how I feel about you."

That text was an obvious message of emotional distance. He wouldn't even address me by my name; I was reduced to just a number. Using the date erased intimacy, lessened the genuine connection, and shifted the personal experience into a cold acknowledgment. He claimed his feelings were unchanged, which was ironic to know because it meant I still held no significance; he still didn't choose me.

My lack of response eventually prompted him to cease contact. My choice to remain silent spoke volumes: I communicated that I refused to engage in performative gestures that lacked meaning. His stop in contact after noticing the canceled therapy appointments confirmed his awareness of the shift.

The relationship had moved beyond repair in his eyes, and in mine, too. The truth lay bare: a lack of mutual choosing defined the space between us, signaling what our bond could never transform into.

The Other Woman

Six months later, when I had forgotten his existence, a stranger direct-messaged me on Instagram with two screenshots of their phones compared side-by-side: a photo of me swinging a golf club saved on his phone and a text message from her wishing him a good time golfing with his friends on her phone. Those instances shared the same time-stamp.

She asked if I had known about it, and if I already did, she was sorry... That "sorry" puzzled me.

She also asked to jump on a call with me but later changed her mind, claiming he didn't want us to talk.

She told him?

I let her know that if she still wanted to talk, I would make myself available. She offered gratitude and additional information: he was living a double life between us. He moved in with her while claiming visits with his mom and grandpa every other week, but in reality, he was alternating living at my place and hers.

So his self-imposed fifty-fifty living arrangement that I had endured wasn't between his family and me; it was between the other woman and me.

Getting into his phone helped her discover the truth. She said she was feeling devastated and expressed regret about not knowing sooner.

That exchange marked the last time I ever heard from her because she deactivated her account the next day, then reactivated it a few days later with an updated profile photo, replaced with their new wedding photo.

He had flown her to Las Vegas to marry her during the days she went offline—that was within five days since she had learned about the truth from his phone and reached out to me. Their marriage ceremony happened on the date of our dating anniversary.

Overwriting

Once again, I had to relive all the memories I had in my head, one by one, "correcting" them with the truth that I know now. Something that I had done in the past… too many times.

She turned out to be the new hire he had to go into the office to train, despite the remote work nature of his job. They started dating almost immediately, and that's the real reason he switched jobs.

The midday beach trip wasn't with his divorcing friend—it was her. Thus, he kept the seashell, treating it as holy.

When he claimed to have brought that same divorcing friend with a pickup truck to haul furniture from IKEA. It was her.

The passenger seat adjustments he couldn't explain away. It was her.

With whom did he dine, indulging in a rainbow sliders dish alongside the take-home rubber duck? It was her and her children.

Why did he conceal his phone in the vehicle while eating with me at that restaurant? He unloaded his frustration on me face-to-face while having an argument with her over the phone.

His new habit of going to the gym to "pop his back." It was to video chat with her. He likely was impressing her with her daily two-hour gym habit, just like he was to me.

Who was he showing the fireworks to when I walked in on his video chat? It was her.

Who did he send those fireworks photos to if not his mom? It was to her.

That golf trip during the Fourth of July weekend? He took her and her children on a trip to NYC.

He didn't spend his birthday with his mom and grandpa. It was a lie he blatantly told me. Instead, he took her to Disney World.

He proposed to her during their Disney World trip over the New Year, the same trip that he and I had taken the year prior.

They celebrated her birthday in the Cayman Islands: the same resort, restaurants, and excursions that we had chosen.

The Disney ears, which he dragged me to seek throughout the parks, declaring them for his mom, were, in truth, for that woman and her daughter, the reason he always purchased them in pairs. I remember asking him to hold off buying them early because I didn't like the hassle of carrying them around all day. He got enraged at me one night when we got to the store after they had closed, which forced him to order the ears online the next morning. He even told me he would never listen to me regarding Disney purchases again.

He felt anger towards me, citing the deadline to vacate, which stemmed from his own suggestion. I later found out the truth: the other woman was also cheating on her partner at the time when they got together. Hence, her home wasn't ready for him to officially move in with all his belongings. He thus rented an apartment temporarily until she resolved her own infidelity.

When he was supposedly homeless, like he told our therapist and me, all four of them actually flew to Arizona and the Grand Canyon for vacation, when he previously claimed that the trip was work-related. I should have known that the import/export company he was working for wouldn't have an office in a city that cargo ships cannot access.

Reality

The other woman was receptive to materialistic treatment and wouldn't question his living-beyond-his-means lifestyle because she benefited from it. I bet she still doesn't know that he has over one hundred thousand dollars of credit card debt, which I later found out.

But would she care even if she knew?

He was living with her in her home, about forty-five minutes from mine—a home she or her ex-husband had bought. That's when I realized his pattern of moving in with female homeowners: his ex, me, then this other woman.

That also explains why he no longer needed the pickup and drop-off at the airport because he was driving his Tesla across the river, not to the airport.

His sudden urge to have children also makes sense now. It came to light that he kept telling me that living with me prevented him from deciding on having offspring, because he needed to have more interactions with children... her children, a son and a daughter. Somehow, my existence hindered his opportunities to engage with them.

Not only can taking her children to Disney World and other childlike activities boost his image of being a great stepdad, but it also soothes his own internal childhood nostalgia. It's a perfect setup.

The truth is, he had already decided that she and her kids were the total package better suited for him, but instead of owning up to his change of heart like a grown, responsible adult, he had to set up the "kiss test" and look for flaws in me to justify his infidelity and convince himself that his integrity was intact.

What's more? While the enmeshment between him and his mom was undeniable, he continued to use his mom as a cover for the other woman, allowing me to believe that his mom was more overbearing than she really was.

The fact that he took part in couples therapy with me while he was also a couple with another woman confirmed my previous suspicion about him having me as a safety net.

His physical presence within my shared existence, along with emotional deceit, revealed his deep entanglement in a double life. His "journey" that I endured was about a guy who was divided in allegiance and love, leaving me with the fragments to piece together later. This late discovery of heart-wrenching betrayal felt like foundational tremors.

Déjà vu

In the end, I wasn't chosen yet again. The reason remained consistent: someone else was selected. But this realization eased my pain after my false reality of not being enough of a partner to a depressed person. Despite his depression, he cheated. That alone set me free of my self-imposed obligation.

That clarity, even though painful, granted me profound freedom. I wasn't responsible for his choices or betrayal anymore. His depression wasn't an excuse for his actions, and it was never my job to fix him or carry the weight of his fractured loyalty.

That other woman received solid proof on his device and requested my clarity, only to withdraw beforehand; it showed they were well-suited for each other. That knowledge shielded me from self-blame's prolonged burden.

It's a brutal lesson in how sometimes love and effort aren't enough when the other person isn't present or honest. But in that realization, I reclaimed my dignity and my right to demand being chosen—without caveats or conditions. My healing no longer depended on him; it began with that truth.

CHAPTER 7: CRUMBS

I believed I had chosen better last time. Turned out, I didn't.

My Level

By this point, others around me echoed what I had already internalized: partners in my dating history weren't compatible with me. "My level" is a concept most people derive from a checklist, including attractiveness, education, financial stability, etc.

Because finding someone with a doctorate who also met other criteria seemed impossible, I lowered my requirements for the "male version of me." But he didn't see himself as my equal, even though I didn't hold his bachelor's degree against him. Earning bonus points for details like his birthday—I talked myself into believing he was my match.

Not understanding how to play the "dating game" correctly, my best friend offered a logical explanation: Practice makes perfect. Why assume dating is unique?

That makes perfect sense! I always welcome self-improvement opportunities.

Approaching dating as a skill, I figured it could be mastered through focused practice.

Swiping

Having deleted the dating app after finding "my person," I re-downloaded it and logged back on.

"I have yet to be found," my profile read.

Right, I almost forgot; that's what my bio stated last time, when I was letting fate control the narrative. But now that fate has proved me wrong, I'm calling the shots this time!

I filtered the age search to be plus or minus five years of mine. My ex was eight years my junior and had proven himself to be immature.

More than half of my matches faded during the initial stage. Several switched to text, then a few to calls, and eventually three requested dates.

One didn't care to know me because he was too self-absorbed. Another appeared refined but lacked truthfulness. Then one's superficiality prevented engaging in deeper discussions. I wasn't picky; I was finally tuning into my accurate barometer. Nobody advanced past the early stages, showing that the majority struggled relating to my level of emotional, intellectual, and interpersonal awareness.

Dating is a distorted system by design because it doesn't value clarity, and that rendered me hidden from game participants.

A Nurse

I then broadened the age parameters to seven years on either side of mine. That's when a male nurse appeared, which sounded intriguing.

I have never dated a nurse.

I had already learned the hard way that a person's relationship with their work says a lot about their outlook on life. So, when he highlighted the love of being a nurse, it ignited something within me because it signaled aliveness.

The preset icebreaker he had chosen was "What's the next thing you're most excited about?"

Without hesitation, I typed, "as little as a cup of black coffee tomorrow morning and as big as my upcoming trip to Australia."

My reply held both the micro and macro of life, and I wanted someone who could appreciate that range.

I didn't have to wait long to receive his response: "I like that. Excited about the big and small moments in life. Australia? For work or leisure?"

His affirming response created shared viewpoints. I was auditioning him for depth, and he passed the opening scene. And just like that, we hit it off. Our messages covered a wide range of subjects... typical dating app fare when both are serious about finding a match.

I inquired whether he spoke Polish, as stated on his profile. He explained that he was the first and only one in his family who was born in the US; his parents and older brother immigrated from Poland. I shared that I had traveled to Warsaw and spent an entire day at the Chopin Museum. His intrigue showed in his saying that Poland usually isn't a popular travel destination and that he walked past that museum without time to go inside. This was an early signal of mutual interest overlap. I was testing for resonance, and he seemed to give it.

We lived only about a twelve-minute walk apart, which added to the illusion of alignment because proximity makes things feel meant to be.

Based on the hunger for someone who could finally meet me on my level, I was already building a narrative with all those details, viewing them as early signs of compatibility.

He felt different, and that "different" felt like hope.

Deeper Questions

He confirmed what he wrote on his profile: he is a go-with-the-flow kind of guy. Also, if his date had a request, he would "likely say yes, so take advantage of that," which I interpreted as generosity. At first glance, he positioned himself as low-conflict—someone I could manage alongside rather than feel dragged down by. He presented as someone who fit what I was looking for: calm and introspective.

But what does he mean by "going with the flow"?

Knowing that a guy who agreed too much might just develop animosity until he blamed me for his exit with flair. So I tested him by asking the exact question that had gone unspoken in my last relationship: whether he saw possible resentment accumulating if he kept agreeing to things he didn't want to do.

I named the dynamic before it took root. He said he didn't see himself doing anything against his will to harbor grudges. A purported honest answer… but his framing still left room for self-deception: the very pattern I feared.

He shared with me that he had been a nurse for eleven years, moving floors to be with his brother, a fellow nurse. He introduced his brother's predicament but deferred details. I did not press because prying into anyone's business is never my intention, especially the first time we chat. I honored boundaries even before trust was earned. Unbeknownst to me, the emotional atmosphere was already tilting as I investigated patterns.

He also shared something he felt was worth mentioning: he sought therapy regularly to help him communicate better. Recall how much I appreciate those who pursue counseling and acknowledge it? I lit up because it made him feel real. I let him know I was glad he found therapy beneficial because I believe responsible people should value mental health betterment. Then, I shared my therapy experience to establish a dynamic of reciprocal vulnerability.

His disclosures felt meaningful, but in hindsight, they lacked depth. The difference was subtle, yet it could be the core divide in a connection.

Deal-Breakers

We had one major mindset in common: neither of us was there to waste time, so we hurried to get the deal-breakers out of the way.

Car. He didn't have one, so that wouldn't violate the car criteria that I had set for myself. *That was easy.* He passed that checkpoint, so I kept going.

Kids. This topic was where the stakes rose. This held weight, originating from my prior relationship. He shared that he had shifted from wanting the full white-picket-fence fantasy with three kids to just one kid and then to a lifestyle without kids, which he felt was more aligned with freedom. While there's nothing wrong with a changing mind, his answer made me feel unstable.

But hearing his declaration of prioritizing a partner over children was music to my ears; that made both of us have the same belief.

Being cautious, I doubled down and pinpointed that this topic was unfair to women: male flexibility around fertility timelines puts women at disproportionate risk. He agreed with my logic, stating that resolution should come before further pronouncements. He responded by acknowledging my clarity without trying to smooth over my fear. But again, I was the one who initiated that level of precision, not him.

Something else he said was also music to my ears: "If you're with me, you're always going to know where I am."

I think he volunteered that stance when I mentioned that my ex(es) cheated on me. I received it as a balm, and he said it too early to be meaningful.

I lacked the awareness of what I was experiencing: emotional leadership without shared labor. The risk was that I would mistake compliance for compatibility. I was already doing the heavy lifting of foresight, while he appeared to be aligned because he didn't resist. However, the absence of resistance does not signify depth. It only looks like mutual understanding, but in reality, it's my clarity mirrored back to me.

My last deal-breaker: I would not be talking about commercial sports with him. And it's unlikely that I would spend every day, evening, and weekend watching them, whether at the venues or on TV. The scores don't matter to me at all.

Commercial sports, to me, represented passive consumption, not active self-connection. My existence centers on purpose: how I use energy. More than just uninterested, I was incompatible with the ritual of it.

I prioritize self-care activities that improve my physical and mental health; isn't that the point of sports?

I have no desire to play that cultural game. Naming this upfront required courage, especially in a country with a default sports culture.

Twice, he tested that boundary, mirroring my significance of the kids topic. Unlike some others he knew, he explained that his viewing wasn't devout and used it as background noise while multitasking, while assuring me he wouldn't force my viewing. While minimizing engagement, he asserted ownership and pride in his jerseys. That contradiction was telling, trying to frame it as casual while holding onto the significance. His identity was entangled with it, whether he admitted that. He emphasized that if I couldn't tolerate that, let's not waste time. On the surface, it seemed fair; underneath, it signified, "Here's the cost of admission."

I once again absorbed the dissonance because it was my choice to stay in the US. American football's social significance makes dating someone unfamiliar with it illogical. So, I softened the edges of my boundaries in the name of realism. Shifting my internal alignment to prevent a premature connection fracture was something I had already been doing.

Perhaps through flexibility, this might persist.

Grown Man

His independence impressed me because he appeared to live in alignment with the life I respected: he owned his own condo (like me), prioritized fitness (like me), and worked in a helping profession he loved (like me). Unlike the guy before him, he seemed to have differentiated from his family structure, which meant fewer inherited roles or unspoken loyalties to default systems.

Considering every broken relationship I had endured by then, I possessed zero desire to shape-shift. What I was offering was my reality. And who knew? Just by being myself, he asked if I was "too good to be true."

Well, sir, that's quite a compliment.

It validated the feeling of "being seen." That line positioned him as the humble one and me as the rare find. However, it was a crack posing as praise. It told me he struggled to believe someone like me could exist in his world without cost—it's subtle self-sabotage. He framed it as admiration, but what he was doing was flagging his own insecurity: his sense that what I brought to the table might exceed his capacity to match it.

> **When someone believes they're dating someone too good to be true, they often start looking for reasons to prove themselves right.**

While I was still being myself, he was already projecting. And that projection was an early fracture, dressed up as a charm.

I was registering the absence of red flags as green ones. The lack of trouble delivered relief, making neutrality appear promising.

Skipping

Time flew; we conversed the entire day. The unbroken flow of conversation halted only because of the adjustment of the clock when daylight saving time ended, signaling a comfort in emotional fluidity I rarely experienced.

He left me with his cell number, suggesting coffee, drinks, or even dinner later that same day... It's opportunistic in a subdued way. He sensed momentum and tried to move the connection into physical space while the energy was high.

Upon waking the next morning, though, my mind raced to him before the morning coffee. That displacement made me pay attention because he violated my inner sequence by jumping the queue, and something in me needed confirmation.

Is this alignment mutual, or am I wrong again?

Curious about his identity, I invited him to brunch as a screening tool for gathering data to see whether my time was being invested wisely. It was a pivotal decision to begin an audit.

Date No. 1

I'm pretty sure he beat me to the restaurant because, as I was about a minute away, I received a playful text from him asking me to let him know if I was watching him from afar. His engaging start aimed to ease tension during an important gathering. Then there he was, waiting for me right in front, resembling the guy I saw in his profile photos. Within the misleading domain of online dating, that authenticity felt refreshing.

I ordered an Old Fashioned and noticed a slight smile on his face as he remarked that I didn't strike him as a drinker. That's another subtle moment where I upended expectations. He then ordered the same; I was unsure if it was a desire to join me on my level or if it was his typical drink of choice. Either way, it placed me as the leader in tone.

But then something shifted. After we placed our orders with the waitstaff, his interrogation began, mirroring the way I had approached the guy I just dated. I don't call it interrogation dismissively, as I recognize the word for what it is: an intensity.

Instead of finding it intrusive, I found it validating. For once, I tasted being the object that sparked interest. I enjoyed the intense curiosity shown; the many questions were refreshing. Most guys focused on themselves, lacking knowledge of me. Also, just by the questions he asked, I could learn a lot about him. I connected with him by answering questions I hadn't heard in a while, reminding myself of my past journey.

Still, I had no reference point to tell whether his energy was genuine or coming from nervousness. Since it was already background information, I didn't need to act on my awareness just yet. We clinked glasses and shared food; it seemed carefree, but this first date was a one-sided high-data extraction… of mine from him.

Towards the end of the meal, he inquired if I had questions for him. But that gesture shifted the power dynamic after his extended interrogation of me. I had already been revealed; the spotlight illuminated me throughout. Thus, I needed to calibrate. Constant messaging the day before had already taught me quite a bit about him. Thus, re-verification of prior discussion felt unnecessary. Because I knew the questions I craved to ask were not first-date appropriate, I pulled a neutral card: hobbies.

He flinched and said, "Well, yeah, I'm not like you, but I think… skiing. Yeah! I'd say skiing!"

That flinch was his body displaying internal discomfort, comparing my countless hobbies.

But that's interesting. Why is that necessary?

That almost imperceptible response revealed that he saw himself as "less than" at that moment. That question landed like a challenge to him. His answer seemed almost defensive, which exposed a power imbalance he already felt. I hadn't accused him, but he had already self-contracted. His perception of me—multi-passionate, expansive, high-functioning—activated something in him that made him shrink. I was being authentic, and that alone created a contrast he couldn't integrate with ease.

At some point, I let my Harry Potter obsession show, and that's when his serious demeanor shifted into a big grin. He then poked fun at me for being a Potterhead, marking his first moment of levity. It broke the tension. I bet he found relief in that amusement: he had finally related to me through something playful. He could meet me there… sort of. I proclaimed that I was a Gryffindor and asked which house he belonged to—a burning question gnawed at me.

Is it his Gryffindor spirit that drew me in?

But he said he didn't know.

Sadly, the brunch was over, and so was our conversation (or interrogation). He stood in front of the restaurant and gestured a goodbye hug, not a kiss… I was disappointed. It felt like an abrupt closure. I was tracking a subtle cognitive dissonance: the emotional investment in the meal didn't quite match the continuity afterwards.

First Impressions

My mind was dissecting the entire date during my walk home. There had been emotional energy, but he lacked even minimal courtesy to confirm my safe arrival home. He had a certain quality that drew me in… but I couldn't specify why.

Hours elapsed with his silence, which activated my emotional foresight.

Perhaps my face-to-face disappointed his expectations? Oh well, it's better now than later.

Out of discipline, I was crafting a mini-emotional exit plan in my head. I had learned how to protect myself with cleanliness.

If he's done, I will match his detachment.

I had already made peace with it by the time he finally texted hours later, asking me to tell him my first impression, emphasizing honest answers only. That open question functioned as validation: a way to measure whether he still had my interest after giving me what felt like a preview of depth.

I affirmed that he had made a good impression and clarified that my lack of questions didn't mean I was uninterested: I had questions, but they were inappropriate for a first date. I also told him it's refreshing that I was being questioned for once. In short, I re-established my depth by providing context without accusing him of anything, mimicking the grounded communication he had claimed to be working on in therapy.

He appeared relieved, expressing a sense of untapped depth, and suggested a second date would enable deeper exploration. It seemed promising on the surface, but looking more closely, it confirmed that he hadn't processed the first date. He mirrored my expressions, not stemming from his desire to revisit it. He was taking my lead, not leaping.

I smiled... a second date was on the table.

Fact-Checking

He disclosed months later that he had researched me on the internet after our first date—that's when things clicked into place: the hours of disconnection that left me rehearsing my emotional exit—he had gone to collect data. That delay was a strategy: he had stepped back to verify me. That level of scrutiny would upset many, yet I felt flattered.

But there's something dissonant underneath that flattery. For me, intimacy is built through shared presence. He retreated to the safety of distance at a pivotal moment to make sure my story checked out before he allowed himself to invest emotionally further. That choice revealed something fundamental: I was truth-tracking while he was fact-checking.

I didn't receive his admission as manipulative because only a few people would admit that they stalked someone on the internet. But even in his transparency, his initial withholding of that behavior curated perception. He had been treating connection as something to regulate, whereas I had been experiencing the moment, trusting my reading of his energy.

Refreshing

In the past, withdrawal had been the first signal of harm: guys who overwhelmed me with intensity early on, only to go dark once my nervous system had calibrated to their constant presence.

I was learning not to build connections out of dopamine highs and to avoid equating silence with threat. So when the silence came after his second date suggestion, I pondered whether it's a healthier pattern.

Maybe he's different. It's Election Day; let's not forget.

On top of telling myself not to be anxious, I also respected his time to rest up during the day, and hence I didn't initiate contact. That marked the clearest evidence of my growth: my peace wasn't coming from his attention. Instead of adapting to someone else's rhythm out of fear, I allowed for the possibility that he had a reason. I gave him grace because I had evolved.

Then the day after, his text finally checked in on me, stating that he had attended a friend's election party. I felt relieved to hear from him… and my nervous system noted it as a sign of continuity.

Gryffindor

I sent him the Sorting Hat quiz as a hint for him to take it because, by knowing which Hogwarts house he belonged to, I would learn so much about him. To me, that quiz was a way to understand his personality framework, and he met me where I was by responding with a screenshot of his result that validated my hunch. I felt seen because he understood why it mattered to me. It meant he was listening on a symbolic frequency most people miss.

Gryffindor!

Gryffindor represents bravery, integrity, and boldness. It mapped onto the presence I hoped he would live into, just like me. I was ecstatic! I had suspected it because we clicked.

Ten points for Gryffindor!

Solo Universal Trip

The following weekend was my monthly Universal trip: something that I had embraced doing solo. I let him peek into my joy in a world apart from him through selfies I sent of the Wizarding World, and he met my passion with lighthearted comments, asking me how many spells I had already cast. He always had a way to make me smile, but part of me tried to stay steady. He had my attention, but he didn't yet have my trust, not fully. I was watching to see if this early playfulness would eventually anchor in depth. I was living my joy and letting him witness it on my terms. That was emotional sovereignty.

Live TV

My imminent solo trip to Hawaii, Australia, and New Zealand was upon me; however, I had a live TV segment the morning before departure. I often do these segments, though that was the first one after meeting him. Awaiting in the Green Room, I messaged him to see if he would like to watch me, as I knew he had just concluded his overnight shift. My invitation was intentional, as if I was saying, "If you want to know me, watch me in my element."

His response hinted at a strong curiosity, likely fueled by my withholding of information about my occasional TV appearances.

It is fair; it's not the sort of query a skilled interrogator like him would have posed during our first meeting.

I rarely share personal details unprompted. Rushing home and tuning in made up his closest approach to offering reciprocal presence. He aligned his actions with my world, on my terms. Still, something in my recounting revealed a subtle asymmetry. I wasn't surprised that he watched, but I doubted he put in extra effort to rush home just for me. Even in sweetness, I was discerning. He sent me a photo showing his monitor with me on livestream, which brought me a smile because he translated curiosity into effort.

He had shifted from passive texting to active observation. That gesture was sweet, yet diminutive. Witnessing someone through a screen differs from real-world interaction.

The real question was, *"Will he be able to meet that version of me off-camera, when it isn't fascinating?"*

Pending

It had been almost two weeks since our first date, and he hadn't asked to see me again, although he had said a second date was needed for deeper discussions. I was leaving for my two-week trip the next day and refused another two-week delay.

By that point, the imbalance between his words and actions had sharpened into something undeniable. He spoke proper words, though silence usually followed, and that silence had gotten heavier. I had respected his rhythm, but if he had desired deeper conversations, he would have secured the time.

My schedule isn't a mystery… I'm leaving the country.

I refused to be carried at someone else's pace while my life surged forward at full speed. His ambiguity—continued attention without commitment—was the most draining form of inconsistency. It gave the illusion of connection without the substance and kept me wondering.

Is he just busy? Or is he just not that into me?

As my trip drew near, I decided against postponement, owing to self-respect. I would not wait in limbo while someone else decided whether my presence was worth scheduling. He had proximity to my attention, but I was waiting for affection alignment. Since it didn't come, I proceeded.

Invitation

When I felt his rest was sufficient in the afternoon, I texted to inquire whether he wished to join me at happy hour, letting him know that I knew I was being too forward.

To my surprise, it didn't take him long to reply. He assured me that I hadn't woken him because he already had an afternoon appointment to attend.

He responded with something that sounded very mature: "To prevent myself from zoning out, I'm going to take a nap for an hour, and I'll message you with an update on how I'm feeling."

I appreciated his transparency; it's like he invited me into his thought process in detail, which was refreshing for me. I had been so used to guys managing my perception; he gave me a brief form of emotional safety.

A little less than an hour later, he texted, "Good morning!"

I. Was. So. Happy.

Someone had finally aligned words with actions. His text was a follow-through: the smallest promise had been kept. Managing disappointment through most of my emotional life made that simple fulfillment of a stated intention meaningful, sounding louder than a flowery gesture.

Date No. 2

Knowing the general area of his home, I chose a location that aimed to shorten his trip—he must have been experiencing exhaustion after his night shifts. Plus, that eatery was one of my favorites. Reserving the barstools at the far end, I formed an intimate space, physical and emotional. Unlike the first date's table barrier, this setting should initiate closeness that had yet to happen.

Then there he was, approaching the bar area as I waved him over. We ordered food off the happy hour menu, something I cherish; it seemed like we agreed on selections.

We chatted… Right! He was no longer interrogating in this instance. I found myself captivated by the endless conversation. His approach to me was warmer this time, signaling comfort. He was inching closer, although it's only physical. His arm draped over the back of my stool—

a deliberate gesture of claiming proximity, which was a body language invitation that I welcomed. I gazed into his eyes and felt a subtle easing of emotional guardedness. At some point, he started tracing the veins on my arms with his fingertips, commenting on their prominence—something that would stand out to him as a nurse.

We wished the evening wouldn't conclude. Unlike our first date, he proposed to drink elsewhere. And while we were debating where to go next, he commented that if he had wine at home, he would have invited me over.

Extension

Retrieving my phone, we reviewed the map together. This transformed into a collective decision about our destination, both symbolic and practical. He favored a place I had desired, towards my part of town.

We secured yet another two barstools, mirroring the prior arrangement. He had to rush to the restroom, which I found endearing, as I share a similar need.

He asked me about my spiritual beliefs again; it's a subject we had already talked about in our dating app chat. It felt like he was testing my integrity, as though he wished to determine whether I would offer him identical information. Obviously, I passed with ease, because my belief system is elemental:

I embrace the Universe, karma, and good jujus.

These are my core beliefs, whether others like it… or whether he liked it. I recall him enjoying hearing it before, which he confirmed in person.

Then he inquired about my childhood once more, centering on the relationship with my mother. Despite the risk, I conveyed the truth, implying his entrance into a territory most are not allowed to reach.

He then leaned in, looked into my eyes, and whispered, "Although I haven't known you for long, I can see you are a very strong person."

First Kiss

My tears started gushing out; I tried to hold them in, not sure why... Maybe I didn't mean to open that door so soon, but I did, and he met me inside it.

He leaned in further to give me a passionate kiss—it was our first, a release that was well-timed and I had longed for. Because I was accustomed to managing others' emotional confusion, that moment created a rare alignment.

He continued to say, "I'm so sorry you had to go through this, but we're here now."

He just said "we."

What I failed to realize then was that it hinted at a premature assumption of intimacy: he acted as if closeness had already solidified.

I wept once more. He grabbed the back of my neck to pull me in closer, and we ended up making out at the bar.

He commented, "You probably didn't expect the night to turn out this way, did you?"

As soon as we stepped outside, he devoured me with kisses once more. I remember hearing cheers from bystanders, but neither of us shrank. I allowed myself to experience being felt, something I hadn't done for quite a stretch until he gave me what others hadn't: presence in the exact second I needed it.

He stood out from other guys: he wasn't scared of my tears but let me cry and made me feel understood.

That moment marked a high point: a convergence of emotional intimacy, physical connection, and psychological vulnerability. It involved experiencing someone who acknowledged my true self.

White Piano

Approaching my condo, we stopped in front of the lobby and made out on the street again. He started being handsy… and I let him because it hadn't crossed my boundaries. I had already let him closer than most by sharing something real that night: my tears.

In one minute of it, he asked if I wanted to show him my white piano at home. His inquiry was coded, and we both knew it. I didn't take offense, but the timing revealed a limit in his emotional discipline. Minutes after I let myself be raw and he held space for my pain, he already transitioned to the possibility of intimacy.

Preserving my dignity, I whispered into his ear, "Not tonight."

He asked if he would just leave me there then, and I nodded. His response was ambiguous: on one level, it acknowledged my boundary; on another, it hinted at a subtle disappointment, maybe even a gentle prod, as if to say, "Is this really where we stop?"

My instinct was to let the moment end where it needed to. It was not rejection but deep self-protection.

Hermès Blanket

He texted me a photo of his Hermès blanket spread on his sofa as soon as he got home—a follow-up on an earlier conversation when I couldn't believe that he owned one.

He also said, "I guess we'll have to wait a little while to do that again [sad face emoji]."

He was naming the distance my upcoming trip imposed, without suggesting going on another date after my return. But without my initiative earlier that day, we would have remained trapped in unspoken potential. Although he wasn't uninterested, he also wasn't moving with the same deliberateness as I was. I had created the second date, and now he slipped back into the passenger seat. He liked the energy between us and took part in it, but he didn't drive it.

The photo he had sent depicted a pleasant residence. I wondered regarding the rest, inquiring about the two big mirrors he had mentioned, if there was a bathtub, and if he lit candles. He answered yes to all of them and added that he also drank wine, though he rarely combined all of those things.

"Boo!!! What if I want to?" I exclaimed.

Those were the minimum number of words of hinting, *"Will you ever match the pace I move at? Or initiate the thing you seem to enjoy? Because if I must summon every time… the dynamic would become off-kilter at some juncture."*

This suggestive exchange captured our way of staying connected even after the physical goodbye—letting the energy linger. I was teasing a domestic fantasy with imagination while keeping my posture still playful, yet guarded. And his witty response matched my tone.

But beneath the banter, I wondered if he would remain attuned after the moment had elapsed.

Airport Bound

The next morning, I let him know I had been tossing and turning throughout the night. My eyes were burning and shut, but I was wide awake. Reflecting on it, my excitement might have stemmed from having just kissed someone who made me feel seen. My nervous system was likely on high alert because something unfamiliar was registered: being both desired and witnessed. I replayed every instance of that evening.

His response, which included a tongue-out emoji, said we should have prolonged our date. I caught that flirty echo, a blend of regret and suggestion. I felt its warmth but tried not to let that magic cloud my clarity.

During the ride to the airport, I conveyed to him the sensation of a forgotten, unknown item.

He said, "Yes, but I always believe we can buy anything we've forgotten because we aren't going to a third-world country."

Are you serious??? That's what I've always told people!

My jaw dropped in disbelief! It startled me because it has always been my way of seeing the world in practical terms. Few arrive at my perspective, yet there he was, speaking my language. Even in text, he mirrored my internal logic.

Surprise

My two-week trip to Australia, which included walking in a fashion show and extending my stay to visit other cities, had begun. It was a trip I had booked after finding out my ex's double life as an act of reclamation to the version of me that predated betrayal: roaming around the world, solo and carefree. This was the phase where my reality and hope braided together.

But before embarking on my solo trip, I encountered this guy. His filling my thoughts during my journey was unplanned, but I welcomed it. Most guys I was talking to would just wish me safe travels and then never speak with me again. Others continued to text, then dwindled out. Their silence reinforced what I already suspected: Most connections don't survive absence.

Except for one: the nurse. Without flooding me with attention, he kept in consistent communication and didn't depend on me to entertain him. He was signaling that I was still in his frame. That consistency without intrusion was more intimate than affection. His unique disposition was shown not only through early interest but also continued engagement.

Given his night shifts and our time difference, I would send him my itinerary and exclusive photos and videos, the kind I withheld from my public feed. His responses with heart emojis were brief, but I felt them. I even shared with him that I didn't pack closed-toe shoes for the Great Barrier Reef tour, so I had to find a store to get them last minute. To help me decide, I texted him the shoe choices. No, I didn't need his input, but I wanted to include him. That's my way of saying, "I see you as someone close enough to matter." And without delay, he provided an answer.

He texted a photo of the Bolognese he had made, to which I commented about how delicious it looked.

"I froze the leftovers, and if you want it, it's yours!" He replied.

He lingered in my thoughts because he didn't pull me off course; he walked alongside it, even from oceans away.

Runway

At the fashion show, I sent him glimpses into my behind-the-scenes reality. He didn't just consume them with passive approval; he queried whether there was a method to broadcast my performance within the hospital. His offer was very thoughtful in trying to enlarge the window through which he could witness me. So I checked with the production team, but received a negative answer.

He inquired about my runway experience the following morning; I could have given a simple response: "It went well." But I chose the higher bar, contemplating sharing with him my deeper thoughts about modeling itself.

"If you'd like to learn more, I will save it for later," I said.

What I was really asking: "Can you hear me when I speak from my core?"

I was offering him the future after my return and seeing if he was interested in depth. The invitation was conditional on his having to choose it.

And he seemed eager and agreed that he would like to learn more. I have never been interested in surface-level admiration and watch for depth readiness in someone who values my experience of what it means to walk a runway within self. He presented something authentic: curiosity towards me, not just my output. That sufficed to hold my interest for a moment.

Emotional Investment

I did not realize how much I had already connected with him on an emotional level... it crept up on me. For example, in response to a sunset on the beach photo I had sent from Hawaii, he told me he'd rather be there than working. Even if he didn't say "with me," it ran through my wiring.

That sounds like a longing he would want to share with someone—me.

Geographic separation created a natural screening process. The early days of my trip clarified that other guys dropped off under minimal strain, but his consistency spoke louder than infatuated words ever could. Both my daily waking and final thoughts were of him. I didn't mean for it to happen that way, but it did.

An intriguing message from him came through at 3 am one day: "So, question, do you feel [sad emoji] that we are waiting this long until we see each other again?"

The timing said everything: he wasn't on shift, but the thoughts about me were keeping him up enough to send something vague yet vulnerable, testing the water without overexposing himself. Using an emoji instead of words was telling: he wanted to express a feeling without assuming the emotional risk of stating it.

I beamed when I saw it, but didn't respond until the next morning, buying myself time to process.

Megan, really take your time. Don't ruin a good thing by rushing.

Unsure of the exact meaning he had meant to convey with the emoji, I asked for a precise explanation, and he told me, "bummed."

I reiterated, "Just so that I don't misunderstand what you are saying, you mean you feel bummed that we have to wait this long until the next time we see each other?"

He affirmed his enjoyment of our second date, then pivoted to question my itinerary, "… but anyway, …"

He could dip into intimacy but not sustain it. I realized he was avoiding going too deep into the topic.

I understand; a month's acquaintance hardly warrants such haste.

Reflecting, that was an emotional breadcrumb he had offered in the middle of the night: one that hinted at growing feelings, then retreated to the safety of neutral ground when being asked for clarity. It signaled his emotional limit. I wish I had not missed the signal that our construction differed in depth and speed.

Suspense

I was about to return from a two-week trip filled with a subtle emotional buildup. He had stayed engaged enough to feel meaningful but not quite anchored enough to initiate a concrete date. His lack of initiative told me that his rhythm was not one of proactivity.

Driven by clarity, I opened the opportunity: "If you were to ask me out on a date for when I get back… I wouldn't say no!"

He jumped at the opportunity and said, "Let's do it."

So we planned a dinner date the day following my return. He showed excitement, confirmed the date, and named it official because that's how he moved: in response, not initiation. That's a dynamic I had already seen: he could meet me, but only after I opened the door.

I had to shift my scheduled light show to accommodate the dinner. I then relayed that information to him, suggesting he could join me there the day after.

He then asked, "So let me get this straight… We are spending two days back-to-back?"

His response revealed mild panic laced with playfulness. That reaction held a micro-truth: closeness startled him. For me, seeing someone two days in a row felt natural; for him, it sounded like suffo-cation.

He didn't decline but flagged it. I also flagged it… as a signal that his pace was slower than the guys before him, although I didn't know what that meant. Not yet.

I gave him space while guarding my peace and replied, "Either/or is fine."

Then we played it by ear to see how we would feel on our third date before committing to the light show.

Date No. 3

Choosing a restaurant from our dating app chats showed he was thoughtful. He treated me to sushi, which was generous given the cost.

He proposed walking together, meeting outside his home, and provided his address. That's when I realized that he lived right across from the eatery I had chosen for our second date. The revealing of his address was a significant advancement because it showed that a level of trust had been established. It's symbolic for someone like him, whose emotional rhythm was cautious, because it meant he saw me as someone who wouldn't misuse access.

He was still seeking entry points into my inner world, but it was gaining emotional color. He was eager to learn more about my trip, especially the fashion show, which was a narrative continuity because he had told me he wanted to learn more about my modeling experience upon my return.

I then asked him about the time he had spent with his family over Thanksgiving. He described a game played with his niece and nephews, requiring extreme physical flexibility. Considering how flexible my body is, it didn't sound difficult to me at all, and he quipped that I should prove it at his place after dinner.

I caught where he wanted to go: testing my boundaries with a smile by blending flirtation with invitation. My line was held, and I told myself not to spoil this. I owed it to myself not to screw it up again. I was stepping into familiar territory: intimacy. But this time, I intended to pace myself differently.

We went to a bar for some beers after dinner, and he rested his arm on my backrest again as if his arm were embracing my shoulders, creating an emotional symmetry with our second date.

And for now, that tenacity, coupled with closeness, sufficed.

History

I inquired about his prior relationships, trying to gather facts by inviting him into the architecture of emotional transparency. I was checking for emotional recursion: how a person makes meaning of their relational patterns and what they carry forward.

The one he dated right before me lasted for about two years. He was in his late thirties when she was in her early twenties. They had met at work—another nurse. He avowed that there's no animosity. Throughout their partnership, she complained about feeling the need for increased maturity to stay with him. He said they had started "flickering" in November of the preceding year, continuing until April of the subsequent year (the year we met). That word—flickering— suggested ambiguity. He was describing a breakup, but what I heard was a slow extinguishing.

He then spoke regarding her predecessor, another nurse. They were friends first, in the same friend group. It sounded to me as if he had let her move in with him when there was an issue with her rental agreement, though he claimed unrelated issues caused their relation- ship's demise. It sounded like he blurred the lines between logistical convenience and emotional commitment. Once again, he was describ- ing a rupture, while I was hearing a fade.

Another nurse preceded that one. According to him, she had unresolved daddy issues because, again, with him being much older, she always projected her hatred of her dad and granddad onto him. He blamed her immaturity, voicing his frustration about her unwillingness to sacrifice short-term comfort (nursing education) for a better long-term gain (higher income). I agreed with his reasoning; our maturity levels seemed aligned.

He concluded by saying that he had only relayed information concerning "long-term" relationships. Instinctively, I asked for his definition, and "six months" was his answer… a timeframe that would be etched in my mind ever since.

His stories offered a clear picture: he gravitated towards much younger women, all nurses, within his professional-friend circle. What he framed as peaceful endings, I sensed as a pattern of non-confrontational drifting. Those relationships either faded or were unsuitable from the outset. There was no reckoning. I didn't hear any stories of transforming from insight, just clean summaries, wrapped in rationality, and sealed with "we have no bad blood."

I was already engaging him from a space of long-view integration; he appeared to bear only what remained useful at the moment and evaded with feelings. He offered neat stories to preserve his image as a "good guy." He never invited his past into the present with reverence, only as backstory; but for me, the past is information that revealed patterns.

Nursing

He blurted a question: "So, you like my job?"

I knew what he was getting at, but I made him rephrase it anyway. He was testing whether I saw the version of himself that emerged at work. And I did. Yes, I had told him before, but asking again showed he was seeking reassurance.

I hold high regard for those committed to such generous occupations. His ICU work highlights the life-or-death impact of every decision, which moved me, along with his dedication and passion for it. I bowed down to his willingness to show up for others in real-time consequences. His occupation reflected a value system I aligned with.

He prompted a revelation that clarified my lack of respect for the guy I had dated right before—the executive with an elevated title—who possessed societal markers of achievement but was devoid of genuine depth. That guy had ulterior motives. I couldn't feel inspired by someone who talked in corporate spirals while playing games in the office. His impact on society, if any, was self-serving.

This comparison was foundational because it's vital for one to respect their partner.

Surgery

I reminded him about sharing a "stupid" doctor's visit that he had gone to while I was in Australia. He revealed he had wanted to consult with a plastic surgeon and finally secured an appointment months later.

Curious, I inquired about his plans. It's something about his eyes… but he dismissed the idea upon hearing the price. He told me it was his ex's idea, and upon his gazing into his dad's eyes, he understood he desired no resemblance upon aging. He confessed to making the appointment during a time when his identity had been destabilized.

When he revealed his ex triggered it, I interrupted the inherited judgment and replaced it with my gaze.

I said, "I don't know her… But you know what? Fuck her! I think your eyes are beautiful. I like them."

That "fuck her" was my defending his essence from an individual seeking to diminish it.

He looked at me with those beautiful eyes and thanked me. It was a moment in his recalibration.

In that instance, I gleaned two facts: he had been susceptible to manipulation—still, he could admit such in my presence. That kind of self-revelation eludes most people, especially guys who were taught to hold things in. Because I remembered, asked, and made it safe, it happened.

Liquid Courage

He asked me how I had been liking our date when defenses were lowered after a couple of drinks. He was looking for reassurance with a soft probe of whether he was getting it right.

I rarely received that kind of straightforward question. That query possessed potential for varied readings; thus, I told him I was enjoying the vibe "so far" that evening. By mimicking the form of his question, I made sure to maintain my boundaries while staying clearheaded.

He gave a slight nod with a smile; it was relief disguised as casual acknowledgment.

He then mentioned the next-day light show that I had previously proposed. He explained that the hesitation he'd had before was derived from not knowing whether I would show up for our date. His admission revealed a crack in his certainty about dating.

Interesting. Perhaps his past relationship experiences were negative, or I have yet to prove my difference.

Feeling the vibe, and after seeing my arrival, he got us tickets. He tiptoed forward from speculation to intent, and I noticed it. Even with his composed charm, he doubted himself until my continued presence.

Just like that, we did end up spending two days back-to-back.

His Place

He invited me to continue the night over wine at his place. I accepted but walked through the door with caution.

Strength doesn't always mean saying no; sometimes it means staying grounded inside a yes.

He showed me around his place: the two walls that he had built, which were impressive because they took skills, both artistic and physical. His place was cozy, and it flashed through my mind at that moment when he had told me during my trip that he had to "get his place in order."

He expected where this might go if things kept unfolding.

The invitation to his home was staged with intent. He showed proof of effort in constructing something himself, ready to reveal it to an individual he might welcome. He knew I would notice everything; that's part of why he liked me: I'm introspective. It's like he was sending a message: "This is where I live, and this is what I've built. It's safe here. I want you to feel that."

Another observation I made was about his extensive wine collection that could not have magically appeared since our second date, when he told me he didn't have any.

First Time

On the sofa, we toasted over wine; we made out, and he led me to his bedroom.

I whispered, "I'm scared," a sound of someone self-aware, trying to steer the moment towards integrity.

He heard me, paused, looked me in the eye, and asked me why. I didn't answer yet as he excused himself to the bathroom.

Upon his return, I confessed, "I like you a lot. I want to do this right."

He responded by saying he liked me too, which was a beautiful line, but it served his timing, not mine. Although he didn't ignore my words, he overrode their deeper weight. He started making out with me and pushing me onto his bed. Although he wasn't violent, he didn't stay in the emotional register I had just opened, either.

Building something layered had taken me weeks of emotional resonance. I had permitted myself to open and feel eager again only when emotional readiness properly aligned with physical desire.

Nonetheless, we moved forward, honoring chemistry, and I permitted it, stemming from the belief that this time it would be different. I am human after all; my body and mind were in different places. Feeling rushed by softness caused me to falter in upholding my boundaries.

And that left a gap, not of regret, because I liked him.

Grounded

He made us coffee the next morning—the way we both liked it—black and strong. He shared his regrets for pushing matters too far the night before.

I said, "Don't be; I enjoyed it."

I have to admit… while my response was true, it's also reflexive. Despite liking it, I had wanted the evening to be more emotionally significant.

Maybe that's why I felt the need to stay rooted, so I brought out my list: a list of questions I had for him to make sure I didn't forget them later. I had planned to inquire about those questions before becoming too immersed, but physical closeness developed faster than emotional alignment could settle.

My initial question involved partner preferences—the qualities he looked for. He said he needed to feel attraction first, which was honest. After that, all he looked for was that she was "grounded."

Grounded—that's an interesting word choice. Knowing I'm the opposite of scattered… Am I grounded, though? I can't be so sure.

That word struck a chord because of its complexity. I saved it to metabolize later.

A grounded woman might keep the emotional tone stable so that he doesn't have to navigate his own deeper tides. And that would explain a lot: why he mirrored my feelings instead of building towards them, why he said "I like you too" while pushing the moment forward rather than slowing it down, and why, the next morning, he felt guilt from knowing he bypassed something I was still holding onto.

He admitted he had pushed too far, which meant he knew he had, and that's the key: I had always been the grounded one. I hold this clarity only in retrospect. It was too soon for him to realize I already embodied the word he used: someone to contain the gravity for both of us, and I now wonder if he knew that wasn't fair.

Hung Up

Wishing to grasp whether he intentionally chose to be with me or if I was just a placeholder, I asked, "Is there an ex you wouldn't mind entertaining dating again if she initiated?"

Notice the way I phrased that question.

He paused, likely debating whether he should speak the truth, and said, "Yeah… one."

I didn't like that answer, but I asked which ex, anyway. He told me it was the one before me whom he hadn't seen for six months.

I remember her: the young new nurse who was in his work friend group, the one who talked shit about his eyes and complained that she needed to catch up with his maturity. Despite all that, he still wouldn't mind dating her again.

So I had to ask, "What do you value in her?"

He started giving me some explanations, saying that their personalities just clicked, she's good-looking, and she kind of challenged him to grow.

I made a mental note of his word choice, "kind of," and sat there in silence to process everything.

He regarded my internal processing and directed the question towards me, "What about you?"

Without hesitation, I told him, "No, no one. I will entertain dating no one from my past again."

I didn't flinch. My "no" was about having grown so far beyond those relationships that they were no longer even on my map. That certainty I carried in my answer was missing in his tone. I enter every space fully or not at all and never multitask my loyalty.

Laying his hands on my lap, he asked how learning what he had said made me feel. I did my best to articulate my thoughts so I wouldn't give him my natural silence when I hadn't reached my internal clarity.

I said, "How I feel differs from what I think. It certainly doesn't make me feel good, but I also don't understand why you're not pursuing her. Are you waiting for her to grow up and then go back to her?"

I know how to hold both truths: the sting of hearing it and the respect for his honesty.

He responded, "I think she's already grown. But I'm not waiting for her; I've already moved on."

He then guided my attention back to his integrity, which was his refuge. Knowing the content might hurt, he hoped the honesty would soften it. He then explained that he had avoided discussing past relationships because each is unique.

While I agreed with him, I explained the reason I had asked: to see what characteristics he was drawn to. His words required me to process both his feelings and their current significance concerning my own.

However, what is spoken with honesty must still undergo consideration of truth: he could still picture an opening for somebody else. That troubles my perception, even to this day.

I departed soon thereafter to assert self-governance. I knew I needed time alone to metabolize what just shifted and to allow us individual time to handle personal matters before going to the light show.

Date No. 4

I returned to his place later that afternoon, this time in my car. The light show, being outdoors in a "forest" at night, was designed to be romantic. I needed to see how he would hold me, now that I had already given him so much.

That night's temperature hovered at freezing. He didn't hold my hand through the forest; our gloves and hands in pockets could have explained it. But the emotionally available would always reach out, regardless of the cold. Physical barriers shouldn't prevent instinctive connection.

Then he photographed me from behind as I was walking in front of him, admiring the beautiful scenery. I caught that in my peripheral vision and didn't flinch. Normally, I dislike having candid photos taken, but this time, I allowed it.

He then caught up with me to show me the photo on his phone, saying, "Here you go, something to post on your Insta."

It's light, almost silly. He saw me immersed in beauty and wanted to preserve that version of me. That marked an early, obvious signal of his attentiveness.

Strolling through the field's twinkling, music-dancing stars, he rested against a tree, pulling me close, and said, "Come here, keep me warm."

At last, he reached for me because the environment drew forth his true nature, revealing itself when romance blossomed in the situation. He afforded me that instance: beneath the frozen celestial bodies, he yielded, however briefly.

He's being sweet… doing this romantic thing that I was hoping he would.

I was smiling inside. That affection without demands resonates in my world.

In Awe

We had fun at the light show before heading for dinner. It was at a brewery that he had picked because he had seen beer flights being displayed on their website, something he had learned that I enjoyed.

Towards the end of the meal, it seemed as if he had to muster up some courage to let me know, "I have two back-to-back shifts coming up, so I need some alone time tomorrow to recharge."

Awe filled me as I stared into his eyes. That moment crystallized his trust in me by being confident that I could receive truth: his desire to recharge didn't diminish his interest in me. Although he struggled to express himself, I found his honesty refreshing because guys I had dated would never be so upfront. That kind of emotional transparency, especially early on, is rare. I respected his boundaries, and mine, as shown by my ability to receive it without spiraling into insecurity. Instead of fearing, I heard, "I trust you enough to tell you who I am, even when it's uncomfortable. I may need space and still care."

I expressed gratitude for informing me, emphasizing the significance of his transparency. I also encouraged him to continue telling me whenever he needed time for himself. That's the moment that created true emotional safety.

That exchange held more emotional maturity than any of my previous relationships had ever reached because I didn't just listen; I honored what was real.

First Initiation

Three days later on his day off. He texted me when he awoke in the afternoon, "I want to check in with you to see about hanging out this evening."

He finally asked to see me after four dates, where I had been building momentum with intention. This marked the initial instance he breached that unseen boundary. The message felt unforced, like he had given thought to my rhythm and his.

I informed him about my ballet class, and then perhaps we could have dinner afterwards. He agreed. Matching my effort at last, it felt meaningful.

Date No. 5

I selected a vegan restaurant because I wanted him to try the menu items that I liked to see if he could recreate them in his kitchen.

On his dating app profile, he claimed he was "always up for a kitchen request," which I had yet to verify.

Over our meal, I let him know about a tradition of mine: I drive to this outlet mall in New York around the holiday season annually, wondering if he would like to join.

It was twenty days in advance, and to my surprise, he said yes! His enthusiastic yes, especially so far ahead, signaled openness to a deeper connection for at least another three weeks.

Giving His All

He had a question for me but would rather wait for privacy in my home. I didn't realize he intended to come in.

Is he asking me to be exclusive?

My anxious mind was running through all the implications, which must have shown on my face as he attempted to provide me with comfort.

He said, "I can see your left brain is running so fast right now. Don't worry; it's nothing bad. I know because I'm the one with the question. Chill!"

After the cocktails we had savored at a speakeasy, we headed to my place. He noticed my worry again on our walk home.

I then admitted, "My right brain had already chosen you, but my left brain is fighting so hard against it."

He replied, "Look. I can't guarantee what the future holds, but I'm giving this my all to see where things go."

Few would dare utter such a forthright statement that cut through the fog of uncertainty with a clear, grounded intention. His calm, perceptive response not only acknowledged my inner struggle but also offered a rare openness that many shy away from.

In that moment, I had a flashback of what he had told me early on: he lacked the mental bandwidth to date more than one person at a time. Coupling it with what I had just heard, I assumed it meant exclusivity.

My Place

Entering my home, he got a brief tour, including my extensive collection of the Starbucks Destination espresso mugs, which I had proudly mentioned during our dating app chat. He resonated with the ones printed "Warsaw and Poland."

He excused himself to my guest bathroom, while I went upstairs to my bedroom to put away my winter coat.

I heard the bathroom door open and footsteps getting louder and louder on my spiral staircase. Before I knew it, he had already started making out with me, pushing me over my bed.

He cut short and asked, "So what are we doing?"

I was unsure of the context he was referring to. Turned out, it was about birth control. I reminded him I was the one who had been standing stronger on the no-kids stance all along. With that reassurance I had provided, he started making out with me again.

I then interrupted by whispering, "While we are on this topic... I don't just fuck anyone."

He responded by saying he didn't either and that I was the first person with whom he had intimacy since his last relationship went south, which, as I could recall, had been about six months to a year, depending on the extent he was lying about.

As it's getting late, we were debating whether he should spend the night at my place. He sensed that I was conflicted because expressing my needs proved taxing, so he pushed me to tell him what I wanted because it didn't matter to him either way.

His offer to stay but deferring to my wishes opened a space for me to hold power over the pace, which was both reassuring and overwhelming for my nervous system.

Weekend

He told me about this Christmas party that he got invited to, mentioning he knew no one except for the friend who invited him. This wasn't a colleague who became a friend, a rarity. They had met on the same app we did.

He let me know that he had social anxiety, so attending was his part to maintain his friendship. On his way home in a rideshare, he texted to reveal progress exceeding expectations, even surprising himself through conversing with a group of strangers. Sharing that level of detail signaled a desire to be known and a measure of trust.

But I found his indifference to my whereabouts peculiar. I had driven out of town to walk in a fashion show one day, got a ticket to the Forbidden Forest experience the next, and had a hotel stay in between.

He finally texted me asking what I was up to after I had already traveled hundreds of miles away. My response was my runway-ready selfie taken backstage, to which he said, "Oh, nice! "

He acknowledged the data, but I felt like an afterthought.

This disparity had already developed: I plumbed depths, while he skimmed the surface. And the most disorienting part was that it didn't look like disinterest.

It looked like presence just shy of full attunement; close enough to feel hopeful but distant enough to feel hollow.

IKEA

He mentioned he might stop by IKEA for some lightbulbs.

"IKEA?!" I exclaimed. "I love that place!!!"

I then detailed my usual IKEA itinerary: cafeteria, coffee, food, chocolate, and meatballs to go. He responded by telling me I was so "cute," an adjective he seldom used.

My excitement didn't cool down. I shared genuine feelings about that place, requested information on the urgency concerning those lightbulbs, and proposed an IKEA date if he could wait.

He assured me, "Lightbulbs can wait lol."

I avoided pressing him for a specific time and date because I was planning to bring it up again.

For the rest of that weekend apart, I kept him posted with photos at a winery that I visited. I even let him choose my shirt to purchase at the Forbidden Forest experience, mirroring the way I had asked him to pick out my shoes in Australia.

That weekend showed where things stood: he didn't invite me to spend time with him on a weekend he wasn't bogged down by hospital shifts. Despite that, I invited him on a full sensory tour of my weekend.

Self-Erasure

I got used to getting infrequent texts from him during his work hours. I imagined he wouldn't be using his phone while attending to ICU patients. Slowly, I had trained myself to be less anxious.

At some point, I shared with him that I tended to over-give in a relationship to the point where I neglected my own needs... not something everyone would admit.

He said, "It shouldn't be okay with you or the person you're with."

That phrasing was neat, which earned him points.

He then added, "You know what that means? You need to be better at asking for your needs. And I'll let you know when I need my physical needs met, too."

It might have sounded reciprocal, but in reality, he rerouted the conversation, redirecting it to a discussion about his physical needs. And that part made me think, but I assumed that his other needs were met otherwise.

But he didn't know my definition of "neglecting my needs." He questioned neither how it might appear, how it felt, nor if I was already showing it towards him. He didn't even ask what my needs were. Instead, he slid the topic towards his own unmet physical desires.

I had been calibrating to him by slowing down my rhythm to match his pace. That took emotional discipline on my part. Maybe the reason I shared with him this piece of information about me was that my body already sensed a shift: he would only hold space for the parts of my inner world that didn't inconvenience him, and I was prepared to find that acceptable.

Wine

One night, he texted me a photo of a bottle of wine in his hand, saying he had missed his bus, so he took the subway instead. That wine was the one I had mentioned to him as my favorite. I read it as, "I heard you; I thought of you; and I remembered."

It brought me to tears—tears of alignment; I was so touched. My emotional structure is built around attunement, so being received with that same quality, unprompted, was rare. A realization struck: this exemplifies my manner of loving and the manner I crave reciprocation.

How did I get so lucky? Am I allowed to trust this and lean in?

I feel loved when acknowledged, and his single act gave the impression that he understood.

But I failed to see that he stopped by the wine store next to the subway station because of transit issues. His thoughtful gesture was circumstantial, not intentional.

Second Initiation

In one instance, he texted me asking, "Didn't we do something the week before, after ballet? You want to do it again?"

I responded almost instantly, "Well, yes! Do you want to meet me at this restaurant? I think I can make it there just in time before happy hour ends. Is it too far for you, though?"

"I'd go anywhere you want me to go. lol I'll see you tomorrow."

He was showing his willingness to follow my lead. This felt like a turning point, since my initiative carried the weight of maintaining emotional cohesion throughout many prior experiences. He not only agreed but also remembered the context, referenced it, and pushed that same energy forward. That's the reciprocity I was craving all along: a clear signal that my presence was wanted.

Date No. 6

"It's raining so bad lol," he texted, and this communication marked our first contact since we had confirmed date number six.

I knew he would show up. He had proved to me he was a man of his word, and I thanked him for it at least once or twice.

I usually pre-book all my Universal trips months ahead, which meant my trip schedule had already been set before getting involved with him. I noticed my Universal weekends somehow landed on those he had hospital shifts.

I shared with him this "fun fact" over our meal, and he said, "That's good, isn't it?"

Does he mean we'd spend our free weekends together?

But he didn't elaborate, nor did I press, because I had already begun self-managing my disappointment before it even arrived. Every time he leaned back into vague responses, it left me in a subtle position of filling in the gaps. That exhaustion was invisible to him, but I carried it.

The rain hadn't stopped during our walk home. He didn't want me to step in the puddles of water, so whenever I was about to walk over one, he would use his strong arm to pick me up by my waist so that I wouldn't put all my weight on it to splash myself or him.

Maybe he responded with his body in a way that showed attunement. However, it resembled a division within him: the external part of him that responded to immediate desires and the internal part of him that withdrew at times. That's what made it so confusing to me.

His Place

We would continue our night at his place. Sharing wine on his sofa, he perceived my worries. I was unsure of what consumed my attention, but I suspect it was the uncertainty of our relationship.

"I want clarity," I mumbled.

He pulled me closer and said, "I can't give you clarity right now, but what I can give you is this," and started making out with me.

His response was telling: he substituted physical closeness for emotional anchoring. That intoxicating sensation missed the key element I required: rational speech with emotional structure.

Does he expect intimacy with every meeting?

Sex itself was not the issue; it's what it represented in the absence of emotional deepening.

Date No. 7

The night before my Universal trip, I had my weekly ice skating lesson. Spontaneity prompted my message to him proposing an ice-skating date near my place after my lesson.

He responded, "Ice skating lesson? You never cease to amaze me! I haven't done it since high school. Why don't you text me when you get back, and we'll see if you still want to do it?"

Right. The ice skating lesson was something that I never had a reason to mention to him before—not hiding it on purpose, but also not blasting it out loud, either.

On my way back from my lesson, he texted me before I did, "Still wanna go ice skating?"

I said, "Yeah! You feel like joining me?"

"Okay, sure!"

A lengthy wait at the rink prompted a lounge visit for drinks. He had two while I had one. He was mistaken if he believed he needed liquid courage to "out-skate" me because I was the one taking lessons —he ended up teaching and dragging me along. He was pulling me so fast that we fell together. As we got up, he would brush the ice off my body. Those slight gestures were tender… innocent, almost.

When I let him know that I had had enough, he said, "Okay, let me go do one more run!"

I was glad that he enjoyed it more than I did!

On our way out, he asked, "Did I impress you?"

That question revealed his boyish vulnerability with a touch of self-deprecation: he wanted my approval but was unsure if I still saw him as desirable.

I responded, "Yeah! Look at you!"

"And they said I'm not athletic."

"Who are they? Not me! I'd never think that of you."

"The people I hang out with, the nurses."

Reset

On the short walk back, he brought up, "You know, we can still do Harry Potter night, right?"

He had wanted a Fantastic Beasts movie marathon; I agreed, having never seen them. But his small tether to shared plans was a method to keep open options instead of a firm commitment.

Approaching my lobby, I stopped, turned to him, and said, "Okay."

He responded, "Okay."

His instant mirroring made me laugh out loud. We made out a little until I said, "See you when we go to IKEA next week, then?"

He replied, "Yeah."

The absence of my invitation to come in showed a subtle boundary set without explanations. I still kissed him and shared warmth, but I ended it where I wanted: on the sidewalk and on my terms. It's my gentle way of recalibrating the dynamic without confrontation. And he seemed to respect it, or at least accepted it without protest.

I walked into my building thinking, *"I hope he knows that it was me establishing boundaries... being intimate every time we hang out is not my intent."*

Date No. 8

On my return day from Universal, I never heard from him until mid-afternoon when he texted, "How was your flight? I woke up late—my day hasn't been very productive. With that said, if you still want to go to IKEA, I'm still down!"

Of course I am!

I collected him in my car, and off to IKEA we went.

We followed my usual IKEA itinerary and first stopped at the cafeteria, where I had to have my usual Nova Lox salad. I convinced him to have the meatballs, my other favorite, the larger portion... so that I could steal some. We shared a lingonberry fountain drink too; it was my idea because of the unlimited refills.

I was letting him into my familiar rhythm that predated him, a subtle way of saying, "Here is where I feel at home. I'm letting you in."

We went up to the cashier with our tray. As usual, he was already pulling out his credit card from the back of his phone. But I interrupted him this time.

"I'll take care of this one. Can I?" I asked.

That offer was meant to balance the relationship, which caused a smile on his face.

"Yes, you can," he responded in a surprised tone with gratitude.

He fed me a meatball with his fork. I perceived it as a subtle moment of hearts drawing nearer—an alignment of deed and purpose.

I didn't need him to say it felt good; I watched it feel good.

Lightbulbs

We then began our IKEA tour—the part where we would immerse ourselves in each model room, imagining life together.

I would suggest IKEA dates for people who are dating... but what do I know?

So, the lightbulbs... we couldn't find the exact match because, I suspect, those were obsolete. We spent a significant amount of time searching for something compatible. I cherished that moment because it's like a quest that we must conquer as a team. That kind of joint task revealed how we problem-solved. I felt that it helped build a bond between us.

As I pondered whether that feeling was one-sided, he gave me a passionate kiss and concluded it with equally intense eye contact. No, I'm not imagining this—I was there.

The way we explored those imaginary rooms together showed how we negotiated choices and aligned our rhythms. For a flickering stretch, we were co-authoring one aisle at a time.

When we walked by the candles section, I found one I liked a lot, despite not lighting candles at home.

He noticed and put one in his basket, saying, "I'll get this for you. It's your candle."

That scent, chosen by me and gifted by him, now held meaning.

Imperfection

When I dropped him off at his place, he invited me in, even carrying the frozen IKEA meatballs I had just gotten, because he said they must stay frozen.

But it's already below freezing outside... Why? How long is he expecting me to stay?

He was very kind, paying for my parking on his mobile app so that I didn't have to. He couldn't wait to install the new lightbulbs, and I couldn't wait to use the bathroom.

As soon as I stepped back out, he inquired, "Can you tell which one is new?"

I couldn't tell, so he opened one of the kitchen cabinet doors for them to project closer.

"Ah, yes, I see. That one," as I was pointing at the slightly dimmer one.

That imperfection bothered him.

Our night ended with me being in his bedroom, where "my candle" had already been glowing on his dresser. As I was lying on his bed, I wondered if it was a signal that I had been folded into his space.

I would have stayed overnight, but I had to prepare for an early morning modeling gig on TV, so I gathered my meatballs from his freezer and headed out.

The sweetest part was that he opted to walk me down to my car in the cold, despite no obligation, as if he was honoring the full arc of our time together from arrival to departure.

Busy

We only texted a little the next day because of his busy schedule. Upon his return home after the last shift, he inquired about the pickup time for our outlet trip the next day.

After I gave him the time, he said, "Okay, it's going to be quite a drive, so I'll have time then to catch up with you."

He planned to give me his time in a space free of interruption, allowing our mutual recalibration. The outlet trip became a designated space to reconnect. I valued that he acknowledged his lapse in communication.

An apology wasn't required, yet that statement served a purpose; the subsequent journey served its reconciliation. And that he confirmed it beforehand signaled a growing emotional accountability. That kind of awareness—especially from someone whose default might lean towards emotional compartmentalization—was significant.

This was him saying, "I'm still here. I know I went quiet, but I haven't forgotten you."

Road Trip

He jumped into my car the next day as I exclaimed, "Yay to road trip!"

Our first road trip was exciting—a mini-test of our compatibility during a full day together. We stopped to get coffee and use the restroom—two things we had established we had in common early on. People show their true selves in liminal spaces: before the caffeine hits, while waiting in line, choosing snacks, and navigating unfamiliar bathrooms. Mundane as they may seem, these moments could intensify bonding.

He shared stories about the hospital, which lit him up. I was curious about his bedside nurse stories, seeking an understanding of his navigation of dealing with hardship. That kind of attention has a cost, but it also leaves an imprint.

In fact, I must have told him at least multiple times, "That's hot," not only on that day but since I had been involved with him.

I saw his value in the field where he mattered most and made him feel attractive for something intrinsic.

My Day

I wanted to make his visit worthwhile because his experience mattered to me. So when we arrived at the outlet mall, I let him know to please stop me if we passed by any store that he would like to take a peek at.

He said, "No, I'm good; maybe I want to go to just these two, but today is your day."

Did he just say today is my day?

He even explained to me his internal dialogue: "I don't go shopping a lot, but she said she wanted to go, so I was like, okay!"

It was an unguarded glimpse into the calculus of his decisions, and his actions reflected his growing buy-in. Such thoughtfulness was unprecedented. He didn't just go along with the plan; he internalized it and made a soft orientation towards me. I was so touched because I was no longer trying to carry the weight of togetherness alone.

Even though it's still freezing weather, we held hands the entire day. He didn't do that back home.

Perhaps he has warmed towards the concept of us. Or perhaps the geological distance from home somehow relaxed him.

Even joy, for me, is processed with precision.

Date No. 9

Guess who ended up making more purchases? He did! I know it's an odd observation to appreciate, but it mattered because I had seen what performative love looked like, having just left someone who squandered his money on useless items for others as manipulation.

However, this guy appeared to lack such an issue. He was living his life alongside mine, and I caught him enjoying it. I was proud of myself for choosing "better," finally.

Shopping with him proved amazing: I got to understand his taste in garments for me. It means he didn't disappear inside my structure; he contributed to it, and that's what I was looking for in a partner.

We conversed with a couple sharing a table at a bar, focusing on the sports games scheduled. He told me "sorry" afterwards, likely because he remembered that I was not a fan of commercial sports.

That was very considerate of him, but I didn't mind it at all. I understood that it's a normal conversation in the American culture I had chosen to live in. But I knew his apology was about attunement; it spoke volumes about his care. One can only attune to what they perceive; he was seeing me.

Plus One

We dined at my favorite ramen shop. As he returned from the restroom and saw that I was checking my phone, I told him, "This friend of mine, whom I have known for a few years now, and I attended none of the birthday parties that she invited me to. I feel so bad. I want to go, but I don't know her other friends; I only know her."

Without hesitation, he asked, "When is it? If I don't have to work, I'll go with you."

"REALLY?"

My eyes lit up. My surprise wasn't just excitement—it was disbelief that someone would show up in my life and insert themselves into my world.

He checked his calendar to find that it fell in the middle of his three consecutive shifts.

He said, "9 pm? That should work. I'll get home and take a shower, and we'll go!"

I couldn't believe it!!! I RSVP'd right away.

The guy in front of me will attend a birthday party with me, despite knowing no one, during his breaks instead of resting.

It held significant meaning since he did it just for me.

His offer was a turning point in how deeply he would extend himself for my sake, even if it meant cutting into rest after brutal shifts.

How did I get so lucky?

Disc Jockey

On the drive back, he took it upon himself to be the DJ. He first looked for songs that he liked and then integrated songs he knew I liked (simple, just Queen and Taylor Swift). And eventually, he just had Taylor Swift on until we got back.

That's the part I had longed for: someone who expressed care in the invisible in-between—that's why it hit me. Maybe the way I lit up reinforced his decision to keep playing her songs. But that's the beauty of it; he paid attention, tracked my reaction, and responded in kind.

He knew what he was doing, and I noticed how the sequence unfolded: he was attuning, adjusting, and inching closer to my emotional rhythm because he wanted to give me something I could feel. It's like he was saying, "Let's drive home through your world now."

Parking

A couple of hours later, I found myself at his residence, spending the night—the norm.

The next morning, he retrieved his phone from the bedside table, half-awake, to pay for my parking. It was unannounced, and that's what made it potent: money wasn't the point—his mental presence was.

That's the care that bypasses language, the kind that says, "I am thinking of you even when you're not asking me to."

Pretending to be asleep, I was admiring his thoughtfulness. I stayed still and let myself receive it. For once, someone met me in the practical ways I usually meet others and kept the small promises I didn't even have to extract.

How did I get so lucky?

Holidays

Each of us had distinct plans over the holidays: he would spend it with his family, and I was going to Las Vegas.

I heard little from him during his family visit; that silence crushed me a bit. But I told myself, *he was with family; it's Christmas.*

In Las Vegas, I reflected upon past partners and my life phases each time I had visited since moving to the US at 20: from being a college student new to this country, to owning a coffee shop, to traveling with past flings who taught me life lessons, to serving as a Marine, to walking the runway, to working in federal law enforcement, and finally to meeting a guy who had potential because I chose differently this time. My reflection was about my entire arc: how much ground I had covered, how many versions of myself I had been willing to shed, and how many lives I had already lived.

I texted to let him know I was mulling, and if he cared to know more, I would love to share later. He struck me as someone receptive to self-reflection; that's why I had no hesitation in sharing with him; I thought he would be eager to listen.

I was testing to see if he could keep that narrative, witnessing my growth through pivotal stages that formed the person he was dating.

Date No. 10

We spent time during the weekend following Christmas. It's one of the very few times that he had initiated, and that rarity held subtle significance.

He asked to do something "chill" and low-key at his place, so he cooked, and we chatted about our time apart during Christmas. I shared with him about my self-reflection in Las Vegas, while he told me about his favorite holiday, Christmas, which, according to him, was "different" but not in a good way.

I didn't press. It's my belief that people will share with me whatever they want to and whenever they feel ready.

He made me his salmon dish, the one that he spotlighted on his dating app profile. We opened up my favorite red wine, the bottle he got for me on his prior subway detour.

Sitting on the sofa while Fantastic Beasts was playing on his TV, instead of paying attention to the movie, he started examining my facial features, even sweeping my signature bangs to the side and combing them with his fingers to expose my forehead. Enjoying that level of intimacy, I allowed it.

After a few moments, he asked, "Have you always had bangs?"

I said, "When I first moved to the States, I wanted a fresh start, so I cut it myself. Why?"

"You flinched when I removed it."

"Oh, did I? I didn't even notice."

"I'm going to do this to you more often from now on."

"Why would you do that?"

"Because growth is uncomfortable."

Finally, a guy who was speaking my language.

How did I get so lucky?

That evening, the lines of my connection were drawn by details: the voluntary reach out, the salmon, the mutual sharing of sensation, and finally, a guy "on my level."

Purpose

I entered this relationship with intention because I believe that

Love is not a feeling; it's a choice.

This one was no different.

This guy showed emotional maturity. So I asked him one question that I had jotted down in the notes on my phone: "What is your purpose in life?"

I offered a question that wasn't casual, because I'm not casual. To ask someone their purpose is to ask if they are anchored in themselves.

I'm not sure why, but he flinched in reaction to it; it was so slight I would have missed it if I had blinked. He then froze, likely for internal scrambling, long enough for me to sense awkwardness.

So I looked him in the eye and said, "I don't know if it'd mean anything to you, but you inspire me."

I was naming genuine, sober respect because I had assessed and found evidence of structure. I don't give respect easily because I see too clearly, often too early.

He looked down, looked back up at me, and softly said, "Thank you," and looked down again.

While I gave it with humility, he couldn't stay in it. That tiny collapse was his retreat. He couldn't hold my gaze in the moment of being seen. That was too bare for him. He folded inward. His difficulty surprised me because he seemed so purposeful.

I might have posed the very question he was not prepared to answer because he hadn't gone there himself. That moment exposed something unspoken—a split between the guy he presented and the one beneath—a fracture line I wouldn't recognize until later. That instance signaled the extent of his achievable depth before retreat.

Toothbrush

The night ended with me in his bedroom with some of my fantasies fulfilled. I was watching the residue of my presence while asking myself, *Do I echo here, or am I just passing through?*

The toothbrush he had let me use last time sat on his bathroom counter, just as I had left it, a silent trace of continuity. I interpreted it as hope—hope that the toothbrush represents my belonging in his world.

I was matching energy with precision and acknowledging my presence in his space. Building with deliberation, I was layering trust to test the mutual foundation. I moved through that space as someone verifying if signals lined up with the substances. But I was already attuned to the fact that even romantic evidence doesn't always guarantee permanence.

New Year

He ended the year working several consecutive shifts over the New Year. Although I wouldn't mind having a New Year's kiss, I told myself that I would not ask because he was going to be working, with the understanding that connection is built by holding space for it to grow.

He texted me on New Year's Eve after work, saying he had planned to visit me on his way home. However, a difficult patient kept him late, and he had drinks with coworkers afterwards to "cool off."

He was candid, revealing his uncertainty about whether to share his original plan since he had already decided against it. It revealed a vulnerable side beneath his professional toughness and how much he valued being transparent with me.

I responded to him with an appreciation of the thought itself.

He then said, "We'll put a pin on it."

I traded honesty for constructing something that might last beyond a New Year's kiss.

Coworkers

The week after, he tried to make amends and took me to an amazing restaurant with delicious homemade pasta.

Waiting for him to get ready at his place, he shared that two female nurses he barely knew invited him on a trip to China a few months down the road. And if the money worked out, he would consider it.

My analytical mind understood his view of accepting invitations for enriching experiences that often lead to wonderful memories. In contrast, my emotional mind protested his planned extended trip abroad with two women.

My right brain's displeasure must have shown on my face because he asked, "What? You have something to say. Say it."

Whenever my left and right brains are not in coherent order, I cannot speak. Different from the silent treatment, it involves allowing time for them to process and comprehension to mature, enabling me to articulate it aloud.

When he asked me to say what's on my mind, my left brain was still buffering.

Why am I still the one earning what they are being casually given?

But for a moment, I let my right brain take over and said, "I feel offended. You'd entertain going on a trip with two females you barely know, and yet we haven't talked about going on any trips together after how many times I have already slept with you?"

My right brain responded first because it was the part of me that had felt everything: the thoughtful parking payments, my toothbrush still in place, and the passionate kiss at IKEA.

The unacknowledged truth I felt wasn't about the trip itself; it was his willingness to dive into spontaneity with near-strangers while staying uncommitted with me, despite all the cumulative ledger of my efforts to respect his pace.

He didn't have an answer for me because I had pierced the illusion that our connection had evolved. I exposed the asymmetry he was still benefiting from: my emotional commitment had deepened, but his had not caught up. I wasn't demanding a trip; I was wondering why the signals I was receiving didn't match the ones he was giving to others through adventure. My words served as a reflection, not an accusation; he could not yet perceive it—but I did.

Date No. 11

We spoke more on the topic of traveling over pasta. I felt like I needed to beat others to inviting him to go on trips, kind of like "first-come, first-served." So I wanted to understand better his mindset about traveling.

Does he travel only upon invitation? Or do initiation difficulties prevent trip planning?

He said, "Some trips I initiate. Like when my family and I went to Poland, that was my idea. And some other ski trips that I went on with friends were my ideas, too."

Then, I explained to him that I struggled to ask for what I want because people in the past had made me feel guilty for asking, "You don't think that I'm being pushy for asking?"

He seemed surprised by my question: "No! Why would that be pushy? You're just asking a question. It's still up to me to evaluate whether I say yes. But asking alone isn't pushy."

That concept baffled me; he had no idea the weight of what he had offered. His answer rewrote something deep inside me: my hesitation to voice my needs in the past was about emotional safety.

Noticing my surprise, he added, "You have never been with anyone like me—I'm not selfish."

His words unlocked something that years of practice hadn't. He named the imbalance that others had done to me. And in doing so, he gave me a new baseline:

My voice isn't too much; it has just never landed somewhere stable before.

Following dinner, we returned to his place, and you probably know what happened next. It was a release valve—something fundamental in my body had unclenched in me over pasta.

Man of His Word

It was in the gap between his second and third shifts that he joined me at my friend's birthday party. That wasn't convenient; it required a conscious decision to hold space for me amidst his own exhaustion. His unresisting participation felt like something beyond mere conduct.

He verbalized his plan to me beforehand: "I should be able to get home by around 8 pm and take a quick shower before we take a rideshare over there. I'll let you know when I get off, so you'll meet me at my place."

Well... YES! Thank you for making my life so easy.

The dress code was white, which is my favorite color, and I took full advantage of getting dolled up. He knew I was a model, but I'm pretty casual in real life; he never saw me prettied up in person.

I showed up dressed in my radiance: fishnets, a white dress, and model poise. My beauty wasn't because of garments; it sprang from an absence of solo burdens. At last, I required no negotiation for care, nor did I ponder if my needs were excessive.

I also shared good news with him: a designer invited me to close her fashion show. Even though the fashion world wasn't his territory, he treated my excitement as valid.

He inquired about the show date; I lacked immediate recall. Retrieving his phone, he accessed the show's Instagram account to discover the date. That consideration held weight with me.

Unfortunately, his upcoming ski trip overlapped with the show date, and his disappointment mirrored mine, a subtle detail that revealed his desire to attend. That mutual longing meant I wasn't the only one marking the milestones.

Birthday Party

This friend of mine had been through quite a bit with me. I became her first friend when she moved into town. We met at a photoshoot and dined together afterwards. Her transformation from teacher to principal unfolded before me in a short time.

We could quantify the duration of our friendship by how many guys (or boys in men's bodies) we had dated. She always helped me cope with repeated disappointments from dating and would always remind me that I'm a "high-value" woman.

Being protective of me, she inquired about my plus one. I shared that he had been treating me well.

Likewise, he was also curious about my friend's story, which I shared on the way to the party. I appreciated that he took an interest in knowing the people whom I care enough to keep around.

Date No. 12

He once confided in me his struggle with social anxiety, something I could relate to. Perhaps that's part of the reason he had offered to be my plus one.

I introduced them at the party. When my friend went for a handshake, he returned with a hug and a "Happy Belated Birthday" instead. He showed up and leaned into social discomfort because it mattered to me.

My friend's hospital-working friends made up half of the attendance, with whom he initiated conversations. I was content just standing alongside him, listening; I never felt bored hearing about an occupation that intrigued me. I didn't realize I was doing my familiar quiet labor: standing beside him, attuned to every micro-expression, and making the moment about him.

A stranger at the party asked, "Are you guys boyfriend and girlfriend?"

Her forthrightness sparked my laughing out loud in reflex; it echoed an inquiry I had been avoiding.

"We are seeing each other," he responded.

That answer acknowledged our bond without naming it more firmly than he was ready to. He offered the bare minimum truth, revealing just enough, yet avoiding greater accountability.

That stranger said to us, "Sorry."

Maybe because of my laughter and his response, she then turned to him and said, "Well, you'd be a fortunate man!"

She did not comprehend the significance of her words.

Yes, he would be, but does he believe it?

He smiled without saying a word. It's polite, grateful, maybe, but not reflective.

That moment stitched together threads that had been floating in tension: my longing for clarity, his social anxiety, and the ambiguity that had been circling for weeks.

What are we?

But it didn't matter that he never said the words I wanted to hear; I had already trained myself to find meaning in subtext and accept gestures as answers.

Bathroom Trips

We were both standing in line for the one bathroom... remember? We had that in common!

When it became available, he said, "We'll just go in together unless you mind."

No, I for sure don't. I mean, how many times have we already seen each other naked?

Although we still needed to take turns to use the toilet, I thought it was cute that he felt so comfortable around me already to do things I would imagine a lot of couples who have been dating for longer still feel self-conscious about doing together.

During her speech, my friend highlighted to everyone my significance in her life: I was the first friend she met who welcomed her with both arms. I then went up and hugged her as she whispered into my ear, "He seems nice, but you let me know if he does anything wrong to you; I'll be the first one to go kick his ass."

That fierce whisper pulled me into clarity for a moment... she had seen enough of my journey to know my pattern of assigning depth to gestures that may not be connected to long-term intentions.

Before leaving, we needed to use the bathroom once more. Without hesitation, he entered with me, signaling our new norm.

In hindsight, physical closeness might just bypass certain thresholds for him without awkwardness because he was in nursing. But at the time, I was smiling inside because I took it as a significant emotional progression. In some ways, it was. But the trust he extended was circumstantial.

And yes, you guessed it: we went back to his place afterwards, where the physical resumed its rhythm. I couldn't help but wonder, *am I the only one keeping count of what this all means?*

Home Alone

I knew the guy he was: practical, measured, and protective of his schedule. He needed to get up early for his morning shift... I had never been "allowed" to spend a night at his place in such a situation because he would rush to get ready for work. However, that morning, he adjusted his inner framework to make space for me; he was okay with leaving me home alone.

Really? He trusts me at this level already?

He was cautious, attempting to avoid disturbance to keep me sleeping. Without adding to his stress of catching the bus, I kept my eyelids closed, attending to his every action. What stood out was the way he let me stay; he curated comfort for it.

He stood next to me and whispered, "You can sleep in and stay," even closing the blinds to ensure my undisturbed rest.

His attentiveness was off the charts. I chuckled inside about making yet another relationship milestone right after the bathroom one the night before.

How did I get so lucky?

But I didn't realize I was the one doing most of the meaning-making because he rarely used obvious declarations.

And while his behavior warmed me, it also left me wondering: *Does he know what he's building with me? Or am I the only one tracing the blueprint?*

Photos

My friend had snapped photos of him and me when we were on her balcony, checking out the view. When I saw them, I caught a rare glimpse of myself from outside of my body in his presence: smitten with no barriers. I trusted that smile, so I shared it with him.

"That's a cute candid," he texted back.

He didn't use the heart emoji… maybe he didn't "love" it. While not unkind, his statement didn't match my depth. I started wondering again because of the emotional asymmetry. I opened a window; he responded by peering through a crack.

Am I the only one feeling the weight of the sweetness?

I then thanked him for sacrificing his rest time amidst hospital shifts to come with me.

He said, "You're welcome. I don't mind showing up when needed."

It sounded sweet, but it made me wonder if his version of "showing up" meant physically or on a deeper level, like he'd be there for me emotionally.

His upcoming week-long ski trip nagged at me. On one hand, I was hoping to see him before his long absence; on the other hand, I was still trying to trust his rhythm.

Without complaint, I gave him the recovery days from work I noticed he needed. That was my subtle way of loving: adjusting myself to what I understood. I was stitching together my security from pieces he left unspoken.

Pastas

I postponed texting him until the afternoon, presuming he had slept in following an extended period of long shifts.

"Hey, remember this place near you that has an unlimited pasta night every Monday? So I haven't been able to get it off my mind since I found out about it and was wondering if you feel like joining me if I were to go tonight?" I texted.

I also explained to him that it took a lot of me to ask, but I had to be better at voicing my needs, like he had told me to. More than just pasta, it was about rebalancing emotional power and my nervous system, learning that I wouldn't have to brace every time I spoke my needs aloud.

"I literally just got up and got myself to the gym… haven't been very productive, but I wouldn't say no. Plus, I think I owe you from the other night anyway," he responded.

He alluded to being dissatisfied with his sexual performance after my friend's party, yet I had given it no further consideration. His statement gave me a perfect opportunity to follow up with a comment that would address my concern.

I corrected him and said, "I never saw it as you owing me at all. Plus, it really shouldn't be transactional."

He gave a long pause here, long enough to break the rhythm.

His text then reached me: "It's not transactional at all. Trust me."

That answer hit the exact nerve I didn't know needed soothing. My subconscious worry that he was only in it for sex had likely been accumulating. He could meet me with gentleness, and his response put me at peace.

Date No. 13

At the pasta place, he was very attentive, seating me away from the freezing window. Upon his return from the men's room, he gently dabbed my back before resuming his seat. I always notice these little nuances.

Somehow, the topic discussed landed on the quality we appreciated most in people.

He told me, "Thoughtfulness," and explained, "That's why the only fantasy I have is you being in lingerie, because that tells me that you actually had to think ahead, and that's thoughtfulness."

He was naming what it symbolized: an inner world turned outward. His fantasy centered on being the focus of my attention, which held greater significance than the image.

He then asked, "How did it make you feel the other day when I texted you a picture of the bottle of wine you said you liked?"

He was testing to confirm whether I, like him, tethered affection to emotional precision.

I gave him the biggest grin, felt a little shy, and said, "I liked it… because it showed that you were thinking of me."

He said, "See! You like thoughtfulness, too!"

I smiled and nodded. My soft reaction showed him he wasn't alone in that wiring. For once, I wasn't the only one scanning for meaning. It created a rare moment of emotional symmetry, like something inside me finally exhaled.

Thoughtfulness

He inquired whether my monthly Universal trip was strictly a solo endeavor. Though unspoken, joy bubbled through me. First, that served as his initiation, even though he admitted to struggling with it. Second, he was interested in experiencing something that brought me joy. Third, that was yet another relationship milestone.

I replied, "No, not strictly for myself at all. I'd love for you to join me. That'd be lovely. I booked it for myself all the way up to next month already. You want to see if you have days off to come with me the month after?"

"My schedule should be out next week, and I know I'll go on a ski trip in the second half of that month. I'll see if I have four days off in a row at the beginning of that month and let you know. How does that sound?"

I smiled and nodded once more; words simply couldn't express my contentment.

After dinner, we walked back to his place. And in what he had said he wanted to accomplish... he performed, in bed. That circled back to when he had claimed he owed.

Was that his way of justifying to himself about accepting my invitation to pasta night?

I believe so.

Because accepting care, in his system, required a frame where he was reciprocating in a way he could control. He needed an "excuse" for himself to lean into spending time with me. The "I owe you" phrase was an attempt to preserve autonomy in the face of intimacy. Those words permitted him to agree to a pasta night... and to everything subsequent.

We both faced early mornings: his, therapy; mine, work. So, I went home that night.

Disjointedness

After his therapy the next day, he confessed he had been feeling disjointed. With his therapist, he discussed diverting his focus to self-care and friendships, which he valued. He blamed his neglect of self and friends on feeling ill and time spent with family over the holidays.

That was him offering me a rare internal truth and framing it in the language of accountability and saying it out loud. I honored it by expressing my appreciation to him for sharing something so personal and told him I understood his shift of priorities.

I felt appreciative of having met someone so transparent; people in the past had kept me guessing. Out of respect for his boundaries, I stopped texting, even though he never named me as the cause. I recognized the delicate balance he was trying to maintain: connection without depletion.

Yet he reached out the following day. It confirmed that my non-pursuit wasn't interpreted as disinterest. He knew the line was still open and crossed it.

So, I took the chance to check his self-care progress and whether he had caught up with friends. That's me saying, "I heard you. I care about how you're doing and remember what matters to you."

My rare kind of attunement showed him that his vulnerability earned more connection, not less.

He shared that he had texted friends, hoping to socialize, but none were free. That likely intensified his awareness that my presence had filled a larger role than he realized. He might have noticed how much my presence meant in my absence.

That was when my restraint created a contrast: he had asked for space, and I gave it. But in that space, he didn't find the relief he thought he needed. Instead, he found me missing.

Needs

My ability to recall events based on the image of a calendar that I have in my brain is a habit that I have developed since I was little. Mapping individual rhythms, mirroring the calendar, constitutes how I love.

With his work schedule being so busy until his ski trip, I knew he would only have time to see me that weekend. But I no longer extended my invites because I didn't want him to feel pressured into hanging out with me when he had already clarified that this stretch of time was one where he needed to recalibrate.

The conflict within me—between honoring his need for space and my need for connection—revealed just how deeply in love I was. But I couldn't put mine over his; I just couldn't. So I backed away out of integrity, but my ache was real.

Will you rise to meet it? Or will I remain here, bearing the full weight of integrity alone?

Balance

When he finally checked in, I inquired regarding his weekend plans for self-care and friendships. He shared that one of the friends he had texted finally responded, and they were meeting for happy hour on Saturday afternoon.

I didn't ask, but he volunteered the information: "It's a she. But I don't want you to freak out because I say 'she,' who was in a friend group I was in on my previous floor, but the group has since dissolved. We haven't hung out since."

I didn't get reactive about "a female friend" because I took it as his trust offering. I reinforced his integrity by once again telling him how much I appreciated his transparency. You should have noticed by now my deliberate effort to show him my gratitude for being open.

I explained to him that I understood he likely wanted to sleep in after his work shifts, so I would be fine if he had to skip me.

To my surprise, he said, "I really appreciate that you said that. I really do. But parts of me, trying to balance my life to feel less disjointed, are not trying to get rid of something; I just need to learn how to be better at balancing everything. With that said, I'd like to spend time with you at some point this weekend. Would you like to have brunch on Saturday?" That's his signaling: "I see what you're doing. I see that you're not making this hard. I see that you want what's best for me, even if it means not seeing you."

His reply filled me with happiness, highlighting that I was in the company of a mature individual striving for a balanced life to preserve their sanity. It's not that he wasn't tired; it's that he wasn't afraid to choose me even while tending to other parts of his life.

I offered to play it by ear, but he insisted with assertion, "No, I'm good with my decision. I'll see you tomorrow morning!"

How did I get so lucky?

Perhaps I really had chosen "better" this time.

Date No. 14

Meeting up for brunch, I would have walked there because I take every opportunity to stay active. But he invited me into his world—navigating with city buses... something he had convinced me to try for a while. He wanted me to first experience it with him so I would feel safer riding alone.

He made it comfortable, and I allowed space for something new to integrate. Knowing my affinity for detail, he even let me ring the bell, which brought me joy.

At last, we arrived at the brunch place I had been wanting to try.

Friendships

His recent mention of rebalancing life inspired our topic of discussion: friendship. Even as a fellow Libra, I don't feel the urge to balance everything as such. It wasn't until I felt him using a measuring glass to give equal attention to every aspect of his life that I truly grasped the magnitude of his intention. I resonate with the importance of self-care, but the idea of placing friendships at the same level intrigued me.

He said he had missed out on being in friend groups in high school because he kept denying invitations until classmates stopped including him. And finally, in nursing, coworker friend groups started forming, a dynamic he valued so much that he missed it after switching floors and coworkers moving on.

He also recalled a desire that had yet to be executed: taking fitness classes to meet people outside of the hospital. I understood where he was coming from because I had met people through such classes that eventually blossomed into deeper connections.

We had previously established one thing in common: we both had the hardest time recalling names. So when I brought up that I intended to track his friends by name, he smiled because he knew it was deliberate.

I empathize with the emotional load these individuals represent within your experience. And if I matter to you, let me in on that structure.

He operated like someone managing connections—allocating time and effort to keep everything upright: work, friends, family, health, and relationships. In contrast, the friends that I care to keep in my life form organically. People who stay on the surface level don't last long with me. I don't multiply connections; I distill them. And depth is how I love.

My system was calibrated for signal clarity, while his was for harmony across multiple orbits. But my emotional depth was already reshaping him, whether he recognized it.

Tongue Bite

He halted a thought while he was biting his tongue and gave me a slight smile with his eyes.

I said, "Okay, you already started it; you have to finish saying it now."

He murmured with hesitation, "Friendships, to me, are a better investment because they last longer. Unlike relationships, where the other person depends on you for other things, like physical needs."

He knew what he was about to say might land wrong, but he said it anyway. What he shared was revealing about the invisible contract he carried into all relationships.

In his mind, relationships were risky, fragile, and costly; their expectations and demands were high—a mindset that situated me as a potential burden. I should have grasped that obvious warning, yet my instinct moved me to trust that I could prove to him my worth.

In hindsight, the real question wasn't whether I was different; it was, "Will he ever let himself recategorize relationships in his internal structure? Will he ever stop managing connections like a budget?"

Check-In

After discussing friendship for a while, he asked, "Is that the kind of deep conversation you said you crave?"

It was a proud check-in, resembling a student query to a teacher. He may not have lived at the depth I did by default, but it showed he was trying to reach towards it for me.

I smiled, nodded, and said, "Yes."

But was it? I mean, yes… that surpassed idle chatter; it's also very thoughtful of him to check in to see if he had met my expectations. But my mind doesn't stop at one level—I keep peeling off layers of insights. So while he was wondering if he had met my depth, I had already reached the point of discernment.

So I questioned, "If you feel the urgency to reinvest in friendships, where are they in this equation?"

My question hinted: If he was the only one doing the reaching, then even his "safer" investments were still solo efforts disguised as community. It would mean that he was seeking control over emotional input and output.

As someone who views friendship as a two-way street, I was listening for symmetry, wondering if that dynamic was another expression of how he carried connection like a self-imposed duty: one more obligation to balance.

And unsurprisingly, silence was his answer.

Passerby

On our walk towards the bus stop after brunch, a guy was approaching us from the opposite direction, pushing a bicycle.

In passing, that guy said to him, "I'm taking my bike into the shop."

As soon as we passed, he said to me, "That was my friend."

That was the coworker turned friend he just mentioned to me moments earlier, with whom he had bonded over an overseas trip a few years back.

My immediate, genuine reaction was, "Wait, that was it? You didn't have more to say to him?"

My instinctive surprise came from a deeper radar: my attunement wouldn't allow me to turn my head away from the discrepancy between what he said he valued and how he acted in real time—something he might not have even done for himself.

Only after putting some thought into it later did I realize that he didn't care to use that opportunity to introduce us. But it wasn't just him either… his friend also kept walking. Two people who considered each other significant became a passing nod on the sidewalk.

That chance encounter revealed that he didn't treat relationships, romantic or platonic, as living things. He related to them more like items on a shelf: available when needed, dusted off occasionally, but rarely nurtured with presence.

So I maintained my core belief and shared, "At some point, self-respect will kick in and say that enough is enough."

I was naming a limit—but I wasn't aware it was my limit that my body was naming. I knew it made him think because he got quiet after hearing it.

As we got seated on the bus, he gave me a gentle deflection and said, "I see that we view friendships differently, and that's okay."

He offered reassurance, hoping to ease my worry that the difference would cause any problems between us. But it sounded like a buffer: the difference was acknowledged, yet he bypassed my discomfort. He was stepping back into his comfort zone, where neutrality was safer than self-examination.

Decision Point

The bus dropped us off in front of his building, where he stopped and checked the time on his watch, saying, "Okay, decision point. I still have to work out and take care of some stuff before I go meet up with my friend for happy hour. So if you come in, it'll have to be at most for an hour."

I was still operating from a place of attunement. Meanwhile, he laid out logistical boundaries, operating from compartmentalization. He was respectful, yes, but sparse in emotions.

I said, "Nah, I'll just go home. I hope you have fun with your friend later."

Knowing that entering his place could signal an interest in physical intimacy, I used my actions to clarify that I was seeking a deeper connection. I started a goodbye hug, but he went for a kiss instead: a long, passionate make-out session on the street. It felt like a contradiction of the aloofness he had been expressing all morning.

I still felt uneasy while departing, though I couldn't identify the reason. Now I know that I felt incomplete because of the dissonance he gave me—moving physically towards me while emotionally stepping away from me. The kiss didn't fool my body; my intuition knew—no matter how passionately he kissed me on the sidewalk—his priority system had declared its allegiance.

My arrival home didn't prompt an immediate "homed" text this time. I later explained to him about my silence: it stemmed from needing space to process my thoughts before communicating.

He told me, "Yes, I totally get the internal processing part."

I had desired companionship beyond an activity partner, but he had already parceled his life into blocks: brunch, gym, errands, friend. My existence slotted in only if it fit his structure. There's a limit to his emotional investment. I kept bringing my reflective self, and he kept side-stepping that weight with a tactical transparency that signaled thoughtfulness but never quite rooted into transformation.

What I hadn't been doing until then was naming the cost of my restraint: every time I adjusted to preserve his balance, I absorbed the imbalance myself.

Solo Ski Trip

He left for his one-week solo ski trip the next day. To me, solo trips are self-rejuvenating; they are like mini life resets that allow me to self-reflect. Therefore, I appreciated that his trip felt well-timed, given his need for self-care.

Even he himself said to me, "It'll be good for my soul."

Intrigued by his trip, I inquired about the details of his planned itinerary. He planned to be at a different ski resort daily, from open to close.

He also added, "And I might go to a brewery to order a flight in honor of you."

While his desire to feel my presence even being apart made me feel warm inside, I couldn't help but worry about our upcoming communication. I had an unspoken promise to myself that I would let him lead the pace, trusting that he was the more stable one between us.

Although I saw his slower pace as healthy, I have to admit that it drove my nervous system crazy.

He never texted me after arriving at his destination, which reflected his priorities. His decision also proved that he could show tenderness sometimes, but he couldn't carry me in his inner world when I wasn't right in front of him.

And my restraint in not reaching out was intentional. First, I wouldn't interrupt his rejuvenation. Second, I had to regulate my anxiety on my own. Third, his independent functioning would then be observable.

I believe in letting someone be themselves, trusting that if they valued me, they will return. I attempted to see whether he could sustain the thread between us when life wasn't curated around the relationship.

Staircase

The night he left, I fell down my spiral staircase at home. Skipping socks on stairs was my habit, but I scrambled to wear them in my upstairs bedroom before rushing out for my ice skating lesson.

It. Hurt. So. bad.

I used to update my partner on such matters for connection. With him, though, I kept silent, stemming from respect. I had disciplined myself to require nothing. It was a conscious act on my part. What I used to do was "too much," so I should tone it down. Hence, I made my pain private, trusted that space was love, and refused to ask for too much.

Secure people love this way, correct?

Adapting to a healthier pace and managing anxious impulses felt like growth. I thought this was how healthy love worked, but I guess healthy love would want to know when I fall.

And let's be honest: my silence was about honoring his limitations. I protected him with my energy, and he didn't even notice. That element caused greater pain than the tumble.

Cold Hands

Before he left, I had told him I would love to see photos. So, he sent me selfies, even a nice photo of a town with Christmas light decorations, saying, "You'd like this little town. It's cute."

That brightened my spirits, believing I was in his thoughts.

I was on my Universal trip a couple of days after he had left. When I updated him with a selfie of me, half-faced, he responded with a selfie, also half-faced. I put an "lol" on his selfie and let him know how cute it was that he was mimicking my pose.

His response was, "Yes, that's what counts as a proper reply."

Mid-trip, I didn't hear from him for a day. I told myself not to reach out; I didn't want my nervous system to betray me again. So I convinced myself that restraint was care and absence was thoughtfulness, because the alternative would have been too harsh to contemplate.

He did send me selfies, which was what I asked.

Again and again, I narrated stories to fill the void he left and gave him the benefit of the doubt, bending logic until it could hold both his silence and my worth together.

Finally, he texted, "Sorry, I haven't used my phone much because it's so cold that I can't even feel my fingers."

Made sense! He was thinking of me, and the story I imagined was correct.

Relief washed over me like proof, but love that makes me constantly reinterpret silence as tenderness is not love I can rest in. The truth is, a genuine connection would stay connected, even in cold weather. I kept filling the space he vacated with hope, but the story underneath it all? I loved him for both of us.

Ramen

He texted me a photo of a bowl of steaming ramen and said, "I need this after a long day of skiing."

It's significant because he remembered my love of ramen. He had trained me not to expect initiation, so when it came, it lit me up because of its scarcity. It gave me the impression that he desired to remain involved with me.

I replied with a photo of the IKEA meatballs that I had cooked for dinner, to which he said, "You and your meatballs lol. I can use another IKEA date soon. I think I want to return some lightbulbs."

Because we had established that he was someone who struggled with initiating, I decided to save his IKEA date idea as a "secret weapon" when I ran out of other ideas, holding onto it as a symbol of hope that there would be a "later." I carried the weight of momentum because I understood his passivity and worked around it like someone coaxing life into a fire that wouldn't quite catch. I was always living a few emotional steps ahead, and that's what made it so heartbreaking: he thought it was casual, but I had imbued it with meaning.

Injury

He texted me more often during the second half of his trip.

He even asked me, "How are you?"

How thoughtful is he to care about my well-being when he is on his much-needed trip to focus on self-care?

With his invitation, I finally disclosed my painful rib injury.

"You broke your ribs. What? How did you do that?"

He seemed concerned, asking me whether I took medication, not whether I saw a doctor. That was part of the draw: I didn't require rescuing; my aching body didn't require a doctor's confirmation of needing rest, and I was glad that, as a nurse, he resonated with my decision.

Home contained various pain relievers; I let him know that choosing one was problematic. He then requested medicine photos so that he could specify my prescription.

My body hurt like hell, but my heart felt so warm.

To make it even warmer, he sent me a naked photo the day before his return, saying, "Just got out of the shower!"

Honestly, I couldn't believe it... this was new behavior for him, given his default of quieter demeanor outside of the bedroom. It was a move that suggested comfort, a desire to close the distance between us after being away, or maybe even a way of reminding me: "I'm still here, still yours, in this nonverbal way I know how to offer myself."

Return

The next day, I received a text from him: "It's so warm here at freezing degrees when I was in below zero all week lol."

Instead of announcing his arrival, his avoidance of vulnerability had to hint at it.

"YAY, you're back!!!" I exclaimed.

We then continued to text back and forth until he said, "Why? You want to try fucking already with a broken rib?"

What is he trying to say? Is he just joking?

Do not gloss over his actions: the guy who returned from his soul-reviving trip chose as his first move a sexually charged provocation that made me question my interpretation of his comment. During a moment where emotional closeness could have been offered, he deflected with crude levity for his protection because, for people like him:

Receiving care means being seen; being seen means being known; and being known scares the hell out of people who haven't resolved their own worth.

He tested my boundaries with a borderline insulting text and then waited. And deep down, I knew it. That's why I ceased texting to have a two-hour internal debate about how far I would bend my own values to accommodate someone still afraid of his own depth.

My right brain recalled the time he had told me about his tendency to take jokes too far, whereas my left brain was warning me that… he had been more sexually driven in this relationship than I had.

Finally, after my nervous system had calmed down a little, I texted him back with tact to re-center the connection.

I said, "I suppose you're good for emotional connection, too, if the physical one is off the table right now. I'd love to hear all about your trip if you feel up for it tonight!"

My reply reminded him that my standard was connection, not transaction. I gave him a lifeline to emotionality, and he seized it, surprised that the window hadn't shut.

He retorted, "Sure, I'm up for it. What do you have in mind?" His instant response was a subtle exhale disguised as engagement.

Coat

It's restaurant week in the city: something that both of us had mentioned we would usually take part in during our dating app chatting stage. He asked me to select the restaurant—something that he had always pushed—for me to choose.

I even texted him, "Thank you for always asking me what I want!"

As I was approaching the restaurant on foot, a smile crept onto my face as I saw him from afar. He also did, albeit smaller. I couldn't hide it even if I tried, which meant my nervous system trusted him enough to feel joy for the way he made space for me to step in. I had spent weeks being cautious about respecting his pace. Part of me was still hoping, tracking for signs of tenderness that weren't laced with ambiguity, and trying to believe that the guy who could make me smile across a city block might also be the one who could finally match my emotional depth.

As usual, he had his hands in the pockets of his big winter coat, which was not zipped up because he didn't have to walk far. And as I came up close, he opened his coat by widening his arms so that I could thread mine through underneath. Here, he was the one initiating softness by enveloping me. I could feel the warmth coming from our hearts touching. That wordless intimacy was instinct—his body moved before his brain spoke. But I already knew he could offer warmth.

The real question should have been: *Can he sustain it once closeness asks more of him?*

Date No. 15

With the restaurant week promotion, we were to select four courses each. He looked at the menu, removed two undesirable options, and handed me the space to choose all eight.

"Really?" I lit up.

He said, "Yes, I want you to get what you want."

How did I get so lucky?

That feeling was born from drought; I was astonished because this kind of baseline care felt exceptional. So when someone finally handed me space without resistance, my first instinct was disbelief. When he did something ordinary, I registered it as extraordinary.

Recollection

Over dinner, he accounted for each day of his trip, even showing me on his phone the app he used to track ski runs. I loved seeing his smile when he was sharing something he felt so passionate about. I do not have experience skiing, but the stats sounded impressive!

And then he recounted that the windshield on his rental Jeep had cracked one morning. So after skiing, he twice drove to the rental place because of tire damage on the first replacement. Frustration flickered when he confided in me, as I finally understood the silence the day I hadn't heard from him. It mattered to me that he shared the messier, less glamorous moments with me.

Although I was relieved, the thought lingered: *If our roles were to switch, I'd have been so frustrated at that moment, and the first person I thought about sharing that with would be him.*

My mind tried to grasp the gentle imbalance.

Perhaps he's wired differently?

I forgave the discrepancy because it felt like grace was the only path forward.

After we had consumed all eight different dishes of delicious food, he asked, "What's your favorite?"

Without hesitation, I answered, "Hearing all about your trip!"

That statement captured my personality: naming the experience rather than material objects.

My answer provoked a grin, prompting him to flinch, declaring, "I meant the food!"

He didn't know how to sit under the weight of being someone's favorite part.

Where did our journey lead after that meal? You guessed it. I forgot about the pain around my ribs because, for a moment, he gave me presence, which was the most potent form of relief. My nervous system felt close to him, since I understood the rarity of such intimacy.

Medication

He looked at his watch and said, "Okay, let's take a walk."

It's his way of saying he was going to walk me home. Granted, we only lived twelve minutes apart, but how thoughtful was he to walk with me on a cold winter night when he was already comfortable at home? Before leaving, he inquired whether I still had medication for my injuries.

I stated, "Yes, I have more."

Arriving in front of my lobby, we paused there and kissed.

Before I walked away, he pulled out a bag with several pills in it, handed it to me, and said, "Take one a day, okay?"

How did I get so lucky?

I couldn't believe it; I thought it was only a casual question he had asked me earlier. I bet he was packaging them while I was in his bathroom. He could have handed them to me after I came out.

From the start, I had been holding space for him. In a flicker, he showed me he was capable of small tenderness. His intention caught up to me on what I deserved all along as my nervous system whispered: *Finally.*

It felt like a reward when the bare minimum finally showed up in a form my body recognized.

Waiting

With no pre-planned dates remaining on our calendar, I admit I was a bit anxious: my nervous system equated his lack of planning to see me as unsafe, but I kept reminding myself that he had already told me about his struggle with initiating, and I gave it room by absorbing the weight of forward momentum so he wouldn't have to. But

One-sided grace is a distortion of effort disguised as compassion.

I paused my anxiety long enough to examine the past pattern: at least one or two days monthly, we had always gone on dates during his time off. I was basically cross-referencing his behavior, schedule, and words until I discovered something stable to rely upon. That was my nervous system misspelling logic to protect my heart.

Restaurant Week continued; I wished to treat him to dinner. But I held off on the invitation because I was offering a gap to be filled by his choice, waiting with dignity to see if he would step into the space I had left open.

Showing Up

The next day, I got a missed text from him when I checked my phone in between ballet classes: "Hey, how are you?"

Rushing into my next class, I retorted, "Hey! I'm at ballet right now and will have to leave my phone. I was wondering if you're up for doing restaurant week with me… if so, it'd be my treat!"

"Sure, where?"

"My favorite restaurant is near my ballet school. I'll see you then?"

"Sounds good! I'll get us a bottle of wine!"

After class, I intended to text him my estimated arrival time, expecting his would coincide, but waiting wouldn't have fazed me.

To my surprise, he responded straightaway. "I'm already here!"

WHAT?

He didn't need confirmation to decide he was showing up—an act that stabilized my system. He had even bought a bottle of wine already!

His recollections possessed subtle beauty: the time my ballet class would end, and my favorite Italian restaurant was a BYOB. These were soft acts of precision, the kind only visible to someone who had been paying attention.

How did I get so lucky?

Needing cash for the cash-only establishment, we stopped at an ATM. But the cash failed to dispense because I grabbed the wrong card —credit instead of debit. My nervous system would normally brace for friction, but my curveball was met with acceptance.

If this were a film, this is where we would cut to his glance at me with a knowing smile, the kind that says, "That's not a big deal. I've been here, too."

Date No. 16

I then proposed a Harry Potter-themed restaurant. The crowd was enormous, so they seated us at the bar, which I didn't mind… Remember? I prefer the physical closeness there.

The atmosphere reminded me he hadn't confirmed dates for our Universal trip.

So I brought it up, "I'm about to book my trip to Universal. Have you gotten a chance to see if you can come with?"

Without saying a word, he whipped out his phone, went to his work schedule, and showed it to me.

He said, "From here to there? It might work!" as his thumb was gliding from Sunday through Thursday.

I then looked at the flight schedule, showing him an evening flight there after his day shift and an early flight back before his night shift.

He plotted his recovery window out loud: "Let's see… I'll still fit in a quick shower before we go… and I'll be able to take a nap, get groceries, and prepare food before my night shift… Sure!"

Just like that, he agreed!!! That energy shift was what my nervous system had been aching for all along.

The airfare wasn't exorbitant, so I suggested, "Would you mind if I bought the tickets?"

His instinct was to reject, but I insisted and said, "You don't wanna sit with me? It's okay. It's not a lot of money right now."

"Alright." He eventually allowed it.

Because at some level, he trusted that my giving came from care. I internally justified it, knowing he'd take care of food and drinks throughout the trip.

He texted me his full name, date of birth, and known traveler number for booking. It marked a milestone because of his previous hesitation to reveal the spelling of his Polish last name when we had first met. His openness now meant the dissolving of the line he had once kept in place.

He walked me to my place, where we shared a passionate kiss outside, signaling his lack of plans to come inside. I viewed it as his way of showing that he didn't need sex to feel close, and that's the part that brought me joy.

Booking

I wasted no time in purchasing our plane tickets for Universal as soon as I walked into my home. Two months of anticipation await.

We've scheduled something exciting!

That eased my anxiety a bit… So I went along with his week of silence that followed. I remained hopeful about the future of our relationship while shifting focus from words to actions, thanks to my past relationships that taught me the emptiness of unkept promises.

He's sacrificing precious rest between chaotic ICU shifts to join my trip. Why should I be questioning his intentions towards us?

I then found out that another fashion designer had booked me to walk in her upcoming immersive fashion show. Since I recalled how disappointed he was that he wouldn't be able to attend my other show, I was too eager not to ask him if he could attend this one.

His response, "I should be able to make that!" told me he hadn't exited on an emotional level.

He also inquired about my job during a significant internal restructuring. But I couldn't communicate those kinds of details through electronics, so I said, "To be honest, a lot has been going on here, but I'll have to save it and share it with you when I see you next time."

He understood my silence, responded to what I didn't say, and created that "next time" by making the space in his home, as if he was saying, "I'll give you a place to exhale."

I also believe he took that initiative because he knew he wouldn't be available that weekend, as he had mentioned trying to find a Super Bowl party to attend. He was never a talkative guy; I already knew that. What helped me stay grounded was his actions.

Date No. 17

As soon as I entered his condo, which was filled with the aroma of his cooking, I thought to myself, *I can so get used to this!*

He already started asking what was on my mind before my coat even came off: "So tell me, what were you going to share?"

I suspected that my emotional landscape had been on his mind. He offered me his wisdom after I opened up to him.

Just like he had made the shopping day "my day," he made this night "my night" without labeling it as such. In just one night, he confirmed that he was the exact man who was worth my time: opening up his home, offering his time, cooking for me, listening to me without interruptions, providing his wisdom, and then even giving me wild bedroom time.

How did I get so lucky?

At last, I found a guy with whom I felt comfortable moving more slowly. His subtle effort to comprehend made me feel so seen, which allowed me to rest for a moment.

However, I perceived discomfort in his response to my candid discussion concerning my office, which highlighted a limit of emotional capacity: he could offer logic, but when I expressed emotional pain, he flinched inward. Perhaps my emotions reached a depth he had not built the stamina to meet. Maybe he was still working on emotional fluency, but I lacked a reference point to gauge whether that was his typical response when discussing deeper emotional topics.

I followed up to see if he had found himself a Super Bowl watch party to attend.

He said, "Yes, I found one, but I only know one person there, the one who invited me; I don't know anybody else."

It reminded me of his social anxiety, so I felt for him. He was stepping out of his comfort zone to keep a promise to himself: to re-enter the realm of friendships, even if it cost him peace. His desire to improve for his own benefit garnered my deepest respect.

Bad Weather

The next morning, another TV modeling job awaited, requiring a three-hour drive through traffic. The weather was around freezing and rainy... or snowy, so road conditions weren't ideal for my sports car and tires.

He had left for work in the morning first before I hit the road, and once he got to the hospital, he texted, "Drive safe this morning; although the roads aren't so bad, you should be fine!"

How thoughtful of him to be thinking of my safety!

What made me feel lit from within was that his attentiveness came without prompting. He wasn't even driving; he rode the bus, so he observed road conditions for my benefit. That act alone cut straight through the surface: most people would just wish me luck, but he scanned the asphalt with me in mind.

I sent him the link to my TV segment, and he told me, "They really just threw you out there, didn't they?"

He clicked the link, paid attention, and recognized the behind-the-scenes disarray that most people would overlook: I was thrown into the fire and didn't flinch, and he named it to meet me where I was.

Once again, his attentiveness was off the charts: watching the weather for me, noticing the subtle chaos, and speaking into it with clarity.

How did I get so lucky?

Rain Check

His favorable comments about lingerie led me to do some online shopping. Knowing that he wouldn't be available on the weekend because of the Super Bowl, I justified contacting him.

"What do you say about Harry Potter night this Friday as I become your personal lingerie model?" My text read.

He said, "Normally, that would be a lovely idea—in fact, I like it a lot. But there is this dinner that work people invited me to, and it was nice of them to think of me when they had one more seat available. Rain check?"

Just a simple "rain check," one that didn't come with an alternative offer to make up for the rejection. Until then, his care had a pattern: if he missed something, he made space elsewhere.

Though he was never expressive, he had met me with moments of soft follow-through. This time, the rhythm broke. A "rain check" without a counteroffer wasn't just a no; it was the absence of a bridge that he used to build. That's why I felt the ache in my chest.

But Megan, remember? He said he needed to prioritize friendships and how eager he was to belong to another friend group again.

And friend groups, to him, always spiraled from hanging out with coworkers.

And hey, we have our first trip together—Universal Orlando—coming up in a month. So he isn't going anywhere... at least not for another month.

I felt my body registering the ache from watching him loosen the thread of closeness before my mind could name it.

Though I had one request for him to make up for his rain check: a picture of his formal dinner attire—we had discussed his penchant for dressing impeccably for such occasions.

But later that night, he texted, "Sorry I was late going to dinner, so I didn't take any photos."

And though his reason was plausible, it still carried the unmistakable air of someone letting the thread loose. It left me holding the intimacy alone.

My nervous system always detects the early signs of absence before absence names itself.

It felt like a small retreat... the kind that people only justify to themselves in private.

Super Bowl

During Super Bowl Sunday, he didn't forget to send me selfies, although he knew that I would mock the whole sports jersey look!

He first sent me a photo of himself in only his green underwear.

It's cute!

However, it also carried a condescending sexual undertone, like a rupture disguised as a joke.

Seeing the other clothing items scattered across the floor, I recognized the underwear photo to be an afterthought. What likely happened was that he had dressed in his entire outfit, but at the last moment, he took off his clothes to snap a kinky photo because he thought it was a more fitting one to send me.

Then came the "real" photo: the full jersey and matching green sneakers. I noticed the intention behind the footwear, so I complimented him on it because he was a sneakerhead! I wanted him to know that I'm trained to find significance in the smallest signals.

I then said goodbye, bracing myself for silence because his phone stayed away when he was with company, showing respect.

Presence

To my surprise, he started texting me not long after the game had begun, and we maintained consistent text communication throughout. He sent me pictures of his view; the host picked an ideal spot in the city for post-victory celebrations. His companionship created a sense of shared presence, but I would have joined him if he had invited me. The truth is… I had been wondering when he would feel ready to introduce me to his friends. I questioned whether he intended to build something lasting and convinced myself that he was waiting for the right time.

If it's meant to be forever, why rush?

To bridge the emotional distance, I was intentionally light to prevent pressure, since pressure would have made him withdraw.

I snapped a photo of my TV showing the score and sent it to him at the point where his team was winning. Perhaps he had shifted my behavior towards commercial sports because his world mattered to me.

He responded with an observation, "You're watching!"

"Yeah, not everyone is popular like you, who got invited to a watch party! (Winky face emoji)."

"I know only one person," minimizing his social importance, maybe to manage my feelings.

His team won! I congratulated him and continued to tease, "Right, from one to twelve now!"

He then sent me a photo of the crowd on the street celebrating the win and said, "Too many!"

He texted me when he got home; it wasn't necessary, but he chose to.

My nervous system found solace within the illusion of progress. He texted me throughout, included me from a distance, sent updates, and even reached out when he got home. He gave me emotional proximity as presence, which made me feel warm because this was someone who didn't normally offer that much, so this counted as "a lot." It felt like a victory because my bar for feeling "included" had already been recalibrated.

Anticipation

Valentine's Day was approaching…

I wonder if he has any plans with me.

Could I have asked him straight up? Of course. But why didn't I? That's the core ache of the entire relationship: I was in something that made me afraid to ask for clarity because I already sensed it wouldn't reflect what I was giving. I wasn't prepared to hear the unwelcome news, so I convinced myself that the longer I waited, the more likely the answer would be in my favor. My passivity stemmed from wishing him to discover matters on his own.

If I mean anything longer term to him, he will... at least ask me out to dinner in his own way, right?

You know, not in the direct "I would like to take you out to dinner because it's Valentine's Day" kind of way, but perhaps something like his usual "Hey, you want to do something low-key... Maybe I can cook, and we'll just watch Harry Potter because it's a Friday" kind of way?

But the news cycle beat him to it: the parade would be on Valentine's Day. An event he couldn't control did what he hadn't: it gave me enough of an answer to stop wishing. It wasn't a direct rejection of me, but it gave him the justification for a deferral that didn't need to be spoken aloud. That compounded the hurt because I couldn't blame him, yet I couldn't feel dismissed either.

The deeper cut was about what I represented in his life compared to everything else; they all had predefined positions in his world. I was still an unknown variable, waiting for him to define it. I felt the truth settle in my body before my brain registered it.

If I had meant more, I wouldn't have had to wonder.

Another Rain Check

I got booked to model on a TV channel in New York City the day before Valentine's Day. Since I would be in the city anyway, I figured I would try my luck to secure last-minute seating at a famous eatery. By some miracle, I received confirmation I had been offered entry, but there's a catch: the minimum party size to allow such a reservation was two. So, I brought up the idea to him.

He replied, "The people at the Super Bowl watch party were talking about going skiing that day because it's supposed to snow, but no one's brought it up again since, and to be honest, I have been feeling out of the weather a bit... not sure if I caught anything during the party or at the hospital. It's my sinus again—it's annoying."

He defaulted to ambiguity and once again didn't offer a counter-plan. He just... floated... into the gray area where he always stayed safe. I opened the door for him into my life, and he stood just outside of it, shrugging.

So I decided for him and said, "Oh yeah, I totally get it. You love skiing and value friendships; of course, you totally should go skiing with them!"

What I did was to pre-reject myself by sparing him from disappointing me. I made his choice easier by handing him an exit ticket because somewhere inside, I already sensed the truth.

If he aspired to be there, he would have chosen me.

And that clarity was feeling louder than the hope.

Recovering

I left just enough space in case he changed his mind, even though he gave me the same suspense he always did: just enough personal context to seem thoughtful.

He then updated me on how intentional he was about drinking more water to recover sooner, and hence the high frequency of restroom visits, something in common that we shared. I found it endearing and told him how cute that was. He shifted the energy to something lighter, hoping it would keep the tone playful so I wouldn't press.

And instead of letting myself grieve the one-sidedness of the dynamic, I redirected my energy towards the next thing I thought he might show up for: the fashion show. I sent the ticket link per his request.

I created significance from scraps, since the absence of harm may appear like care when someone offers just enough contact. But what I was doing was shrinking my needs.

Griffin

One of my model friends texted me out of the blue, telling me she had just moved to NYC and asking if I wanted to meet up. I informed her of my restaurant reservation, and she jumped right at the opportunity.

So I texted him, "How's your sinus treating you? No worries about coming to NYC—I found someone else to join me at that restaurant!"

But let's be honest: I wanted no one else at that table.

He responded, "OMG, that's great! I have been feeling so bad because that restaurant would be a place that I'd enjoy, and I didn't want to cause you to not be able to go. I actually even looked up the train schedule—just so you know how seriously I was considering it. But I have to be honest with myself that an NYC trip is something that my body should be up for one hundred percent."

"That's so sweet. I understand. Remember, I have an annual hotel reward that I need to use soon to claim my free night? I say it'd be much better if you came with me and stayed at a boutique hotel for a night, so that I'll have time to show you my NYC. I hope you have fun skiing with your friends."

He put a heart emoji on my message, but I did not know which specific part he loved about... Because he only responded to the skiing part, "Yeah, skiing is not happening because apparently it's snowing everywhere else but on the mountain."

I let him feel included in my NYC visit by sharing a photo of Griffin at the Harry Potter store, to which he responded, "Of course you would lol."

In my defense, I said, "Apparently, my friend is a Slytherin, so I had to take her there!"

"You getting along with a Slytherin?" His words echoed, as though he didn't decline an invitation intended to bring him closer to my existence.

His tone floated above the deeper truth I didn't want to say out loud yet: he was the one who kept himself a visitor while I had been ready to give him a home. And that's the disorienting part: he stayed emotionally available enough to remain present in the surface-level tether. But in anchoring something meaningful with weight, he disappeared into polite half-reasons.

V-Day

As Valentine's Day was replaced with Victory Parade Day, I wanted to see if he would at least text me "Happy Valentine's Day" when there was already no expectation of seeing each other.

Without hearing from him by midday, I texted, "Remember a while ago you asked me what my favorite holiday was, and I asked you to revisit that question at a later time?"

I had withheld the answer to avoid pressuring him when we first started dating.

I continued, "Well, today is the day because it is a day I tell people who I care about how much they mean to me. So, I want to use today to let you know how much I appreciate you because just by you being you, you inspire me to be a better version of myself every single day. I hope you have fun at the parade with your friends."

I gave him my most generous self by introducing vulnerability, the kind that says, *I know we haven't labeled this, but I care about you. And I'm not hiding it.*

Sitting with his nonresponse for hours, I convinced myself to believe that he was taking the time to metabolize what I had said. Maybe my morning comments had burdened him too much.

I finally heard from him late afternoon: "Today is the day? You have an interesting take on today. You're introspective—that's what's cool about you."

His response was… superficial, like someone who wasn't ready to meet me at that depth. He acknowledged my message the way someone might comment on a painting, not the way someone would respond to being seen or when their presence in another person's life has inspired growth. His reply skimmed the surface, complimenting me for being "introspective," as though my emotional clarity were a personality quirk rather than a doorway he was being invited through.

He gave me vague praise, then withdrew, hoping I wouldn't notice the difference between contact and connection, but I did; I always do.

Amendment

Despite Valentine's Day not being over yet, he didn't invite me to meet up. At this point in our relationship, three-and-a-half months in, there was zero acknowledgment of emotional investment.

I kept asking myself: *Is this because of something I did? Or someone before me?*

But it didn't matter. I showed up as myself—attuned. He also showed up as himself, but as a guy who benefited from my clarity without ever matching it.

He finally initiated time together after denying me two and a half times but laid out his busy schedule: family time with his brother and nephews and some last-minute planning with his friend for their upcoming ski trip.

This was his method of explaining why Sunday evening made up the only opening within his timetable he could offer.

I found comfort in his offering because, at least, he had thought about making time to see me during a brief break in his busy schedule.

It's the thought that counts, isn't it?

Except… I had my monthly Universal trip planned, which he forgot about.

"It's very sweet of you to offer to spend time with me even after your long hours of work. I'd love to, except it's my Universal weekend," I said.

There was a pause in response on his end until he said, "Okay, your show on Thursday it is!"

Weeks ago, I had already predicted this outcome, attempting to avoid it via invitations. But with his repeated rain checks, I celebrated crumbs like meals, holding up both sides of the relationship, alone.

Ticket

And then it was my Universal weekend. I sent him photos of thrill rides with the caption "You'll be doing this next month!"

He knew I was going to help him get his ticket, but what he wasn't aware of was my intention to get him an annual pass just like mine. To me, it's a difference of sixty dollars… which served as "insurance" to invite him again, aiming to eliminate money as an issue. I would keep it to myself until he entered the park, holding the annual pass instead of a three-day ticket.

But beneath the surface, a dread persisted: *perhaps he will change his mind about coming with.*

And even now, as I'm writing this, I'm still managing the reveal of my heart and orchestrating moments so that he might one day catch up to what I already knew:

A genuine connection requires equal effort.

Dominatrix

I yearned for his first attendance at the fashion show, though I wish it were a conventional runway presentation instead of an artistic immersive experience. I was "Madam V.," a fictional dominatrix the designer had always envisioned me to be in every one of her collections. To be honest, I'm flattered because it brings out the vibe I instinctively have beneath. I wanted him to see what it meant to step into my world and witness how I commanded the space, hoping that he might finally encounter all sides of me.

"I have a request," I teased him. "I usually starve myself the entire day until the show is over. Will you feed your dominatrix after the show?"

"LOL," he responded. "Do you mean cooking for you? Or eating out at some place?"

"I don't believe I can last until we get to your place. I would eat a human if I could by that point! Let's just find a place by the venue!"

"Deal!"

A few hours before the show, he texted, "I should be there on time. If the bus doesn't come or is late, I'll just take a rideshare."

"Please don't waste money on a rideshare—the show likely won't start on time anyway. I'd feel bad. Just take the bus."

As predicted, he arrived before the production even allowed guests in.

He texted, "I am here. I'm not going to lie, this is out of my element, but I guess there is a first time for everything."

"I put myself in your shoes and realize how awkward it must be for you. It means a lot that you came to see me!" I responded.

I worried about his comfort and empathized with his awkwardness because I was managing both sides out of instinct: my spotlight and his nerves.

Date No. 18

I then transformed into a dominatrix. The artistic immersive show fostered natural audience interaction when appropriate. His height made him easy to spot. He was already using his phone to record me, something that I had asked him as a favor.

I was "equipped" with a whip—that's right! At one point, I approached him and wrapped it around his neck. That moment was a layered collision of personas: the private, soft-spoken me that had tiptoed around his slow pace for months, and the embodied, in-control me, performing a kind of power I rarely got to own in my daily life.

257

I was enjoying being in my character, especially when he was the only one in the audience that I cared about pleasing on a personal level. Judging from the smirk on his face, that enjoyment was mutual.

Perhaps he likes this side of me.

And yet, beneath my dominatrix persona, my stomach was empty. It mirrored the deeper dynamic: I gave him access to the most vivid parts of me while often operating on depletion. I hungered not just for nourishment; I yearned for him to reciprocate the care I contributed to our connection.

Feeding

Finally, the show was over! He pre-researched our dining choices. It's so refreshing that he had a plan in mind.

Yes, please! Tell me where you want to go; I'll follow.

I often assumed the leading role in relationships, even though deep down I desired someone else to take the lead. My constant planning highlighted my disproportionate investment. So when he said he had an idea, my nervous system unclenched a little.

Sadly, the show ended so late that the two places he took me to had already stopped serving food.

Oh well. I guess I can get full of alcoholic beverages?

It landed like an echo of the deeper imbalance: my consistent preparation versus his casual spontaneity. I always had mental tabs open: every signal his body and schedule gave off. And when he offered something planned, it still fell short.

Frigid Night

We had started dating when it was going into the winter, so he always had his hands in his pockets. I couldn't help but wonder if he would hold my hand once pockets were unnecessary.

On this frigid night, he had his hands in his pockets as usual, but he welcomed our arms being intertwined. When he saw that I was about to thread my arm through, he would make room with his elbow to allow it. Much like wrapping his arm around my waist to lift me from puddles as he did in the past, that physical attentiveness was when his body said yes, even if his words often lagged.

How did I get so lucky?

I kept noticing the "little things" because they were all I had. I was hopeful… trying to make the picture whole when I could only see fragments, and to my nervous system, fragments can feel safer than voids. It's something to hang onto and to decode.

With no communication, he walked into my condo with me. And then there was the sex, as if we already had an unspoken agreement that physical intimacy would be the "finale" of each date. To be fair, I played my part in initiating the script by hyping it up earlier with my dominatrix act.

But the flaw in his pacing was undeniable: sex represented closeness, serving as the currency when emotional intimacy was absent. I knew that was his way but kept giving, hoping that if the body could keep him close, the heart might follow.

Pills

Before things got too heated in bed, I handed him a jar of "pills."

For each of the sixty nights prior, I began jotting down on a small piece of paper one thing I appreciated about him or a sweet moment I had recalled. Rolling each one up into a small capsule, they formed sixty pills, stored in a glass jar. That was me giving him a private archive of where I saw him when he might not have even known he was being seen. A physical object that carried more intimacy than most couples share in a year—I had built it by tracking gratitude.

"Sixty?" he exclaimed. "That's the sweetest thing."

His response was observational. Appreciative, yes—but passive.

Much like when I handed the guy I dated before him my handwritten letter, the list of I-statements, and finally the book, he was also amazed at my "sweetness." It's a distancing move: a way to admire my warmth without standing in it. They say "you're sweet" because they don't know how to say "this makes me feel something I wasn't ready to feel."

Setting aside the glass jar, we started making out. He ended up spending the night... I had asked him to because I wanted the warmth to linger longer.

Taking Pills

A couple of days later, I walked in a fashion show in which I was the bride, the one that he couldn't witness my walking down the aisle... I mean, runway. It was his travel day for a ski trip with his friend.

He texted, "Sorry, it's been hectic. I barely made it to the airport."

In the message that immediately followed, he stated, "I didn't have time to read all the messages. I only opened up a few, and they were sooooo sweet!"

He could have left it at "Sorry, hectic," and disappeared into the logistics of his travel. But he reached back towards the jar and told me he had read my words, even if just a few. Despite his chaotic last-minute preparations, his effort to connect warmed my heart because, for one, it was in a separate message that he had typed, which signaled intention, and for two, he wrote "sooooo" with exaggerated o's, which told me the ones he had read touched something real.

That's how I operate: I picked up on the buried signals he didn't know he was sending. That's what makes me feel so much more than others: my listening goes beneath the surface.

Ski Trip

I knew who he went on a ski trip with: the boyfriend of one of his female best friends. They were all nurses, and he had trained this friend as a new nurse. Later on, all of them were in a bigger dynamic of the whole nurse-coworker-friend group.

He had hoped to find a couple to accompany them so they could all split the expenses four ways.

"How come she wasn't going with?" I naturally asked, referring to his travel buddy's girlfriend.

He described her as not an all-day aggressive skier.

I could have hung out with her, and there would be four of us to split the costs...

But I buried this thought under my well-honed sense of restraint cultivated from the emotional discipline that has been my survival mechanism since childhood. I believed honoring his pace was more important than risking the loss of connection, knowing that questions with a pressure undertone would have pushed him away.

Compared to his last solo ski trip, the updates I was receiving this time were thinner. I interpreted his silence as typical, given that he had company.

Friendship: that's what he valued more than me, and I had learned to accept it with grace.

What's remarkable is that I made peace with being secondary. I thought I was loving him on my terms, but what I didn't realize was that I was honoring his nervous system at the expense of my own by adjusting my instincts and rhythm to preserve something that already had an asymmetry built in. My grace became the thing he relied on... perhaps even took for granted.

Thinking About You

My workplace underwent a major, newsworthy restructuring while he was gone. I refrained from bringing anything up to him not only because it would be inappropriate but also because I respected his boundaries.

He's out there having fun doing what he loves; who am I to kill his moment or interrupt his mood with my "bad" news?

A text from him popped in: "Hi! How's work? I was thinking about you watching the news here, wondering how you are doing."

He noticed the news, connected the dots, and then thought of me.

I kept fixating on those three words—thinking about you—re-reading them again and again. I also pinched myself.

YES! He's thinking of me. I'm not dreaming.

Those three simple words pierced through everything. He was a man of few words. I didn't overinterpret; I knew the difference between habit and intention, and this was intention.

Okay. What was he saying again? Oh, right! He asked me about work.

And what did I say to him? "It's incredibly sweet that you were thinking about me. Work is alright, but I'll have to wait until I can share with you in person."

This marked his first time reaching towards me in an unsolicited manner from within. I felt seen.

Shoulder

He told me on his last ski day, "I dislocated my arm. I am fine. Long story. I will tell you."

"OMG, are you okay?"

"Yes, I popped it back in place."

He was short but clear; that was him telling me not to worry in the most minimal language possible.

I wasn't that surprised about his arm situation because he told me before that he had dislocated his shoulder while learning how to ski a few years prior.

I can't deny it; I feared he was using that excuse to avoid our up-coming Universal trip. His actions offered no cause for such reflection, but guys from before had trained me to expect it: the slow backpedal hidden behind acceptable reasons. I had lived through too many worded exits and sudden shifts from closeness to distance disguised as "unforeseen circumstances."

I didn't accuse him of anything, but my body kept checking the exits. I was waiting to see which version of him would come home.

When he texted that he had landed, I welcomed him: "You're back? Welcome back!" Simple, open, no accusations, but the line carried restraint because by then, the part of me that always offers softness was withholding as self-preservation. I was waiting for proof that he differed.

Third Initiation

Guess what? He requested to see me again! I said yes, of course. I was hyperaware that he struggled with planning, so his offer already felt like a miracle, and I returned his effort with acceptance.

But the day he originally had in mind proved difficult; a grueling workweek culminated then, and stress consumed me. I braced for the subtle shift that usually follows when I need to change plans, knowing how much weight a reschedule can carry when someone is fragile in their effort to initiate. In my past, "Can we move it?" could risk their canceling plans altogether. But I proposed an alternative and explained to him my reasons.

Without hesitation, he replied, "Of course. Let's do Wednesday. Always put yourself first, no matter what. You have to take care of yourself."

His response mirrored my core ethic: prioritize self-care. That's usually what I say to people, so it's a strange yet refreshing feeling to hear it from someone else. More importantly, that someone else was him—we agreed.

I was overwhelmed with stress, and he diffused it without making it about him. The absence of consequences elicited a bodily exhalation. For once, someone absorbed my needs without making me earn it.

How did I get so lucky?

Date No. 19

A couple of days before our planned date, he texted me, "So I was thinking I'd swing by your place tonight after work to spend time with you if you'd like."

I surmised that it was something I had to negotiate because my nervous system had been trained to brace for the trade-off.

If they say "yes" now, it's only to soften a future "no."

So my reflex was to assume it had to be "either-or." It never crossed my mind that I deserved to be seen both times. That was the way care had always been rationed in my past.

So I asked, "Do you mean either tonight or Wednesday?"

But he corrected me and said, "Both tonight and Wednesday, if you want."

That shook something loose because "both" didn't just mean two nights; "both" meant I was worth the effort twice. His action served as direct opposition to the idea that my needs were too much.

I was ecstatic and said, "That'd make me so happy!"

"Okay, so say 8 pm, and I'll be at your place, if that works for you?"

"Yeah! Actually, I'll pass right by you, driving home from pole. Can you let me pick you up? That'd make me feel so much better. I don't want to inconvenience you to make you walk."

"I can walk. Chill. Tonight is a bonus. It's supposed to be stress-free."

That told me the subtext I didn't expect: "You don't have to brace for this. I'm just showing up."

He captivated me that evening. Even with a dislocated shoulder, he gave his all, not just physical presence, but also encompassing intention.

How did I get so lucky?

He didn't stay the night with me because of work the next morning. He normally wouldn't even have seen me between work shifts like that. But he transformed that night into a "bonus night" and gave me what I never believed I could ask for: bonus care, bonus time, and bonus warmth.

Coming Around

Like a typical Libra, he cherished balance in all aspects of his life. He mentioned receiving similar comments from his female friends, who were enthusiastic about zodiac signs.

The prior month was off; I wasn't imagining the imbalance. I interpreted the "bonus night" as self-correction on his part.

Maybe he reflected and saw the lag.

He appeared to have recalibrated. That shift mattered a lot to me, whose core ache is being unreciprocated in presence. I had hoped that he would finally see that a romantic connection required tending and awaited his eventual realization to prioritize us.

All of his inexplicable actions were developing towards my desires. Maybe without the jar of pills, he otherwise wouldn't have even realized that I noticed the smallest things.

Still, part of me was cautious in my hope. I understood that inclusion on his schedule differed from integration within his life.

I asked, "You think you'll still be able to come with?" Referring to Universal and his dislocated shoulder.

"Yes, I think so. I'll just hold up one arm like this."

It was an inside joke: he had asked me what kind of rollercoaster rider I was—the both arms up, no screaming type—as he resonated with me.

I understood that night as him realizing that he hadn't nurtured our relationship, so he decided that he would pour energy into it now. That wasn't nothing; it was an intentional follow-through. And for once, that felt like enough.

After weeks of waiting, accommodating, making space, and softening disappointment with understanding, I finally felt him move towards me.

Date No. 20

He again met me following ballet classes and this time, presented three preselected destinations.

I liked it when he took charge, and he even did it without explicit instructions.

How did I get so lucky?

The restaurant was full, so we were seated at a tiny coffee table in the bar area. To be honest, the environment wasn't ideal, and I didn't conceal my discomfort or pretend to be chill. I have always been the "take me as I am" type of person.

I noticed the people at the next table over were paying the bill, so I asked that we move over after they left.

But he said to me, "You're fine."

No, I wasn't fine, and to suggest otherwise felt like he wasn't seeing me.

I think he meant to reassure, but what he offered was dismissal, a moment of misattunement. It's not the table that mattered; it's the deeper contract between us—that he was someone who didn't blur the edges of my needs.

He stepped away for the restroom; I then moved to a vacant, larger table. I had taken care of my body's discomfort myself without making a scene. He came back to find that I had re-situated us, and I tapped the space next to me to signal him to sit.

I re-centered the moment: my comfort with emotional transparency gave me a fluency he didn't yet speak; he was still toggling between support and subtle shutdown. The table might be petite, but my feelings weren't. I took up full emotional space with no apology, adjusting and watching whether he would follow. That's the real partnership I wanted: responsive and present.

Packing

Over dinner, he shared, "I laid everything out."

I repeated, "You laid everything out…?!"

Because of military service, my hearing is impaired, resulting in frequent misinterpretations requiring repetitions of the speaker.

He clarified, "Yeah, for Universal."

I smiled because I heard care delivered through his forethought. He had taken our shared trip on Sunday with enough care to prepare early on Wednesday, arranging travel plans despite his workload. The military may have left me with trouble hearing, but I had flawless emotional reception.

He sought my view concerning packing, thus bringing me in. It said, "I trust you to lead in what you know. I want your input." It represented a brief yet significant acknowledgement of equity. As a pro at handling the unpredictable Florida rainstorm, I warned him to prepare for getting wet.

Per usual, he walked me home, and I asked him, "Would you like to come in?"

He agreed.

I posed a simple question, hoping to see if he would make any unwarranted assumptions of physical intimacy.

After he walked in and got situated, I said, "I got good news. My period just started… which means I won't be on it during our Universal trip."

I was reading the subtle barometer of his emotional presence. He then hung out a little longer, and my heart softened because finally, his actions told me he could hold space without demanding more. Perhaps he eventually understood that my emotional language did not always require physical conveyance.

Universal With Him

Unlike the mindset of many who go on vacation, I don't go to Universal to escape reality, and I aimed to show him why Universal brought me joy. I was giving him access to the sacred, playful, and structured part of me.

Traveling often reveals people's true selves; thus, he was going to experience firsthand how down-to-earth I was. I knew the adrenaline would bond us even more.

We would build a new type of memory together—another milestone in our relationship. Anticipation, vulnerability, and hope layered my excitement.

He texted me to confirm our plan to get to the airport, and I used the opportunity to express my gratitude.

I said, "Don't worry about waking up early; I want you to get rested."

That was my instinctive caretaking, a reflex I didn't even filter.

He then responded, "No, I'll be fine," which was his version of gratitude. It's his way of saying, "This trip matters to me too."

Because his ski resort routine was like my rope-drop-to-park-close style of visiting, he honored it. He did not wish to disrupt my system and sought to prevent significant plan adjustments only for himself.

This first trip together was also my unspoken request: *Will you meet me where I am?*

I didn't need him to be perfect. I just needed not to be alone in what I was building.

Rideshare

He would usually take public transit but offered to pay for a rideshare because that's how I usually commute to the airport. That gesture was meaningful because I'm usually the one smoothing logistics. When we were standing there with time ahead of us, bags on our shoulders, and shared rhythm finally syncing, I caught a glimpse of him finally meeting my internal pace.

He inquired about my airport ritual: whether I would be there hours early or last minute before the plane door shut. I let him know about my three-hour-early habit so that I could enjoy an airport lounge and remarked that I was waiting for the new lounge to open.

"Oh, it's open now!" he said.

"When??? I was just at the airport two weeks ago, and it wasn't open yet!"

"I think last week. How did I know that... Oh yeah! I follow the airport's Instagram and saw the post."

His offhand, almost sheepish admission held a kind of accidental intimacy.

I lit up, suggesting, "Let's go! Do you want to go? I want to go. Let's go check it out and get some drinks and food!"

I was inviting him into my spontaneity, and he agreed with instinctive yeses.

Sapphire

Settling at the lounge, he researched the restrictions for entry using his credit card.

"Annually," he told me, then exclaimed, "Great, perhaps I can visit when I travel to Poland solo."

Going to Poland by himself?

That new, unannounced information slipped out, but I caught it. Though I didn't press, it reorganized my mental landscape. That's how my mind works: cataloging details until it's right... or until the silence becomes too loud.

I also casually made a comment that I lacked cash for a bartender tip because I didn't expect to be stopping at a lounge. I wasn't sure if he heard me because he didn't speak of it.

But moments later, he pulled out a five-dollar bill and set it on the counter, saying to the bartender, "Here, this is for you."

That was the language he spoke best: subdued actions that showed acknowledgement of my concerns, and I was fluent in enough subtlety to hear it.

How did I get so lucky?

He drank more than me to help him sleep on the plane, a topic we had talked about. In contrast, I am someone who can fall asleep anytime, anywhere, except in my bed when it's time I am supposed to rest. We both leaned into each other's tendencies, letting them merge without resistance.

Flying

We boarded the plane, and even though my preferred seat was by the aisle, I chose the middle one without asking him. I wanted him to feel as comfortable as possible after his long work shifts.

But I had one question in mind: *Will he be all lovey-dovey with me?*

Neither of us dropped the armrest between us. I offered my hand to connect, and he reciprocated by interlocking my fingers. I rested my head on his shoulder because the moment felt safe enough to, and he welcomed it. Although he didn't initiate the intimacy, he allowed himself to receive.

That might appear insignificant; however, for someone reserved like him, that was something. I created an environment where tenderness could surface with ease. It's genuine, even unspoken.

How did I get so lucky?

Date No. 21

Arriving in Orlando, he let me know, "I am your slave on this trip."

It sounded playful—devoted, even—but something in me felt the edge. Instead of obedience, I was hoping for co-creation, demonstrating investment in our shared experience.

"I like how that sounds!" I responded, "But I want you to let me know if there are things that we pass by that you'd like to stop and do because I go there all the time, so I get complacent, and I rarely even notice new things."

He insisted, "No, I won't have anything that I would want to see. We'll do everything that you want to do."

It sounded sweet, but his lack of opinion meant he was only coming along for the ride.

Deep down, I wished that he would have input because it would show me he liked it too. I had made space for him in a world I already loved and wanted him to engage because that would mean he was choosing to be a part of building new layers on top of it. I wanted a co-authorship that deepened emotional commitment. As someone who already carries the weight of noticing everything... it felt like yet another space where I would be steering alone.

My plan was for a relaxed park visit at a deliberate pace, showing him things I would usually do, so he would resonate with my experience when I returned there again without him. My wish was for him to enter my world. It's a subtle form of devotion: embedding him into my routines, landscapes, and sense memories.

Spider-Man

Poverty marked his childhood; a family sponsor enabled his only previous visit to Universal. I aimed to customize the trip for him, providing a full experience, going on rides that I wouldn't usually do, and the parts I had grown numb to.

It warmed my heart when he told me he delighted himself by recalling childhood memories of the Spider-Man ride. Touching something of his own, he experienced a spontaneous flicker of belonging. For a brief second, his inner child reached out and held hands with mine, which revealed he could let himself feel connected if he allowed himself to.

In Sync

The long waits for rides did not bother me because of the perfect opportunity we were given to embrace each other. He would often lean against a railing and clasp me in his arms. Otherwise, we would hold hands, interlock fingers, or swing our arms together.

He would gesture for me to hold onto his hand while navigating crowds, ensuring we stayed together, a silent agreement that we moved as a unit.

His body was answering a question my heart had been asking for months: *Will you move through life with me, or will I always be one step ahead, turning around to see if you're still there?*

His reaching for me, claiming closeness in public as instinct, reflected a kind of physical attunement that I had been craving. We were finally in sync in the embodied rhythm of real time together.

I was content, reasoning his lack of hand-holding stemmed from the cold weather back home.

That must be it! Just look at what he is doing in warmer weather!

In those moments, the friction of my colder, more uncertain past faded.

Queues

Standing in long queues, he reviewed photos from the ski trip on his phone, saying, "I haven't had a chance to look at these photos since I took them."

After a while, he asked, "Is this bothering you right now?"

"No, not at all," I responded.

"Let me know if anything that I'm doing is bothering you, okay?"

I couldn't believe what I just heard, so I repeated it back to him just to confirm: "You said if you're doing anything that is bothering me, let you know."

He was asking a minor question with enormous subtext: "Am I safe to you? Is my presence kind? Am I making this easier or harder for you?"

It hit me so hard because he made space for me by noticing my noticing, which means he was attuned and that my experience wasn't something he would bulldoze past or minimize. I had long calibrated myself to be the one who noticed when others checked out, even while they lingered close. Yet, he assessed whether he acted that way towards me and initiated the bridging, positioning himself as someone accountable for our shared dynamic.

HOW. DID. I. GET. SO. LUCKY.

Drugstore

As soon as we got back to our hotel, he said, "I'm going to take a walk to the drugstore next door. Do you want anything?"

I was like, "Wait, you are? Can I come with you?"

He hesitated for a few seconds, so I said, "Oh, is it your me time? Do you want 'me time'? If so, it's okay; I won't go. I want you to have your me time."

"No, come."

I asked what he needed there; he got a little embarrassed and said, "It's a bad habit that I picked up skiing with friends... I rarely do it, but right now, I have been drinking, we've been having fun, and I'm in the mood."

"You can tell me anything. I have been in the Marine Corps, so I don't think there is anything that anyone does that would surprise me anymore. Is it dip?"

"No, not dips. It's different. Let's just say that Marines who are in the Corps right now would be doing that instead of dips."

The way he tried to preserve his dignity over the nicotine pouches was vulnerability in disguise. He permitted me to witness something diminishing, perhaps even causing shame.

But I wasn't surprised at all, especially since I had already noticed a package or two at his place. I just never mentioned it because it wasn't a deal-breaker.

Upon our arrival at the drugstore, he motioned for me to explore the aisles alone while he dashed to purchase them before joining me.

Around Easter, I crave soft-centered chocolate eggs, something that my parents had denied me. As an adult, I have always gotten them for myself. I found them in the candy aisle and shared the story with him.

He said, "See, now you can get as many as you want."

I grabbed two of them and asked, "Will you get them for me?"

Sure, I had money, but for the sentimental value behind them, I wanted him to get them because they symbolized my longings being undeserving. Perhaps I related that action as caring, and he understood enough to say yes.

Vitamins

The checkout counter displayed vitamin mints, an unfamiliar item to me. It's buy-one-get-one-free.

He noticed my interest, took two of them, and said, "One for you, one for me."

That's an instinctive pairing: he just split the offering in two, because something inside him assumed that we were in this together.

En route to the park the next morning, he combined the electrolyte mixture he had brought with a large bottle of water that he got from the drugstore. I'm guilty of never hydrating… and he was well aware of it.

So he made me drink it with him, saying, "See? Now we are hydrated!"

It may seem minuscule to many, but to me, it was anything but. He was joining me in something small that said, "I see that you neglect yourself, and I'll help you remember."

His tending was proof that he was tracking my tendencies, and that's why my system kept whispering:

How did I get so lucky?

Frustration

Our last morning at the park frustrated me, as I had difficulty securing a ride that would not quit in the middle of waiting.

I voiced my disappointment: "I'm sorry, I'm really feeling defeated... I feel like whatever I choose for us to do is just going to be delayed or shut down because I was the one who chose it."

He then consulted the park's app and told me, "Okay, if this ride isn't coming back up in the next five minutes, we are going to go do that instead. What do you think?"

That moment created a subtle shift: from "I'm tagging along" to "I've got us now." He took the reins to lift the burden I was carrying alone. My breath then descended within my chest because, for once, I wasn't the one holding it all together.

I felt like my weight was off my shoulders and ran to the restroom and burst into tears. To me, someone who had always been a mental project manager, his intervention was revolutionary. It mattered even more when it originated from an individual lacking initiative.

How did I get so lucky?

Express

The rest of the day redeemed itself as it got smoother, especially when we were the lucky couple who received a random giveaway of express passes when we re-entered the park.

Of course, we would use them to get on one of my favorites: the Hagrid Motorbike Adventure rollercoaster. He showed his sweetness by refusing to sit on the motorcycle of the ride vehicle; my earlier enthusiastic expression of preference for it explained his refusal to ride it.

He said, "I want you to take the bike. I haven't gone on it, so I don't know what I'm missing. I'm okay in the sidecar."

How did I get so lucky?

But was it luck? Or was it his stepping into a role I made visible by holding the emotional scaffolding of the entire experience? I had been queuing in my head for months, downplaying patterns. So when something finally flowed, it felt miraculous.

Hidden Urges

Throughout our park visits, he would check in with me to see if we had fulfilled all my wishes. Whereas for him, his only request was to visit Weasleys' Wizard Wheezes in Diagon Alley.

I later found out he had hidden urges only through the questions he posed afterwards: "Why didn't we see the dragon breathing out fire?" and "Why did we only ride Gringotts once?"

He didn't speak up, letting me guide the ship, only hinting at his unmet wishes masked in questions. That's withholding paired with scorekeeping.

To be honest, I had already witnessed the breathing fires countless times, and the Gringotts queue was always too long to justify riding it one more time without knowing his preference.

Mind-reading isn't one of my skills. His silence handed me a puzzle without the pieces, and then he questioned why I didn't complete it. I felt like I had failed him…

I didn't, though. If anything, he failed to meet me on the level of shared responsibility when building the experience together. I was operating with incomplete data, which was unfair to me.

I had carried an invisible load of planning and adapting, even offering autonomy, which would have only worked when someone used it.

A real partnership requires two active participants, not one emotional overfunctioner and one silent evaluator.

Return Flight

On the way to catch our 6 am flight home, a two-hour delay text came through from the airline. Despite that, we headed straight to the gate for confirmation with the gate agent before heading to an airport lounge, where I continued to monitor the flight status.

Out of nowhere, the status switched from "delayed" to "boarding," so we rushed back to the gate. Arriving at the gate, as he was busy trying to compact his "one personal item," I noticed no one was there, not even the gate agent we had spoken with. I drew his attention to what I saw as other passengers heading our direction, surprised by the same situation.

That same gate agent finally approached us, checked the gate monitor and the door, and stated the obvious, "The door is shut," as the flight's status changed to "departed" right in front of our eyes.

This cannot be happening, right?

That was the first "chaos" I had encountered with him, marking his first time experiencing how I would deal with unpleasant situations.

Have I mentioned that I'm cool as a cucumber?

I didn't collapse, but I did something else: I over-owned, translating airline errors into my failure, stemming from my childhood experience. I was trained to misplace responsibility.

It's all my fault. He must return home, allow ample preparation time, and report to the hospital for his evening shift.

But I did not hold up the flight, adjust the gate monitor, or close the door while travelers stood present. The airline's incompetence and the agent's deflection were out of my hands.

He, who possessed the ability to decline, had also agreed to come along.

Homed

I booked us the next flight home with another airline before sorting out any refunds. Not causing him any more delay was my primary concern. We then revisited the lounge for round two.

He commented while drinking, "It's unbelievable my patients tonight are oblivious to my current drinking."

His deep thoughts were one reason I was drawn to him.

Our fingers were intertwined as we sat beside each other on the plane, and we both slept during most of the flight.

At one point, he woke up, looked at me, and murmured, "Are you okay?"

This soft question in the air was the climax of our shared story arc. I nodded and laid my head on his shoulder as we fell asleep together again.

I called us a rideshare home and included his place as an added stop so that he didn't have to walk. He told me not to, but I insisted. My goal was to end our trip well by making the return to his world easier.

It wasn't a perfect trip, but it was a bonding one. Our experience yielded considerable mutual understanding; we faced both triumphs and setbacks together. The original goal was adrenaline, but what we got was more intimate than thrill rides: sharing a window into how we each navigated chaos. It gave me hope that our connection would go up from this point.

The trip revealed what our connection looked like when tested by reality. My instinct was to soften the edges; his was to show up in slight gestures: switching plans without pushback, checking on me mid-sleep, and letting me lean in without resistance.

At the beginning of the trip, he told me, "I'm your slave," but the irony is, I was the one structuring the entire trip around ease for him.

Lack of Silence

Following our farewell, I expected his silence because his habit involved recharging after companionship with me; I adapted to his quiet, like one develops calluses—initially sore, eventually numb.

To my surprise, he texted me not long after he got to the hospital: "How long did you end up taking a nap for?"

His text followed up on a topic I had raised earlier: he advised against long naps when I asked him how to combat my insomnia.

That initiation was rare for him. He reached for me when there was nothing at stake, which, coming from someone like him, translated to, "I'm still carrying the conversation we started when we were sitting next to each other in that lounge. You're still in my thoughts as I clock into work. You matter to me—enough for me to check in before I disappear into routine again."

His text might not scream significance to most, but it was gold in my emotional economy.

Night Shifts

I then received no more communication, which was unsurprising given his nighttime work schedule.

A day later, he texted, "Sorry, I had to take some time to recharge after a lot of socialization."

It didn't bother me, and I expressed my understanding. But I also noticed he always began his texts with "sorry" following his extended silences.

It cannot be because of me, right? I never got mad or accused him of not texting me.

They were likely preemptive apologies to women from past dynamics: exes who may have punished him for silence or left him guessing about their internal state. But I didn't do that; I created the conditions for him to try again without fear of backlash.

My growth includes expressing appreciation and its rationale to those whom I value. As I reflected on our last morning at Universal, when he saw my defeat and took the lead, I sent him a text of explicit gratitude: I named the moment, identified my internal experience, and credited his role in it. That's the delayed affirmation that teaches someone like him that initiative is worth it, even if he's uncertain.

Did this trigger him to initiate? Maybe... maybe that's why he invited me to dinner after a series of night shifts. And when I let him know that it would work better for me on a different day, he adjusted his schedule to accommodate my needs.

Struggles

As soon as he saw me when we met up for dinner, he explained to me how he was still trying to figure life out, and it's difficult—he emphasized "trying."

I couldn't help but wonder if he truly grasped my genuine compliments the way I had intended, which were rooted in the granular evidence I had been gathering through presence. I don't dispense them easily; I mean every single thing I say.

Basically, the pattern was: he was just being his normal self, and I would dissect his actions, realize the good qualities, and reflect them to him.

I now realize that he was uncomfortable being seen in a light he hadn't yet earned for himself, so he needed to dim it by reminding me —and maybe himself—that he was still "figuring it out." He hadn't internalized those same traits as part of his own self-image, so my reflection of them felt like an overexposure.

Someone without inner reflection might find accurate observation threatening.

That's why he would always come back with some kind of struggle that he was going through to sort of "even out" the greatness I saw in him, to balance my compliment with a confession. That was his way of staying in control of how he was perceived. Every time I tried to hold up a mirror with specificity, he would reach for a reason the reflection must be flawed.

I was loving him by showing him who he was becoming, which required a level of self-acceptance he hadn't reached. He couldn't handle the weight of being seen mid-transition. He might not have realized that my gift wasn't blindless praise—it was precision: I witnessed his growth before he could. And instead of planting himself in that ground, he pulled back into the safety of struggle because it's familiar.

Date No. 22

We went to dinner at a sushi place that I had mentioned during our dating-app chatting phase. He asked me to explain the runway casting that I had just come from, which mattered to me because he was acknowledging the world I lived in.

He then shared that his brother's divorce had been weighing on him. That disclosure was an inflection point because he had held back the detail when we first met and finally allowed me entry, an act I interpreted as our closeness transitioning to something mental. I took it as a good sign.

He trusts me more.

I imagined it was because our Universal trip had marked a major milestone in strengthening our bond.

My Treat

After dinner, I treated him to a bar in our neighborhood, one that he had yet to visit.

Over beers, he showed me an app on his phone, saying, "You wanna see something really stupid that I do?" That statement felt disarming, as if he was saying, "I trust you enough to show you a part of me I rarely spotlight."

I met it with curiosity; it was a sports-betting game. He explained how it worked and how lucky he had been with it. His actions held intimacy because they displayed something that felt personal. I was listening with a smile on my face because, to me, it's his way of inviting me into his world.

We went back to my place afterwards, and you already know what happened next.

Rain poured, so I suggested that I would drop him off, but he insisted on getting a rideshare. He wouldn't even let me walk him outside to join the wait with an umbrella because he said I was already comfortable at home. That was him protecting my warmth, even if it meant his stepping out into the rain alone. In his world, that counted as affection. That is a prime example of how he showed care in his way: being considerate, although he didn't know how to wrap it in the symbols that meant love.

Fog

However, the very manner also disoriented me because it required constant decoding on my part. For example, my solo trip to Bermuda was approaching, and although he inquired about my return, it served as a breadcrumb of care within his otherwise silent behavior. The scrambled signals created foggy confusion within me.

Unsure of my position in his life, I fixated on any sign that I held the place I desired and did what anyone with emotional precision would do: I started parsing every detail for meaning and looking for anchor points.

What made it harder was that I wasn't wrong to feel close to him. The sidecar instead of the bike, the electrolyte water, and the interlaced fingers suggested a connection. But without being introduced to anyone in his existing ecosystem, I remained drifting within a region that felt legitimate yet unanchored.

Typical Silence

He didn't contact me the day before my cruise; I didn't expect him to because I had already lowered the bar for closeness so far that emotional absence had become normal.

But I had a weird feeling that I couldn't explain away: *he would use the physical distance between my cruise and him to further emotionally distance himself.*

I could not quite pinpoint what gave me that feeling, but it's unshakable. On embarkation day, I experienced extreme anxiety. Despite understanding his rhythm, my body was screaming.

This time, the distance is not neutral. He knows I'm about to cruise, yet he remains silent.

Receiving my boarding pass at the pier, I finally received a text from him: "Sorry, I was taking time for self-care. I hope you enjoy your cruise. You're probably boarding now."

His message, while gentle, was pre-cleared of wrongdoing. He had gotten used to absenting himself, and I had learned to expect nothing extra.

I responded almost instantly with a photo of my boarding pass sitting on my lap. That photo served as a bridge to keep him close while I was about to be far.

He responded, "Just make sure they don't leave without you lol."

He picked up the thread just enough by returning an inside joke from a few weeks back when the plane took off without us. It felt like proof: shared memory, which gave me temporary permission to believe I had a place. It signaled, "I'm still here. I haven't vanished." I clung to it for inclusion, since it was the only option available. And that flicker of connection meant everything for the ache underneath.

Cruising

After boarding, I messaged him pictures of the jacuzzis because I had told him hot-tubbing was on my to-do list.

He responded, "Nice! I wonder what it'll be like with many people... I wonder how many."

His engagement with curiosity was just enough back-and-forth to soothe my nerves before my offline period, but I was self-aware enough to know that it wouldn't sustain. I was looking for the tiniest evidence to disprove my instincts.

That's the most painful kind of denial: when my mind insists on being fair, but my body knows it's already bracing.

I then sent him a photo of my dinner at the buffet: a full plate, or two, of all protein items (I had just begun my protein diet, which he knew about). But for hours, I got no response until I lost signal.

At sea, I rationed my cheapest Wi-Fi package to protect myself from the very experience I ended up having: waiting, hoping, checking, and finding nothing.

That unreturned message hit harder than silence usually would because this time, I was holding the dread that he might use the cruise to shift away from me. My picture traveled to remain connected, to convey, "I'm still thinking of you, even here." I provided him with a vivid glimpse of my trip, trying to involve him in what could have been solitary moments but ended up with an empty space.

He didn't owe me constant communication, but I was making space for someone who never stepped into it, and what I kept receiving back were fragments that never settled me.

Bermuda

As the cruise docked in Bermuda, my cell signal resumed. I took photos of the scenery but refrained from sharing them because he still hadn't responded to my dinner photo from two days ago.

"Look at all the proteins lol." His text finally arrived. "I forgot to hit 'send' after I typed the above message lol."

Okay, so that explains it. He didn't mean to ignore me.

His attention deficit hyperactivity disorder (ADHD) prevented the follow-through. It's a relief, but ADHD was also a neat label that justified the silence in a way that honored who he was and allowed me to resume the story I wanted to believe.

He cares but just can't always track.

I then sent him the photos of Bermuda and other updates in small doses. I was strategic with the frequency of texting because the way of his responses shifted... he was not as engaged. The thread between us was still there, but loosening. I was tugging on it, hoping it would tighten.

My nervous system sensed that the active connection between two individuals fresh from traveling together had faded, but my logical mind rationalized the shift.

This is my solo cruise trip, and I'm sure he is just respecting my boundaries.

While the story I told myself was kind to him, it asked me to swallow my feelings. I interpreted every shift through a generous lens, even when it cost me clarity.

The saddest part was how quickly and instinctively I moved to cover up his silence. That's an absence of boundaries wrapped in the language of respect.

Nag

A nagging, unsolved feeling I couldn't reason with prevented me from enjoying the cruise. My body knew something was slipping, even if the surface stayed polite. I had just shared a milestone experience with him at Universal and was still attempting to stay connected.

His long night shifts, overlapping my return, made immediate contact impossible. Still, he updated me on his hospital duties; I had always enjoyed hearing about them because I found his heroic occupation fascinating.

I commented, "You're ever so humble, daily saving people's lives, and you're taking it like a champ."

He took time to process my praise—the response came only the next day: "Honestly, not doing my best. There are a lot of things on my mind at the moment."

I was still hoping that something real was unfolding—that he was unfolding.

Assuming he was referring to his brother's divorce, I stated, "I am sure it's a lot. Thank you for trusting me and sharing it with me."

His increase in openness with me felt like a positive omen, so I kept filling in the blanks with the most generous interpretations I could summon and stayed hopeful for the door to open further, but what I didn't see yet was that he had already started closing it.

What disturbed my peace was the fact that his retreat had no shape, confrontation, or rupture. Just a slow fade, leaving only polite texts and glimpses of depth.

Anxiety Attack

Upon my return, I waited until after his full day off to text, "I miss your face! I can't wait to share with you about my cruise!"

He didn't respond for hours, which was out of character for him. I was at work… and grew anxious. I recognized my anxiety symptoms: the need to take deep inhales frequently to compensate for shallow breathing. My body was screaming what my logic couldn't yet confirm.

He's pulling away, and I'm the only one trying to hold the thread taut between us.

Finally, he responded, "Sorry, I woke up late and went to the park to walk their dog with my friend, which turned out to be a much longer hike than I had anticipated. Then we came back and grabbed food and drinks. I literally just got back and walked through the door. And yesterday I was dead to the world."

Well, at least he texted me first thing as soon as he got back.

But what was stopping him from texting me earlier with just a simple, "Walking dog with friend, will text you soon"? His worded deflection wasn't cruel, nor did he disappear completely, but that's what made it harder: he gave me just enough to blur the boundary between explanation and avoidance.

And I knew it was shielding something he didn't want to name because he had chosen "their" as the pronoun on purpose.

For the first time, I didn't cushion his explanation with my usual understanding. It's a subtle refusal to betray myself for the sake of "being understanding." My integrity wouldn't let me keep pretending that this was mutual.

Coffee

My anxiety attack made it clear to me I couldn't work the next day, and because catching up with him in person was my priority, I asked, "Would you like to grab a coffee tomorrow morning?"

In retrospect, I wanted an in-person check to gauge whether he remained the attentive person who once made me feel like the luckiest girl alive. I was attempting to handle the delicate balance between my desire for connection and my need for self-preservation.

"Sure, what time and where?" He responded.

"Anywhere between you and me would be fine. And whatever time you get up in the morning would be fine with me, too."

"Okay, I'm going to set my alarm for 8 am, and I'll text you and see where we wanna go."

"As long as you're not setting your alarm for me. I want you to have as much rest as you need."

My words were generous but firm, offering flexibility while holding space for my own boundaries.

"It's for both you and me. I need to adjust my sleep patterns back to day shifts anyway."

His response showed that he cared, even amid exhaustion, and a willingness to meet me halfway.

Coming Through

"Good morning. Where would you like to go?" He texted me the next morning, a little after 8 am.

I replied, "Can you just meet me at my place, and we'll walk to a coffee shop together?"

"Sure, if that works best for you."

"Yes, it does. Thank you!"

"Okay, I'm leaving soon."

I needed more time to get ready, and I thought he meant "leaving soon" casually.

Not long after, he texted, "Here, outside by the stairs."

"Oh, I'm so sorry; I need a little bit more time."

"That's fine."

He wasn't being impatient, while my quick apology showed my respect for his time. This felt like a delicate dance; both individuals attempted to meet in the middle through subtle, meaningful displays of consideration alongside patience.

Date No. 23

Approaching from afar, I reminded myself that *he's here, I can touch him, and he is real.*

Giving him a long, warm embrace, I allowed my nervous system to calibrate to physical proof. I needed to feel his body against mine as a way of answering the question I didn't dare ask out loud: *Are you still here with me? Or is it all slipping away?*

Proximity was reassurance; it's my way of feeling anchored again.

He asked, "You don't have to work today?"

"I took the day off today," I said with a sigh, one that already carried more weight than any explanation I could have given.

To move forward, I needed to see for myself if my feelings were still true.

Request Number One

Expecting him to be vague, I asked, "What are you doing on the 24th?"

To my surprise, he said, "I'll probably be flying back from Poland."

"Oh, okay. That's crazy; I didn't expect you to know exactly when that date is, coming from a person who doesn't live longer than two days ahead."

I wasn't bashing about the "two days ahead". It's something he had told me before, word for word.

"Yeah, I remember because I actually had to type that date in when I looked up the flights. But I don't know if it's possible because I messed up my work schedule on my personal calendar, so if I can't find someone to switch with me on the day I'm supposed to go, then I won't be able to. We shall see. Why?"

"Oh, it's the annual open day at my work, so that's the only time we can bring outside people in to look at our workspace."

That invitation wasn't casual for me—it's a subtle offer to be seen in a space that held meaning for me. But his gesture fell flat, and I had already written the idea out of my mind.

Cafe Number One

I took care of the bill at the coffee shop because the date was my idea. Over coffee, I shared my cruise experience and told him how many people felt surprised I took it alone—something I thought he would resonate with. He listened, but his posture gave him away: something in him pulled back with a slight but unmistakable touch.

Request Number Two

I then pursued my second request: "This coming Saturday, would we be able to do a Harry Potter night for real?"

Turned out, he had already planned a family visit but promised notification if plans changed.

I was also secretly planning a "cafe hop," because it was one of his interests listed on his dating app profile… I remembered, just never brought it up. I was extending myself in ways that said, *I see you, and I want to keep seeing you.*

I had envisioned ample time for shared activities, but in that instant, I hurried... since I sensed something departing: I was trying to place something solid beneath my feet before the ground gave out.

Request Number Three

Coffee mugs were emptied. Not ready for us to go our separate ways, I proposed visiting a different coffee shop as my last ask. It's my third request that morning; I was counting. Following my anxiety attack, I reminded myself to be more forward about my needs.

He responded, "Sure, I definitely can use some more coffee. Where would you like to go next?"

I chose the coffee shop that was our Plan B for our first date.

He said, "Okay, let's go there. You ready?"

"Yeah. And it's like cafe hopping."

Finally, I let it slide in.

He swatted the intimacy away with humor and said, "Not as cool as bar hopping."

"Well, someone said he liked cafe hopping... whether that's true or not."

That was my way of saying, *I remember who you said you were. Do you?*

In fact, I wasn't sure if he even knew I was referring to his early blueprint, the version of himself he had curated when trying to be chosen.

I was asking, *are you still in this with me? Do you still remember how this began? Are you still interested in developing something real?*

Divorce

I wasn't shy anymore... I threaded my arm through his elbow on the short walk to the next coffee shop. Not only in a physical sense, but

I was also striving to narrow the growing gap between my efforts and his participation.

He explained his earlier attempt to distance himself from his family's issues, which proved ineffective. Thus, he did a one-eighty, started showing up for his brother more often, and dedicated his weekends to supporting him and his kids. He mentioned his intention to travel to Poland, where he would be inaccessible, to evade everything, because the weight of his brother's divorce had taken a toll on him.

I said to him, "Oh, I'm so sorry, I didn't know. When I asked to do Harry Potter night on Saturday, I wasn't aware of your brother's situation. Please, go spend time with your brother. We'll do it on some other night."

What I withheld—but desired to voice—was, *Would you return to me afterwards? Will I remain within your domain when the crisis concludes?*

But those questions remained suspended because I always made it easy for him not to answer them.

His pattern was becoming clearer: he wouldn't volunteer information until my requests revealed his silence. He let me carry the emotional burden of attuning and rarely brought me in.

I distinguished myself through a swift retreat that arose from prioritizing his desires over mine. That's how I had been loving him all along: softening in advance any friction that might make him pull away.

I didn't realize I was writing a love story alone.

Cafe Number Two

Over the coffee and my chocolate-almond croissant that he had paid for at cafe number two, he shared about his upcoming trip. I, having traveled the globe solo, experienced inner peace for his sake. I hoped for beneficial change.

He'll take his time to self-reflect and realize that our relationship is the one thing that he hasn't nurtured, and I'm sure he'll come back around when he comes home.

I could tell that the clash of his work schedule and travel plan was bothering him because at one point, he showed me his work schedule on his phone, explaining, "This is how complicated our work schedule is… I really don't wanna ask this older lady to switch with me, but I'm afraid I might have to. If not, I'll have to call in sick, but I don't really wanna go there."

The subtext was, "This is hard, so please don't expect too much of me."

And of course, I didn't. As usual, I validated, made it easy, and kept hoping his eventual return would be a moment of recognition: "She was the one thing that didn't make it harder."

"What's the downside of calling out sick?" I asked.

"I wanna be able to talk about my trip when I get back, so I don't wanna lie."

I admired that integrity. But it also told me he had no problem choosing honesty with his coworkers, yet with me, he defaulted to vague, polite distance.

His trip was going to happen over Easter weekend, so I asked what his Catholic parents thought about it.

He told me, "Yeah, I ran it by them first. They said because of what happened with my brother and his wife, they are probably not going to do the normal church morning and then a meal over the afternoon into the evening. They support my decision to do this trip."

Something told me that his brother's divorce had changed the vibe of family gatherings over holidays, and so he would rather be away. That's why he had told me that Christmas was "different" for him.

Caring

He shared with me that he spent his weekly therapy talking about his family issues instead of his own.

I looked him in the eye and said, "It means you care so much about others."

Turning his head away, he then glanced back at me, signaling his unease with a sideways lip gesture. His nonverbal cues hinted at his discomfort with the accuracy of my statement and its weight on him. This reflex mirrored the one he gave me when I had told him he inspired me months before.

As usual, he downplayed my compliments about his inner qualities by telling me all the internal struggles he was having. This time, he admitted difficulty in planning.

So I asked a grounded, specific question: "How has it been working out for you?"

"At this point in my life, I don't see how I would drastically change myself." He answered.

Interesting. Where did that come from? That does not relate to my query.

The answer given was not what I had expected. I sought to understand whether his struggles continued to extract a toll or if he had found peace.

What he heard was a challenge, and his reply was a veiled confession: "I'm overwhelmed, I'm stuck, and I don't want anyone expecting me to be more than this." It bypassed the present altogether and leapt to a permission slip to remain unchanged. Instead of engaging with my clarity, he closed the door with that sentence.

I mirrored back acceptance and said, "The reason I asked was that, if it's been working out for you, then why change?"

It's the same dynamic again: I reflected his truth to him, he flinched, and I cushioned the moment and kept the connection intact at the cost of my own emotional footing.

His family situation may have drained him, but the real erosion was subtler: the way he redirected vulnerability into distance. He took my recognition and countered with self-limitation. Despite that, I kept making space for him to grow because I kept hoping he might one day walk into the self I already saw in him.

Excitement

His redirected query regarding my eagerness about Universal's new park.

I understood his reference, and yet I replied, "Our Harry Potter night."

He smiled and said, "No, I'm talking about the park."

As this second cafe visit ended, he hugged me goodbye, but I went for a quick kiss on his lips.

"Please don't worry about Harry Potter night," I reiterated, reassuring him not to stress about the plan.

But he assured me, "Let me talk to my brother, and I'll let you know. Hopefully this weekend, okay?"

That promise offered some hope. He was trying to manage his duties and the connection, even if it felt delicate.

I allowed myself to walk away with a moment of peace amid uncertainty, knowing that sometimes connection wasn't about immediate answers but the willingness to keep trying.

Break

When he finally had a moment to relax at work, he considered my whereabouts and texted, "Did you end up going to New York?"

I had mentioned my agency had put me on hold, yet they could release me at any moment.

"Thanks so much for checking in with me, even though you're busy at work. No, I ended up being released, so I went to happy hour with my friend instead," I responded with a selfie of me and my friend—the same friend whom I had introduced at her birthday party.

"Nice, looks like you're having fun. Yeah, I finally got a moment of quiet to sit down."

Despite his exhaustion, he carved out space to check in with me. It was a subtle yet clear sign he cared, that I mattered enough for him to break away from his duties just to connect, even briefly.

How did I get so lucky?

My Friend

My friend inquired about us because she knew about the guys I had dated who mistreated me. She was always there to remind me, "Megan, you're a high-value woman. It's their loss."

I wanted to believe her. I mean… I did, with my intellect.

But why do I always adjust my behavior to please guys?

Because that unconscious urge to please was rooted in old survival mechanisms I had developed long before any guys appeared in my life. Seeking approval had been a habit since childhood.

"He has been so good to me. I honestly have no complaints. Promise… I'm even consciously looking for red flags, but I can find none. Honestly, I feel so lucky," I told her.

"Cheers to that, Megan. Finally, a real man!"

Those cheers weren't just for the relationship but also for the powerful woman I had become. We toasted my achievement: finally finding someone on "my level." Now it's about letting myself believe it, feel it, and stand in it without the old, automatic scripts pulling me back.

I was navigating unfamiliar territory with this guy; I had yet to understand whether his slower pace represented good intentions. I convinced myself that my awareness of his pattern already put me far ahead of where I had been in the past.

Harry

The next day, he let me know: "There has been a lot on my mind, and I have decided to go see my brother on Saturday. I feel bad because you wanted to do Harry Potter night, but I plan on coming back Sunday afternoon. So will Sunday night work?"

His suggestion felt like gentle solace: a familiar comfort during his current difficulties.

"Are you sure you don't want to just chill and relax after you have given so much to your family? It's really okay that we'll do it another time," my response gave him space while expressing care.

"No, I'll be fine. It's nice to have something to take my mind off of that anyway. I wanted to pick up an extra shift on Monday, but I had my therapy session scheduled, which I don't wanna move. I'm thinking I'll use Monday as my me time."

It sounded like he had a solid plan to balance his commitments and personal space while still wanting to stay connected with me, so I agreed.

He texted me to let me know on his train ride back on Sunday, "On my way back. Bolognese sounds good?"

"Sounds perfect!" I responded.

"Around 6 pm, you think?"

"Yeah!"

Date No. 24

Eager to spend time with him, I arrived early. Sitting on a barstool by his kitchen island as he was cooking, I savored that my man was fixing a meal for me, and it's something that he loved doing. He wasted no time in starting the first of the three Fantastic Beasts movies. Honestly, I was still admiring him and wasn't ready to dive right into the movie yet.

I loved his cooking, even when he over-salted the pasta, like he always did.

He asked, "On a scale from zero to ten, how salty is it?"

"Oh, it's definitely an eleven! Lol!" I teased.

"You're eating it, though."

"Yeah, I still like it! I want more of it!"

"You can take the rest home!"

"REALLY??? I will!"

I found his salty pasta to be adorable, and it didn't bother me much. He fed my tummy, and I loved every bit of it.

I didn't need perfection; I just loved the entire intimate experience. It was a subtle celebration of connection, where even the salty pasta became a sweet symbol of care.

Facial Hair

We cuddled on the couch to watch the movie. I mentioned that he was my first bearded boyfriend, which intrigued him. Somehow, my hand started caressing his soft facial hair as he nipped my fingers as they neared his lips. Stopping the movie with the remote, he fixated his seductive gaze on me, a perfect blend of tenderness and desire.

I asked with a smile, "What?"

He locked eyes with me as his fingertip pressed on the 'play' button on the remote.

I then looked back at the screen, but he paused the movie again and asked, "Don't you want me right now?"

His question was a raw announcement of our electric connection.

"Is that a trick question? When do I not want you?" I asked as he began kissing me, and as always, he thrilled me... until he couldn't.

Then, just as the anticipation crescendoed, he introduced a bittersweet admission: "I think this is it."

That's a fleeting edge of vulnerability within the closeness.

I had already alerted him that I intended to return home rather than stay.

He packaged the rest of his bolognese for me and said, "I'll walk you halfway."

It was a gesture that felt considerate, but it wasn't the norm; he had always walked me all the way home.

Halfway

Once more, I linked my arm with his elbow. And it was at the halfway point between his place and mine where he gave me a goodbye hug, but I went straight for a kiss on the lips without knowing why it wasn't already instinctive on his part.

Maybe he's tired? Perhaps chilly weather prompted an early departure?

But I didn't let those subtle shifts bother me long because I was walking the rest of my way home with his bolognese in my hand—a tangible reminder of the connection I was holding onto. Gratitude enveloped me for what remained: I was just thankful that he even walked me home at all.

After getting home, I received his text, "Are you home?"

The warmth of his care still lingered in those small moments.

I responded right away, "Yes <3," which he never acknowledged.

Usual Silence

By now, his habit of recharging following our shared activities had become a norm to me. During his silence, I got myself a preview ticket to the new park when Universal Orlando released them for passholders. It was an arduous process of enduring the virtual queue for hours, and my instinct was to share with him the joyous experience.

Trusting that he would receive it well, I broke the silence and texted, "Hey, guess what? I secured an Epic preview ticket. I really didn't mean to bother you, but I was too excited not to share!"

"Lol, you can bother me! That's great! You got what you wanted." He responded almost instantly.

It felt like a soft invitation wrapped in humor, signaling that he was open to my reaching out.

But did he realize what he was inviting me to do?

I believe he spoke knowing I would not overstep his boundaries, based on my track record.

He also added, "Sorry, something has been weighing on me heavily."

I'm sure it's his way of maintaining honesty without making me feel like my excitement was a burden.

He valued my openness, yet needed boundaries to feel safe. He allowed me in, but on terms he could manage.

TV

I could feel the increasing weight on his mind, so I texted, "My priority is your well-being and not crossing your boundaries. Please take good care of yourself, and just know that I'll always be here holding space for you."

My increased empathy and lowered boundaries came from a genuine place, wanting to support him through his mental load. Yet, that very compassion often made me vulnerable to emotional imbalance.

The next morning, I had a live TV modeling segment appearance again, but, of course, he forgot about it. I didn't remind him either; I had noticed he went from being enthusiastic to avoiding watching it over the course of our relationship.

This shift felt like a withdrawal, especially given how much I had invested by holding space for his struggles. I had stayed steady, becoming even more loving, but the way he "forgot" my live appearance suggested a distancing that wasn't about me changing but about him pulling back.

What changed? Not me. I'm still the same person.

Actually, no, not exactly. If I were to be honest, my understanding deepened the longer we had been together—increased empathy resulted in compromised boundaries.

Meanwhile, his engagement seemed to have receded.

Full Stop

At 7:45 am on a Monday, he texted, "Good morning."

That's odd... he has never sent me a good morning text before.

His use of punctuation was also new... he put a full stop there. Those shifts suggested he strove to become more deliberate.

Since I hadn't responded, he texted again: "So something has been weighing heavily on my mind and heart lately. Not only everything that's been going on with my family, but also, I think it's time we have an honest conversation. I have been doing a lot of reflecting lately and just trying to figure out my current thoughts and emotions and all."

"Thank you for letting me know," I responded. "I can tell you've been carrying a lot, and I really respect you for being honest with me. I'm here, and when you're ready, I'm open to whatever you want to share."

His silence that followed left me in suspense, so I texted later that day: "So I've been spending all day reflecting since your text this morning, and I realize I also have some things I'd like to share. Let me know when you're home, and I'll swing by if that's the most convenient for you."

"Yeah, I do think we need to have a conversation. Maybe I can take the subway home and swing by you. Are you going to be home at eight? Or a little before?"

"I have been home. But you've worked all day and have so much more to do; I can go to you."

He insisted on coming by, mentioning a grocery stop, a minor discrepancy I had overlooked. Later, I recalled no grocery store connected my place with his.

The Night

I already knew he had bad news to deliver when I saw him from afar, walking up. As he got closer, opening up his arms to hug me… just a little longer and tighter with his palms on my upper back, squeezing harder than usual.

Walking inside my home, he kept his backpack on, preferring conversation while standing.

He murmured, "You also had something to say?!"

He was returning the emotional burden to me. But I declined to go first because, deep down, I already understood the script; I was just bracing for the lines.

He then opened with, "You're a good person, and you didn't do anything wrong," placing me on the pedestal of moral safety: an emotional courtesy that revealed the avoidance.

I knew the conversation was going someplace I didn't want to, so I offered him the stability he was denying both of us and said, "You wanna sit down? But earlier you said 'briefly'."

I showed that I already grasped what was happening. I wasn't confused but was collecting the dignity of truth in real time.

I had already read the room before he began to speak. His body gave him away: holding me tighter, lingering longer, standing instead of settling in, and keeping his bag on like he didn't plan to stay long. Those didn't seem like actions from someone intending to grow a connection. They were the soft choreography of someone trying to cushion an exit, and I knew it.

Speech

So he took his backpack off. He wanted me to sit in my only chair in my living room, and he sat on my coffee table in front of me.

Beginning with a compliment, he started again: "You're a good person… and I have nothing negative to say about you and find you attractive. You haven't done anything wrong, and that's why this is so hard. But I have had one foot out the door. This has been weighing on me… I spent my last two therapy sessions asking how to break this to you. My therapist told me there isn't going to be a right time, and I just need to start talking, then thoughts will follow. I don't even think we should be friends."

His words sounded rehearsed. The praise wasn't about me but about sparing himself from guilt.

If you're telling me that nothing went wrong, then why are you doing this?

His texts from the morning mentioned an "honest conversation," but the afternoon's texts reduced it to a "conversation." I was tracking the entire pattern, shifting from implying vulnerability to distance in real time. I saw that he used the word "conversation" as a shield—a neutral word that made the situation sound mutual when, in reality, it wasn't. He wasn't looking for my input because he had already decided for both of us, alone.

So I questioned, "Did you mean for it to be a conversation? Or have you already made a decision and then came to tell me?"

"Yeah, I came here to do this face-to-face, or I could have texted you about it this morning because I owe you at least to do this in person."

"I don't think you understand what I'm asking: Have you made your decision already? Or is it a two-way conversation where my input matters?"

I was trying to restore honesty by insisting that he name what he was doing: choosing and declaring. My question cut through the noise and reached for the actual truth, not the softened version he was trying to deliver. It forced him to confront what he was avoiding: that he had staged this as closure for himself, not clarity for both of us.

And when he couldn't answer… that silence was a confirmation: he wasn't there to explore a shared truth but to present the one that he had arrived at in private.

The Feeling

He left me in a fog of confusion, so I just had to ask, "Then what's not working?"

He explained, "I don't even know if I'm supposed to have this feeling or what, but people say it's like a fairytale. I reflected on my past relationships, and some of them had that. Some came instantly, and some a little later, but it never took this long, and you know I always go with the flow, so instead of having this conversation three months down the road when I still don't have it, I'd rather do this now because your time is valuable and so is mine. Plus, I feel like I need to grow."

Instead of engaging with any specific, relational truth between us, with my direct, grounded question, he defaulted to the abstract "a feeling," mythical and unverifiable, as the lone reason he couldn't continue. He wanted the exit to feel justified because of something missing, but he never articulated what was missing beyond a vague emotional benchmark borrowed from fantasy. He made it sound like the "fairytale" was the goal, but what we were building was reality: I had brought genuine effort—and he bypassed it to chase a feeling that may or may never return to him.

That ambiguity protected him. It allowed him to exit, naming no failure of effort, compatibility, depth, or willingness. It burdened the passage of time—time he needed to shield.

But whose time had he wasted?

His claim of needing to grow was an evasion, not an insight. If he had meant it, he would have remained in the uncomfortable, expansive work of relational growth with me through the unknowns. But he used "growth" the way people use escape routes: to exit. And beneath that narrative was something far less magical: he wasn't willing to grow in my direction, only to name "growth" as a personal pursuit that now required my absence. Instead of a revelation, what he delivered was a retreat disguised as reflection.

He concluded his rehearsed speech by offering, "If you have questions, in a few days we can talk again. I'm open to it."

In hindsight, that offer was in fact his way of softening the blow of his decision: he wanted to appear generous while maintaining all the control.

So I stated, "For what? Closure? I don't understand the point of talking after this."

Even if I couldn't name it then, my body knew that I didn't need a follow-up conversation to "understand" because I already did: he had made a private decision and delivered it with rehearsed language about feelings. I didn't get a voice, only a front-row seat.

He looked disappointed and said, "I'm sorry you feel this way."

I was challenging him at each step: exploring the conversation's aim, gaps, and follow-up. And his truth unfolded: he had checked out, desiring escape while presenting a positive impression.

He didn't want my truth, understanding, or grace, but a gentle exit without having to confront what it meant to be loved by someone emotionally available.

The pressure of being seen by someone who required presence was the actual weight pressing on him, not confusion, timing, or absence of a fairy tale.

I questioned his initial long-term vision. He was still standing by his initial claim of having the intention to "give it his all" to see where things would go when we first met, and he was waiting for the feeling that never came.

Spills

I expressed uncertainty about sharing my thoughts because he didn't inquire about them. It was apparent that he was there only to deliver his speech, not to receive my thoughts. But knowing it's our last conversation, I spoke my mind anyway.

The irony: I told him his desired feeling was a red flag to me because all my previous partners gave me that fairytale feeling before turning out to be unhealthy relationships.

I let him know that I had been dating three other guys when we had first met, and it was during my subsequent trip to Australia that I had time to reflect on how he differed from the rest: it was his steadiness, not his spark, that made me choose him.

Because his balanced approach to life was something my nervous system wasn't used to, I had to rewire my inner being to feel safe. I gave language to something he never expected me to name: his version of love wasn't wise, safe, or grounded. That likely unraveled him because I held up a mirror that provided a profound recognition: I saw him clearly and chose him despite my anxious wiring. He told me he wanted a feeling—but when I described what it took for me to feel safe with him, he couldn't handle it because it was too real.

I also shared that I lacked clear direction on what to write for my book (this book) until I met him because he helped me understand what love should look like. That was the truest compliment he had ever received, and he couldn't metabolize it.

Sharing that information caused his emotional collapse. While he appreciated my sharing, he felt overwhelmed and was unable to discuss it further. He proposed picking up our conversation within a few days; this made up his second offering.

In hindsight, that was an evasion tactic: he wished to dismiss his discomfort, deferring digestion of my communication. But I didn't cling to the open loop or collapse to accommodate him, because my body saw what he couldn't: he had already shut the door emotionally, and now he wanted me to help him feel okay about it.

That's why I delivered the truth again: "I don't know what we'll have to talk about; what's the point?"

I let my presence speak louder than my need for reciprocity. With this action, I reemphasized the depth from which he departed.

He had spent the entire relationship drifting in and out of connection, giving pieces of presence and then retreating, always hedging and protecting the exit ramp. He thought I wouldn't notice; I did... but I also trusted him.

He also shared, "And you know I have difficulty expressing my feelings."

But what he really meant was, "I don't know how to handle being the object of someone else's truth. Especially when that truth reveals my absence in the story."

He said he didn't know if he was supposed to feel the fairytale. But I had given him a genuine love story, and he backed away the moment it asked him to meet it.

And here's the brutal truth: he wasn't waiting for a feeling; he was actively avoiding one—the feeling of being seen, needed, and held responsible. And the closer I got, the harder he scrambled for an explanation for himself as to why retreating felt safer.

Confusion

He told me that dating me was different because I allowed him to work on himself and his friendships, which he valued.

He also told me, "You're a very interesting person, and there are still many other aspects of you I have yet to explore." Though he continued, "We're kind of different people. That's not a bad thing!"

These were the reasons he gave for leaving. His logic collapsed on itself, which is why I left that conversation feeling like I was standing in fog.

He invoked mutual growth as a neat way to close the chapter: "You've challenged me to grow, and it sounds like I have challenged you to grow too, so we have learned our lessons, and we move on."

He explained it as if it were a college course we both completed. But my experience wasn't academic; it's a real investment from my nervous system. I lived in that relationship, and it's not a clean arc of "lesson learned," at least not for me.

He credited me with being a catalyst in his growth, with helping him refocus on his friendships and internal life. He admitted that being with me was different. I expanded on him. And still—he walked away.

At some point, he had to elaborate again, "You really are a good person. You did nothing wrong. That's why this is so hard."

I said something like, "This is the hardest thing I have had to go through, and you know what I have been through. This is worse than when people used to tell me I was too much, I was not enough, or anything like that."

"You want me to tell you that you're too much? Or not enough?... I'm just kidding."

But I wasn't laughing. That cruelty cloaked in humor was emotional cowardice dressed up as playfulness. When I told him how deeply his words impacted me, instead of staying with that gravity, he reached for levity to diffuse his discomfort—not mine. The laugh was of his relief, not my pain. That line blurted out, but it revealed what he couldn't regulate: my emotional truth had more weight than he was willing to hold.

He told me he wanted to have that conversation with me in person because he cared. But care without clarity isn't kindness; it's confusion. His stated act of care might appear thoughtful, but it left me with emotional wreckage that I had to sort through alone. His delivery gave me graceful words without grounded answers; I was left having to decode them because he didn't stay present enough to own what he meant. I suspect he intended to make me feel better. But after hearing about everything, he left me very confused. I was met with contradiction wrapped in politeness.

I was confused because he couldn't hold a consistent truth in his own mouth. And every time I challenged it, he couldn't meet me. I asked whether this was a conversation or a decision, what wasn't working, and expressed my truth. Soft words and vague gestures, coupled with a variable exit strategy, comprised everything he possessed.

The contradiction in his goodbye revealed someone wished to evade the portrayal of villainy upon their exit. So he flooded me with niceties and contradictions. He said it's hard because I was a good person, as if my goodness made it harder for him. At that point, even my virtues reflected his challenge, not mine. He aspired to be seen as kind, but if he had respected me, he would have come clean with the truth instead of cushioning it with fragments. He gave me no space to co-create the ending: he just delivered it, already packaged, while pretending it's still up for dialogue. And when I asked whether my input would change anything, he went silent. That was the answer.

So no—he didn't end things in person because he cared; he did it to appear righteous. And in doing so, he bypassed what I needed: clarity that didn't leave me with the burden of interpretation.

I deserved a partner, not a riddle.

Composure

My composure held until he stood and offered a hug; I was squeezing him tighter and tighter, and I cried even harder. That collapse was the exact moment when my nervous system finally stopped trying to negotiate with his ambiguity. My body felt the finality, even though his words kept the door cracked open. I ceased deceiving myself regarding his true nature.

Before my cognizance, my body knew: This embrace would prove the ultimate. Everything I had held back during the conversation broke through the moment we were close again.

He whispered, "Please don't cry."

He then left me to go for a few seconds to grab me a tissue and then resumed the hug.

I then cried more and squeezed him even tighter.

All he said was, "You'll be okay," as if he needed me to recover fast so he wouldn't have to carry the weight of what he had done.

He then repeated, "You'll be okay," a few more times, and I gave him the same response every time: "I'm not okay. And I won't be okay."

Those repeated phrases were about his discomfort; it's a way to wrap my pain in a neat bow so he could walk away with less guilt. But I refused to shrink my pain for his relief. It's dignity in the face of someone who delivered heartbreak with performance rather than presence.

He concluded his departure with, "This isn't necessarily the end. We can be friends down the road, but not right away because each of us needs to process this."

Notice the shift from "we shouldn't be friends" to "we can down the road" and how he walked back even within his own boundaries. These contradictions weren't invitations—they were emotional escape hatches, ways to exit without full ownership, and ways of cushioning the blow without stepping into the wreckage.

He also, for the third time, told me he was open to answering questions in the following days if I had them, and again I told him, "But there's no point."

My clarity was unwavering even in heartbreak; I refused the false comfort of "maybe." This wasn't open access. It's a guy trying to leave with clean hands.

Pivot

Right before he stepped out, he gave me the last hug and whispered, "Bye," like someone who wanted to linger in my emotional world without staying in it. He wanted softness in his exit, even though he hadn't offered me substance in his staying.

But I didn't echo the goodbye as reclamation: I refused to give him the closing line to a story he unilaterally ended.

He exited as I held the door. You know that when someone leaves, they would just keep walking, but he pivoted around.

I used to stay at the door, holding it open when he walked away in the past. That gesture mirrored how I kept my heart open—attentive, available, and hopeful. I would watch him stroll away, trusting he would return.

Maybe part of him hoped I would stay the same—the under-standing one, the forgiving one, the woman who kept the door cracked even after he had chosen to leave—the "grounded" one that he had claimed to be looking for.

But this time, I didn't need to read between the lines of a half-turn; I had already seen everything I needed to see. The moment I stopped negotiating with his absence, I left him, even though he was the one walking away.

Unsure of his intentions, I didn't wait this time. As soon as he stepped out, I had already shut the door in his face with no need for another glance. I wasn't standing there anymore.

That wasn't coldness; it was clarity: I no longer needed to witness his departure; I had lived it already, long before he said the words. He noticed it, turned around, and continued to walk away.

I knew what I was doing: the door didn't close because I was cruel; it closed because I was done holding space for someone who couldn't hold space for me.

Drawer

After locking that door, I dove into bed: headfirst, hard. Silence grew without resistance, even though I wasn't sleeping, and pain flowed.

I wasn't collapsing but was clearing space: lying there to allow my physical body to feel the pain while my head had as much time as it needed to process everything—not only to make sense of what had happened that night but also the entire five-and-a-half-month relationship, which was two weeks shy of how long he had defined a "long-term" relationship. I bet it's calculated; for someone who did not function off of a calendar like me, it signified the intentionality through instincts of how urgent it was—he couldn't allow himself to file our relationship into the "long-term" drawer.

He might have avoided labeling the relationship as long-term, but that didn't change what it was. My nervous system knew the rewiring it required to feel steady beside him. The loss hurt like something real because it was, no matter what drawer he filed it into.

The entire architecture behind it was real: the way he calibrated his exit down to the calendar, held back just enough to make sure our bond never qualified as "long-term," and my body registered the emotional severance long before my mind finished the sentence.

I didn't try to fix it, rewrite it, check my phone, or beg the past for a different ending. The hardest thing I did was stay present with the truth. I wasn't looking at the clock or forcing myself to rest.

I didn't have the urge to contact him, which was likely my all-or-nothing mentality at work: I love with my whole heart, but I also withdraw everything to preserve my dignity. I didn't have to announce, "I'm done." I just was.

A few rays of sunset and sunrise peeked through the window screen when my feet finally stepped on the path that led to my bathroom, and that warm shower felt good. The feeling I had that I felt for the first time in my life whispered, "Megan, welcome home."

That's a feeling of victory: returning to a home that does not need to prove itself to anyone, but the home I carry in my bones when I stop making myself available to people who can't stay with me in the depths I had awakened in them.

Instead of a heartbreak, that was homecoming.

Consent

It's apparent in retrospect that he had planned to flood the following month with just enough sound to prevent self-reflection. His day shifts, Poland trip, and night shifts, lining up one after another, were tempo designed to mimic regulation.

He was intentional about keeping himself busy post-breakup because pausing would induce quietness that would have made his internal voice seem louder. He wanted to convince himself that the breakup was clean. Despite the lack of communication, even elaborate distractions cannot conceal the body's wound.

Now I know he had already planned his exit for at least as long as he had planned his solo trip. Which means he led me to his bedroom on our last date, knowing he had already made up his mind to exit. That realization made me feel betrayed because, by withholding crucial information, he stripped me of the ability to give informed consent to an act I otherwise would not have.

I feel violated.

Outlier

I was the odd one out—someone who didn't already exist in his ecosystem. None of his friends or family knew about me. He never integrated me into his "real life" because doing so would require real inclusion on his part—where someone new isn't just present but witnessed by others, and witnessing is where the risk begins. Integration held no allure; it would have involved excessive effort and threatened to render them too authentic, jeopardizing his well-being.

Recall his "best friend," who saw us together on the street by chance... I likely got explained away, even if I was brought up in a later conversation. That's when I realized he already had an exit plan before he entered "us," if "us" even ever existed in the story he told himself.

That's why he kept his exes close post-breakups: not out of affection, but because they were already conveniently integrated. They didn't require effort or alter the story of who he was; I would have. He couldn't fit me into his pattern, as I wasn't at work and therefore didn't belong. I moved through the relationship as someone who already knew her worth, which meant my presence in his life made the stakes feel higher.

That's why the ex-girlfriends that he allowed to file in his "long-term drawer" share something in common: they were all already embedded in the larger friend group that originated in a work setting to begin with. To him, proximity was a much safer type of intimacy, the only type his nervous system could tolerate for a little longer... six months or a little beyond.

Perhaps those "lucky ladies" gave him the feelings that he was waiting to develop with me, but the existence of the feelings still did not guarantee the longevity of their relationships, because if they did, what then made him flee? The collapse wasn't just of his logic—it was of his blueprint. He desired to feel but was wired to flee; he craved intimacy, but only if it's pre-approved by proximity; he wanted to fall in love without the risk of being changed by it.

That's when I realized that he had run away at the first sign of his true feelings being developed with me. Sadly, that's the paradox his nervous system functions on without his conscious knowing: he will never receive the feeling that he claims he is waiting for when his body avoids it. And that's what his body rejected: not me, but the possibility of transformation. He mistook emotional depth for danger, love for chaos, and regulation for control. And once he felt something genuine, his body sounded the alarm.

His structure, I perceived, existed for confinement, a secret he would not own. The more something stirred his actual emotions, the faster he coded it as a threat. He departed, not for lack, but for the existence of depth.

His three offers to answer my questions during the aftermath seemed to be an exaggeration, not as an act of care, but as a reflex—like muscle memory from past relationships where the women clung to the loose ends he had left behind. That's all he knew: to him, we as partners always relied on him for closure, didn't we?

His insistence wasn't about my need for closure; it was about his need to feel needed. He expected me to orbit his gravity the way others had.

My complete silence post-breakup was new to him. This confirmed an earlier notion, originating from his assertion that friendships provide superior returns compared to relationships. I told myself, *he never dated me before; he doesn't know that I'm not like the others.*

I bet he does now.

PART V: THE RESULT

CHAPTER 8: CLARITY

Life one month post-breakup remained challenging. Despite that, I continued with my monthly Universal trip.

Light

A rideshare driver picked me up at my hotel to take me to the park. Her eyes were kind and possessed an unspoken strength, hinting at inner riches. Somewhere between traffic lights and small talk, she told me about her daughter, who had lived for twenty years and found fullness, boldness, and meaning in her brief life. The driver's voice, calm with pride, conveyed her statement, the kind that survived losses.

I breathed, "Life is about quality, not quantity."

She looked at me through the rearview mirror, held my gaze, and said, "Yes! I keep telling people that."

I told her I didn't think it was a coincidence that she was assigned as my driver... maybe the Universe arranged it just so I could hear her story. She didn't dismiss or laugh it off; she just nodded, as if she already knew.

It was a quick ten-minute ride, and as I was stepping out, she turned to me and said, "Girl, don't let anyone dim your light. You keep shining!"

I hadn't told her a single thing about me—not the heartbreak, the silence I was living in, nor the ache I was wearing under my skin—all I did was listen. Despite that, she blurted out something that hit my soul, as if she saw it... as if she saw me.

Her words gave me a sensation of realignment within my body, and they still cause tears to this day. She saw me comprehending suffering, having survived the loss that had rewired me. Recognizing the form of concealed sorrow, she understood being bound without being seen, requiring no elaboration.

I also gave her a gift: my listening made space for her daughter to live again, even for just ten minutes, between stop signs and traffic lights. I didn't interrupt or redirect; I just let her talk. Perhaps that was sufficient... Perhaps that encompassed everything.

What transpired exceeded mere kindness; it was recognition.

Grief knows grief, and light recognizes light, even dimmed.

Those tested by hardship often possess exceptional clarity. It's not what you say; it's what you don't. Your hidden ache resonates, and someone who has suffered can perceive it as music.

She didn't know my story, but she sensed my energy. And some blessings aren't random; they're earned and passed down from one survivor to another. What she said wasn't a compliment; it was a hand-off and guidance from one who endured hardship yet illuminated others.

Reflecting on my life, I was always asking to be seen: to be known beyond what I could offer, fix, soften, or endure. And for years, I mistook being "chosen" for being cherished. I thought attention meant safety, and survival meant love. My emotions were never excessive; it's just that nobody ever reflected them to me. I was never clingy; I was starving. I was never weak; I was just alone in a world that kept asking me to apologize for my strength.

And each time someone erased me, I resurfaced. Every time something reduced me, I rebuilt myself clearer, cleaner, and more exact. I had often felt invisible, wondering if anyone could see the full sky inside me, even in silence. This driver proved that I was seen and heard; even in stillness, my light spoke. And when someone sees it—

sees me—I'll remember it. Even if it's from a stranger, even if it only lasted ten minutes.

Primal

So where did my light come from? I believe that it's primal, not cognitive. I argue that I had already developed the ability to find a center within myself before I was born.

My mother never wanted children and was trying to abort me when I was in her womb. I suspect I had already sensed I was unwelcome before taking my first breath. Thus, even as a fetus, I was given two choices: give up or live. And my mother was right; I had insisted on choosing the latter.

Entering this world feeling unsafe, I had frequently pondered human behavior to decipher motives and intentions. I kept questioning societal norms, even though it was hard for me to express as a child.

The kindergarten interview was a key moment. My parents and that teacher tried to make me fit in, but I have stayed true to myself since then and throughout my life. At only seven, I questioned why people reproduce. Many people expressed the belief that I would alter my stance with passing time, an accurate prediction indeed: my convictions shifted towards increased assurance regarding my child-free inclinations.

My childhood was marked by seclusion, emotional neglect, and transactional attention. I felt shame and isolation and was punished for being human. I was taught to suppress my instincts and control my inner world. That's not just restrictions but also psychological constraints arising from having emotions, crushes, or curiosity as a normal child.

Despite those challenges, I somehow found the strength within myself that helped me endure. No formal instructions could have taught me how to survive. My nervous system became a surveillance system that was always on alert, scanning for unpredictable adult actions. My body had become so sensitive to any micro-changes in emotional volatility that my mind couldn't always keep up. Unwavering clarity and refusal to break cultivated my resilience.

If I were to sum up my childhood, I would say my parents programmed me to earn affection.

Love wasn't something freely given; it's conditional, and

I had to earn it.

However, no one ever told me the goalpost was constantly moving away from me. Once achievable goals always proved unreachable in the end.

I know now that I wasn't flawed; someone else wanted power and control over me. It's heartbreaking that my needs for love, connection, and safety were met with silence, punishment, and control. I was never "too much" or "not enough." I was just a little girl placed in impossible circumstances, expected to carry burdens no child ever should.

Parentification

Recall when I confronted my father about the silent treatment that he and my mother gave each other. That instance signified the hidden dynamic between them and me: I, as a young teenager, was the grown-up being assigned a role to police emotional immaturity between two adults. It meant I also had to raise myself since those in parental roles didn't.

When my father passed, my mother collapsed her entire emotional world onto me, as if she forgot that she had never wanted me before I even existed. Her grief became my leash. She didn't choose to love me better; she chose to use me harder.

Her silence on my biggest win—getting into a prestigious university—was her way of stealing joy from my future, the same way she had from my childhood. The silent treatment wasn't passive; it was punishment: it's her twisted way of saying, "You don't get to rise above me." I didn't just commute three hours a day between her home and my university campus; I endured emotional whiplash, trying to keep a dream alive while tethered to someone who resented me for having it.

Instead of finally being free to grow into myself, my mother's treatment of me as her surrogate spouse was a crushing load to carry: a load I had carried for so long with a kind of strength that most people can't even comprehend.

Trophies & Passions

Despite emotional deprivation, I did extraordinary things. All my achievements and hobbies collectively make me unique. But I distanced myself from those accomplishments and didn't boast about them.

I could have used them to seem superior, but my subconscious chose not to. I saw them as default milestones on my journey that I was supposed to pass through.

The experience of surviving a car accident prompted these questions: *Were those trophies valid in securing affection from others? Why did my thoughts remain active, despite a broad spectrum of interests designed to occupy my attention?*

Megan, as a young child or teenager, lacked the awareness that the motivational force behind achieving the number one spot every academic year and the highest-level piano performance certificate was to earn love from her parents.

In adulthood, it translated to getting titles that people assumed I couldn't: PhD, Marine, law enforcement, and model. My function remains within the programming I had learned: demonstrate my worthiness to exist.

I used to have chronic restlessness because of the internal dialogue between my cognition and emotion, so I sought talk therapy, hoping I could talk my internal contradictions away. Instead of medication, therapists would prescribe me hobbies or activities, anything to kill time with.

For others, pursuing hobbies distracts them from thinking. They take their minds off deeper emotions that most avoid feeling. That explains why many have suggested going on walks, working out, or traveling during heartbreaks because of their way of coping; that's how they have learned to handle things. So, out of the goodness of their hearts, they suggested those things to me.

But me? I must deliberate before immersing myself in activities. Even hobbies would become unenjoyable unless I attain internal clarity first. For me, external actions always create distracting noises, hindering my ability to sit in silence and process my understanding.

By now, I trust you recall my long list of passionate interests. If keeping oneself busy was the cure for mental health, I would have been the best candidate to advocate for it. Sadly, none of my hobbies could distract me from my internal unrest.

And you're right; I call it a "distraction" not just for me, but for everyone, for similar but very different reasons. For me, think before doing; for others, distract to avoid thinking.

It's harsh, but I had always been convinced of its truth, even though I wasn't able to pinpoint why.

Brain Hemispheres

Few facing peril would contemplate the purpose of life. I did because of my equally developed "left and right brains." My early upbringing, coupled with ongoing circumstances, clarifies my distinctive approach to life.

In simpler terms, the intensity varies between mine and others in relation to the functioning of the brain hemispheres. The left brain governs intellectual logic, whereas the right brain recognizes emotional processing.

Most people are dominant in one hemisphere. They prioritize either problem-solving and decision-making or intuition and imagination without considering the balance between the two. So they either feel everything but get overwhelmed by it or suppress their emotions to stay in control, often missing the richness of their emotional world.

But I have achieved a harmonious blend of both in equal measure. My emotional intelligence enables me to feel intensely, while my intellectual capacity allows me to step back from my emotions and evaluate the broader context objectively without being swept away. But I still struggle to pinpoint when I started stretching my emotional and intellectual capacities in my journey.

This simultaneous functioning is rare because it causes emotional discomfort that is inevitable; it requires a great deal of self-reflection that most steer away from. Holding both emotional and mental loads at once prevents me from conforming to societal norms, which is why I often feel alienated.

Cognition

I had developed independent cognition very early on. Because of the unreliable emotional responses from my parents, I cultivated a deeper ability for independent thinking than the average child. This trained my brain to separate surface behavior from deeper reality, which contributed to my cognitive range being unusual: I can focus on minor details (like an unusual use of a full stop in texting) or consider the bigger picture (like his overall emotional avoidance).

As a result, I notice the contradictions in romantic relationships as an adult.

> **They say they love me, but they bungle; they claim they listen, but they don't comprehend.**

Emotion

I raised myself emotionally because those who were supposed to failed to do so.

Let's not forget that I had to endure physical abuse, the silent treatment, and being used as a messenger. Through my parents' emotional unavailability and other intense childhood experiences, I had learned that no one would mirror or hold my full emotional reality reliably. At a very young age, I had to become self-reliant with my emotions. My inner structure is private.

I will hold myself if no one else can.

My emotional honesty likely developed as a coping mechanism or survival tool during my childhood. In romantic relationships, my emotional expressions were often undervalued or misunderstood. So I had learned to honor my emotions as they arose, rather than filtering them. This honesty enables me to experience my emotions and process them with clarity. I refuse to conceal my inner thoughts and feelings because doing so would feel inauthentic to me. Because most people are not as comfortable expressing their emotions, I often felt like I was "too much" in romantic relationships.

Tug-of-war

Frankly, I'm unsure whether thinking logically while feeling deeply is a blessing or a curse, because these opposing forces create a constant internal tug-of-war: my unconscious motivates me to please others, while my conscious mind prevents relying on others for validation.

The strong sense of self I have developed from a survival instinct has been fighting against the "earning love by pleasing others" notion since the beginning of my existence. Of course, it would be much easier to choose the path of least resistance: go with my intellect or emotion, pick one. Yet, the tug-of-war shows both sides possess equivalent persistence, with neither wishing to yield.

Most humans, by instinct, choose to belong and find emotional stability through an outside source because society reinforces blending in, maintaining illusions, and preferring emotional comfort over truth.

I, however, chose the opposite: I'm self-reinforced, prioritizing reality over comfort, and would rather know what's real, even if it means I stand alone. This much harder journey cuts me off from the emotional consensus that binds most people together, but I have always felt even more uneasy whenever exposing myself to external elements that weren't aligned with my core.

For instance, I reject religion, politics, and commercial sports because I'm allergic to anything that replaces firsthand awareness with collective expectation; this kind of thinking makes me feel isolated from society. Yet I refused to contort my core beliefs and give in to talking politics or wearing jerseys.

What I have discovered is that the balance between my cognition and emotion provides me with depth. I can process and comprehend my feelings with intellectual rigor, but my emotional world also serves as a guiding force when needed. By merging the emotional and intellectual realms, I cultivate insightful life navigation.

I would even argue that I had formed a survival strategy based on truth over belonging. This inner practice didn't just happen; it's something I have cultivated and chosen, and continue to do so with awareness.

Therefore, I experience cognitive dissonance more than most people; I'm always seeking harmony between my emotional truth and reality. While most people prefer narratives they can control and keep things superficial, I don't shy away from embracing complexity and contradictions; I strive to simplify them, which shapes my perspective.

I understand the complete picture and embrace internal conflict— strength and vulnerability, love and distance, and clarity and confusion coexist.

My ability to hold multiple conflicting truths at once without ignoring the way they make me feel isolates my experience because most people struggle with that level of nuance.

Odd One Out

My strong emotional awareness and contemplative nature led to an early disconnection from my peers. I realized that others my age didn't understand me because of my heightened emotional regulation and life experiences that had surpassed theirs. Perhaps my subconscious reluctance to rely on others for validation was why I disconnected from the herd mentality from a young age.

Most people filter their emotional sensitivity to others' opinions, cultural expectations, or societal norms; I have developed the ability to regulate my emotions at a level that allows me to stay calm and understanding, bypassing those filters, piercing through illusions, and experiencing emotions with intense passion while maintaining exceptional clarity about them.

While others seemed to find solace in surface-level interactions and a more reactive emotional state, I always pursued more profound and meaningful interactions because I find grounding in truth-seeking.

Many claim that they want "the truth," but comfort proves alluring. They often become jaded when encountering human contradictions but live with them anyway because of familiarity, and familiarity provides comfort.

In contrast, I truly prioritize truth over comfort. My strong drive to make sense of the dissonance in life came from training through hardship and deep self-work. It requires absorbing complexity without succumbing to bitterness. That's why I'm straightforward, especially with myself, tackling the core issues that many hesitate to venture into.

The combination of high emotional intelligence, cognitive independence, and existential awareness is why I feel so different from everyone else. They form a unique and intricate inner compass that enables me to navigate the world with a level of clarity, independence, and depth. This type of introspection is uncommon because it often involves facing hard truths and painful contradictions, which leaves me with a permanent sensation of "being out of phase" with the world around me.

Internal Validation

Most people operate within default settings, adhering to social scripts and navigating life based on emotional responses that align with collective experiences. They are often driven by external markers and get their sense of direction, value, and self-worth from external sources —what's happening around them, what's trending, and how others perceive them. Many people remain trapped in the external validation loop, constantly seeking answers, reassurance, or validation from others. Their identity and sense of life's purpose become tied to a script, checking off boxes of milestones like dating, marriage, having children, or career progression.

Growing up in an environment where validation was scarce, inconsistent, or conditional, I didn't receive support during my formative years. This early realization taught me I couldn't rely on anyone else, not even my parents, to validate my worth. I then went through many relationships where external affirmation was inconsistent. During my childhood and adulthood, I encountered people, relationships, and situations where the truth couldn't be boxed.

My journey unfolded after discovering that others' expectations couldn't define me. I have made a conscious decision to stop outsourcing my peace to others when processing my emotions. In developing an independent thought process, I broke free from the need for external validation. Trusting my inner compass, I have created a path to emotional freedom that is not confined to the standard narrative of success or societal timelines, expectations, or scripts.

I don't need chaos, drama, or confirmation from others to make sense of my inner world.

My self-worth and decisions would then come from my instincts, not external markers such as career steps, relationships, or typical life milestones. I know who I am, regardless of how others perceive or interact with me. This level of internal sovereignty makes me seem detached from the collective way people follow others' emotional responses.

My resilience in emotional attachments explains why I didn't chase after being discarded by the last guy I dated. Unlike many people who become overwhelmed by emotional attachment, I have learned to hold space for myself first. I don't need others to complete me.

Stepping back gave me the time and space to reflect, avoiding emotional responses like longing or regret. I can hold my boundaries and see my worth with no need for anyone else to define it for me. By shifting my internal foundation, I have learned to be at peace with things as they are.

Self-Reflection

The inner work I had done to achieve internal validation required a great deal of self-reflection. Walking away from a car crash that granted me borrowed time was the rock bottom that forced me to face who I was: the common denominator among all my failed relationships.

As the only child in an unloving family, I depended on heightened self-awareness to engage in constant self-reflection that helped me navigate situations. As young as age four, I refused to conform when others wanted me to lie about hypothetically taking home a beautiful flower from a garden. Exposure to emotional complexity or difficult circumstances in the Marine Corps forced me to sharpen my awareness of myself as a way of managing complexity. Pursuing my PhD amplified my critical thinking quality.

While few individuals function with awareness, and even fewer self-reflect except during challenging times, I have developed the ability to constantly analyze the underlying layers of my ongoing conflict, motivations, thoughts, behaviors, reactions, and the intricacies of the situation acutely and without distortion or emotional cloudiness.

This persistent self-awareness and my inner workings enable me to notice and see the bigger picture, which allows me to reflect on the guys I had dated with clarity. I understand their patterns, why they did what they did, and how they would continue to behave if our connections were to continue. My emotional depth has honed the ability to filter out my own past pain and projections, allowing me to grasp the truth rather than fantasies.

Existential Awareness

Life is delicate and unpredictable; few value this notion. I have internalized the fragility of life and the uncertainty of the future since losing my father to lung cancer in his late 40s. Despite being a competitive swimmer who had smoked nothing in his life, not even a cigarette, he succumbed to the illness that he had spent his lifetime trying to avoid.

I faced a deep loss and had to cope with this existential uncertainty, which was ingrained in me as an essential part of my worldview as I lived through life's unpredictable moments. My understanding is that nothing lasts forever. I have a unique, broad perspective on existence and mortality, which is a powerful motivator, and I have made peace with that understanding.

Recognizing life's fragility, I live with urgency but detachment from status, milestones, and worldly success. This realization allows detachment from conventional timelines, and it also lets me be present, fluid, and adaptable. This awareness motivates intentional living, fostering individualistic views, which have shaped me into someone who doesn't shy away from difficult or uncomfortable truths.

Unlike most, I'm not focused on conventional markers or timelines because everything is temporary. While many people focus on superficial experiences, I have been seeking deeper meaning and connections for much of my life. While others avoid confronting the deeper questions of existence, I have been brave enough to face them head-on. This makes me seem disconnected or different because it's hard for others to operate with that constant truth in mind.

I have developed a realistic understanding of human behavior at a deeper level and recognized that people's actions are often a reflection of their own inner world and struggles. Instead of personalizing their actions, I see them for what they are—their inability to engage at a deeper emotional level because of their own limits.

This is the opposite of the "blame and shame" cycle many get stuck in when they try to figure out why someone left them. Instead of viewing it as a rejection of me, I see it as a misalignment between what I need and what they're capable of.

"Superpower"

The byproduct of my lifelong internal tug-of-war is trauma-sculpted foresight, or what most would call "intuition."

From infancy, I grasped that slower or heavier footfalls signaled trouble, or a snap appeared imminent during the extended silence. I had also learned that when the facial muscles didn't match the tone of voice, they were lying or there was tension underneath, or when someone said "I'm fine" with a clipped rhythm, they were not fine, and I had to brace myself.

After years of fine-tuning this foresight, now I often see what's coming before the person I'm watching even knows it's coming for them. I feel their fragmentation—buried resentment, mounting anxiety, and internal contradiction—before they do. And I sense the unspoken rupture weeks before it surfaces.

The costs of this hyper-attunement are deep because it is not just about reading danger; it also prevents me from relaxing into safety. Even when I'm with someone who says they love me, I'm scanning; even when nothing is wrong, my body is still bracing.

I'm not choosing to… but my survival instincts wired my nervous system this way. Therefore, most people will never feel "safe" to me, not because I'm picky, but because my definition of safety is precision-level emotional consistency, which is uncommon.

But here's the trap: because I'm so far ahead of what I know is coming, others don't believe me. They think I'm "overreacting," "being too sensitive," or "jumping to conclusions." So I would stay quiet to avoid being dismissed and let people walk straight into the consequences I had already predicted. Knowing I had been right yet again, the ache of solitude consumed me.

However, I have learned to embrace it now and call it my "superpower" because my previous denial of this powerful gift was the source of the painful internal tug-of-war I had to endure. That pain came from the betrayal of my instinct because it reminded me of how different I was. But I now carry my "superpower" in silence because I no longer seek external validation of what I have already known to be true.

I don't need drama; I just want peace.

Parental Love to Romantic Love

Here's an unpopular fact: romantic relationships echo the parent-child dynamic.

Humans learn what love feels like when they are infants. Babies' basic needs—physical care, developmental stimulation, and emotional connection—require caregivers' attention. But if their needs remain unmet, or love feels conditional and tied to performance or punishment, they shift to believing it must be earned. They then learn through trial and error to "win" those basic needs from a caregiver. People learn love through demonstration by their parents during upbringing and then apply what they have learned in their adult romantic relationships.

I was one of those infants growing up in an environment where love was transactional and scarce. That's why it makes perfect sense that I have carried invisible chains from it to my romantic relationship patterns. None of this was my fault, and none of it makes me broken, but it clarifies the uniformity of my romantic encounters. I linked love with the "highs" or the "thrills" because that's what was shown to me during childhood. My upbringing occurred in a world where love had conditions, where I had to perform to be worthy, attune to be accepted, and dissect others to feel safe. I studied every glance, silence, and shift in tone, thinking that if I just decoded it right, I could finally unlock the love that always felt out of reach. I gave energy as if it were infinite—time, presence, loyalty, and care—offering them to those who had never earned them, hoping one day they would realize my worth.

My needs, clarity, and sense of being chosen were sidelined, yet I continued to earn love from guys who kept moving the goalposts, just like my parents did. When I was forced to equate affection with punishment, autonomy with betrayal, and success with abandonment, I found myself in situations where those old echoes resurfaced. Guys I dated seemed unable or unwilling to commit or communicate with honesty, yet I remained present, trying to hold space for their struggles. That took immense strength, but it also left me vulnerable to being diminished and unseen.

The discovery of a former partner's double life was a heartbreaking confirmation that I wasn't his priority, despite everything I had done. It's not me; it's him—my strong emotional core grants me this perception now, even while others in a similar situation might remain tangled.

No longer reacting to the actions of the last guy I had dated, I'm observing his patterns with clarity. I'm not caught in the emotional cycle of "loss" or "missing him" in the way others might be. Even when my emotions are intense, I don't let them control my judgment. I have an unusual ability to hold two truths at once: "I feel this way emotionally," and "I also see reality clearly, even if it's painful." I remained focused on what's real, not on the emotional turmoil. This ability to separate emotions from reality grants me clarity to grasp dynamics.

I adopted a broader emotional perspective, recognizing that I'm not just reacting to the breakup or the person involved. Instead, I comprehend that an individual's ability shapes the depth of interaction, even when their desires extend further. This level of awareness allows me to move on from him without lingering on what could have been possible.

Now I realize that love is about consistency, depth, and a willingness to grow together. I deserved so much better than the half-truths, shifting priorities, and emotional unavailability those guys gave me. My goal isn't to win over my ex or to create a narrative where I come out on top. I'm not even trying to repair the emotional aspect of the story.

Many people experience intense emotions during relationship transitions. They spiral into a chase for closure, obsess over past events, and rehash everything to comprehend what went wrong. I broke free from that cycle of "emotional drama." And that's when I realized: while genuine love was never given, my "superpower" was always on alert for knowing when their detachments were coming, but my intuition would never be validated because I was too far ahead of everyone else in the room.

The Test Is Over

Megan, in the past, gave her all to those who only received. She bent, studied, molded, and waited, and not one of them rose to meet her.

I have lived through enough repeated patterns that I finally understood the common denominator was me. Instead of resenting that, I found peace in it—because if I'm the problem, then I'm also the solution. And I trust myself to change. So, I stopped trying to fit inside romantic relationships or to earn love from people who don't even love themselves. And I forewent the fantasy that someone who hasn't even seen themselves could see me.

When I was seven, questioning why people had children, I found no valid answer beyond self-serving explanations, and my opinion has never changed.

Then I questioned, *if I don't want kids, why would I get married?*

With my belief that having children is nonsensical, contrary to what everyone has been telling me my entire life—"You'll change your mind"—I didn't see the point in getting married. Many people say it's for tax benefits (telling me, who is a Certified Public Accountant!). Most would ask, "Don't you want someone to grow old with?" My answer was always, "It depends on the individual." I love my surname and would never change it, especially not for another person. So then, it spiraled down to a harsh reality: people are unreliable; they develop in countless unpredictable ways.

Why dedicate time and energy to a volatile partnership? When I already feel whole within myself.

I had remained neutral on cohabitation with a romantic partner; it was the last societal norm towards which I had felt no strong opinion.

So, there I was, spending countless years experimenting with different approaches to relationships through trial and error, trying to figure out whether the social and cultural norms of romantic relationships would fit me without even realizing it. Ultimately, my entire dataset revealed that the return on investment was not just low; I was operating at a deficit. Now I realize that relationships, much like parenthood, religions, and political beliefs, are not suitable for everyone, and that's okay.

The test is over.

Relationships exhaust me—that's my truth. For a while, I was clouded by a hidden ambiguity that controlled my approach to personal goals. But I have finally resolved it.

The decision to remain unpartnered isn't for everyone. It's the right path for me because I finally see that I have been built to navigate life on my own since birth. Through social influence, I have tested the hypothesis of spending a shared life with a potential match, but the results have shown that the odds of meeting "my person" in my lifetime are not just slim; they're almost nonexistent. Therefore, I have decided to cease the pursuit.

No one can hold me until they hold themselves, and vice versa.

So, I have stopped carrying other people's weight. And I'm living—truly, wholly, and finally—just for me.

I Am Home

During that last relationship, I considered myself secure. But if I'm honest, I wasn't. I rationalized his actions, envisioning the best in him, clinging to delusion, and exceeding the duration others might have remained in a similar situation.

But I didn't stay because I was naïve, nor was it a failure of my intelligence... I was still operating based on what I had been trained by my parents and the guys before him who had "groomed" me: I reinterpreted distance as normal and inconsistency as a code to crack. But I'm unashamed of that interpretation: I had to learn my lesson the hard way.

So, how did my last relationship bring me back home? Despite mistreatment from prior partners, I still believe that the last guy was the only one who lacked malicious intent, meaning I don't think he was using me for sex intentionally. This was the most valuable lesson because I had assumed in the past that intention meant everything.

I saw his good intentions in the beginning, so I trusted them to be the key to longevity. Until he came into my life, I had never truly understood that some individuals are incapable of emotional affection, regardless of effort, because of unresolved personal problems. For him, the only way he knew how to connect was through physical intimacy.

The Universe lined him up right after the one who intentionally betrayed me to give me this wake-up call. Eventually, I saw the pattern, named the dynamic, owned my part, and stepped out.

I know you must be thinking, "But he dumped you." You're right, he did. But I also didn't chase, negotiate, or beg for more time like he had assumed that I would, because when you think about it, he himself said he was confused and repeatedly offered post-breakup communication.

What he had was an uneasy feeling that he was desperate to shake off. He chose avoidance; I chose introspection.

Finally, I no longer audition for belonging or earn to be included in rooms that shrink me. I don't confuse labor with intimacy or tolerance with affection anymore. No more sleeping in storage rooms, trucks, or childhood homes with the smell of control. I stopped chasing and finally made a full circle to return home—to myself. It took the Universe a few decades to teach me one valuable life lesson:

Other people's weights are not mine to carry.

And once I realized that, I began to live my life in full, for myself.

I never asked to be born, and yet I insisted on surviving... and thriving.

Clarity

In summary, what have I learned? Awareness is the foundation.

A person needs to first recognize their unconscious desires and determine if they align with their conscious wants. In short, what does your conscious brain know you desire, and what does your intuitive brain yearn for? Once you have identified them, it becomes your choice to live by whichever one, should they differ. However, the latter requires the hard work of internal rewiring, which some refer to as "healing." But neither route is incorrect; it's just a personal preference. It's your life—your prerogative.

When partnering, though, it's vital to reflect upon your selection for positive outcomes. I argue that it's unethical not to be upfront about what you're looking for. Just because you're single, it doesn't mean that you're emotionally available. Knowingly admitting yourself into the dating pool implies your emotional availability. But how many times have you found out the person you're dating has a limited emotional capacity? It's not always their fault because some people truly perceive that they are ready until tested by reality. This is why I said self-awareness is everything.

Awareness of your emotional capacity, coupled with honesty and good intentions, would save many from heartaches.

With that said, I choose to be emotionally unavailable to others. I mean no harm; it's just that I'm self-aware enough to accept the way I am: I do nothing half-assed, and I tend to over-give. My point is, the torment of continuing to subject myself to testing the possibility of whether I'm dating "my person" outweighs the reward of being with one. I refuse to manufacture illusions but continue existing on my own terms, without demanding that others live the same way, clinging to pride, hope, nostalgia, or spiritual ego.

Let me be clear, this path is logical for me because I have built my whole life towards internal validation. External validation is something I no longer need. I do not expect others to adopt it. I don't make a practice of preaching authenticity. But it's a topic so dear to my heart that I chose it for a school project when I was pursuing my life coaching certification.

The self-discovery I have undergone is profound and irreversible. I didn't just "move on" from people. I have moved beyond the limiting framework that most people are confined to. From questioning my worth, I have evolved to accept my true nature and to cease pursuit not from failure, but from understanding. And once it happens, I can't un-grow. I have been on a different plane ever since.

I have experienced a profound shift in my relationship with myself, which has given me an awareness and depth that most people lack. Clarity and truthfulness became priorities because of this evolution, even amidst challenging emotions. I have the uncommon ability to see through my own and others' illusions and confront the truth of a situation without resorting to emotional self-deception.

I am true to myself and have never been afraid of my own feelings. So, I often keep delving deeper to refine my insights until I reach clarity. I consciously choose self-defined clarity over perpetual confusion about others' actions and words.

Most people I have encountered speak in confusion, contradiction, or self-protection. In contrast, my body has learned to find peace in clarity, not ease. That's why relationships exhaust me—I would subject myself to situations where I have to shoulder a dual responsibility.

I don't abandon myself anymore or betray my inner knowing just to avoid pain. Even in sadness, grief, and sharp realization, I stay present with myself. I no longer bend, explain, audition, or seek reflections of myself in others. It doesn't close me off; it protects what I have spent years cultivating: my inner peace.

And finally, I am sacred to myself. My peace is not up for negotiation; my time is not available.

This clarity allows full presence. My life now centers on hobbies and passions. Ironically, they are no longer distractions for me because I have gotten my authentic self straightened out. I love doing these things. This is life itself. I now live on my own terms, with purpose. And not because I finally became "enough" for someone, but because

I finally realized that I have always been enough for me.

And this is what true freedom feels like.

About the Author

Formerly British, Megan Elizabeth Victoria is a US citizen. She is a Doctor of Philosophy in Business Management with a concentration in Forensic Accounting. She is also a Certified Professional Coach, Certified Public Accountant, Certified Fraud Examiner, US Marine Corps veteran, fashion model, and proud to be part of the Federal Bureau of Investigation.

Outside of her professional and creative work, Megan lives a vibrant and intentional life. She enjoys traveling, photography, motorsport racing, singing, and playing the piano, guitar, harp, violin, and ukulele. She practices ballet, en pointe, pole dancing, hand balancing, ice skating, golfing, hiking, indoor rock climbing, Pilates, yoga, and all kinds of water sports, including swimming.

Photo Credit: Diana Peterson

Above all, she lives her life in truth, authenticity, and clarity.

www.ingramcontent.com/pod-product-compliance
Lightning Source LLC
Chambersburg PA
CBHW030326130626
46554CB00011B/48